THE
COLDMAN
COMETH

Also by Bob Durr

Down in Bristol Bay:
High Tides, Hangovers, and
Harrowing Experiences on
Alaska's Last Frontier

On the Mystical Poetry of
Henry Vaughan

Poetic Vision and the Psychedelic
Experience

THE
COLDMAN
COMETH

A

Family's

Adventure

in the

Alaska

Bush

BOB DURR

THOMAS DUNNE BOOKS
St. Martin's Press New York

THOMAS DUNNE BOOKS.
An imprint of St. Martin's Press.

www.stmartins.com

Book design by Kathryn Parise

LIBRARY OF CONGRESS CATALOGING-IN-PUBLICATION DATA

Durr, R. A.
    The coldman cometh : a family's adventure in the Alaska bush /
Bob Durr.—1st ed.
        p. cm.
    ISBN 0-312-31179-6
    EAN 978-0312-31179-7
    1. Durr, R. A. 2. Durr, R. A.—Family. 3. Pioneers—Alaska—
Biography. 4. Frontier and pioneer life—Alaska. 5. Alaska—Social
life and customs—20th century. 6. Wilderness areas—Alaska.
7. Alaska—Biography. 8. Talkeetna Region (Alaska)—Biography.
I. Title.
    F910.7.D87A3 2004
    979.8'04—dc22

                                                    2004040966

First Edition: July 2004

10 9 8 7 6 5 4 3 2 1

*Dedicated to my family
and the memory of my late wife,
Carol*

Whatever it is, it's still there. . . . This thing can reach into the human world, haltingly, hesitantly, but plaintively, probingly, trying to bring us back, calling us to some kind of return. . . . And this is what is the cause of all the nostalgia for paradise . . . and all the utopian yearning.

Terrence McKenna

Contents

Acknowledgments

My two sons, Steve and Jon, have been invaluable in correcting and clarifying my memory. For the past year or so just about every morning over coffee we put our heads together and compared notes about those bygone days when we were first settling into the Alaska bush. This memoir isn't in the nature of a documentary or report, of course, but the memories they revived in me helped immeasurably in filling out the story with the kind of details that can breathe life into a narrative. So it's a pleasure to acknowledge their help here.

It is also a pleasure to thank the people at Dystel & Goderich Literary Management and my editor at Thomas Dunne Books, Pete Wolverton, for their support and encouragement. To Pete Wolverton I owe a special debt of gratitude for his close reading of the manuscript and his many helpful suggestions.

Introduction

This one's not getting away.

In 1991 I published a book, *Down in Bristol Bay*, describing the adventures, misadventures, and perils involved in my effort to prove up as a commercial salmon fisherman in Alaska's Bristol Bay. I kept at it, returning to Alaska summer after summer, taking my knocks and risking my life (commercial fishing is counted the most dangerous of occupations), because I saw salmon fishing as the best way for me to earn the money I knew would be needed, at least the first years, for my family and me to make it as greenhorn settlers in the Alaska wilderness.

However much I appeared the fool to most of my friends and relatives for wanting to do that, giving up my comfortable position in society, I wasn't fool enough to think we could just walk into the woods and start living off the land. So becoming a fisherman was important, the necessary first step to moving us into what I was sure (most of the time) would be a better, because more natural, life.

Mainstream America for me was too commercial, too aberrant to human nature—and too quietly, smilingly desperate. That an entire society can be aberrant (insane), and not just some of its members, isn't an observation that originated with me. From Nietzsche ("Too long has the world been a madhouse") to Erich Fromm *(The Pathology of Normalcy)*, from Joyce ("History is a nightmare from which I am trying to awaken") to Paul Shepard *(Nature and Madness)* and Ken Kesey *(One Flew over the Cuckoo's Nest)*, and so many other thinkers and artists, it's a given.

How could I live from my real self, or even be aware of its existence, in such a distorting social environment? If you're living in or near a swamp and keep coming down with malaria and then one day you discover the cause to be all those millions of mosquitoes, it behooves you to move away to some healthier location. For me, city and suburb and even the mental life of academia were the dismal swamp and all their influences the malarial mosquitoes. These intuitions were operative in me long before I consciously realized it, long before I thought it through.

But I was ready to leave, I was already walking. On summer vacations while I was still a professor instead of making pilgrimages to Europe to genuflect before the icons of civilization, as did my colleagues, I took my family north and northwest camping and probing for a passage into wilderness. Living in the country as we did was much better than living in the city or suburbs, but the hand of man nevertheless was apparent everywhere. The land was tamed, carved into squares and rectangles, laced with asphalt lines from city to city. I was still in the asylum; it was just a bit more bucolic.

The aboriginal was what I wanted, the primitive—*primus,* the primary world—the untamed wild, where maybe I could hear the voice of my human nature blowing in the wind, where in any event I wouldn't be constantly distracted by the psychobabble of modern times, and where my family and I would be immersed in a brave new world of trees and bushes, wild animals and fishes, lakes and rivers, rain, snow, wind, and, yes, mosquitoes and subzero temperatures, all real, all speaking truth.

My readings joined forces with my stubborn inchoate yearnings to turn me away from modern society and face northward, toward

wilderness. That's where, over the course of evolution, human nature had been formed and where, in its natural habitat, maybe it
could once more flourish.

I was still a tenured professor of English at Syracuse University
through the first four fishing seasons of *High Tides, Hangovers,
and Harrowing Experiences on Alaska's Last Frontier* (the subti-
tle of *Down in Bristol Bay*), but then in 1968 I took the plunge. I
resigned my professorship, sold or gave away most of our possessions, and with my wife and our four kids set out for the wilderness area of Lake Iliamna, where my fishing partner, Gene Pope,
lived. *Down in Bristol Bay* touches on but doesn't delve into the
reasons why I did that, and it doesn't tell the story—the "family
saga," as we call it—of the trials and triumphs we experienced
trying to settle into the bush and make it a home. This book tells
that story and is in a sense the sequel or complement to *Down in
Bristol Bay*, and it goes much more deeply into the why of it and
what we found and what it has meant to us—not expressed in dis-
crete essay form but embedded in the narrative, emerging as the
tale is told: meanings integral to the story.

Because this is the memoir of a family's experiences, and not
just mine, I thought it would make for a fuller, more interesting
account if sons Steve and Jon, who live right here on the lake (my
daughters are living elsewhere), entered bits of their own vivid recall into the narrative; for surely they would have seen some things
differently from the way I had and noticed other things I hadn't.
So whenever the flow of my narrative triggered a particularly
poignant memory in one or another of them he wrote it down in
his own words and I inserted it, using italics to set the passage off.
And just as I had supposed, they did remember events I had forgotten or been absent from and experienced others differently
from the way I had, to the enrichment of the story.

This book covers the first six years of our venture into wilderness, counting the first year at Lake Nerka in 1964–1965, when
I was on a sabbatical from Syracuse University and had been

awarded a Guggenheim grant to write a book. Everything was new and exciting (and sometimes fearsome) to us through those years, and they involved us in every aspect of bush life, so that this memoir will take the reader into all the essential ingredients of that life, even though we have now lived in the bush for a total of thirty-seven years to date.

Cabin raising, fishing and hunting, exploratory expeditions into new territories, encounters with bears and the most dangerous entity in the north woods, the Coldman (our personification of subzero temperatures)—all are here described in detail and living color.

The story's setting includes four distinct wilderness areas of the Great Land where we have lived, three of them for only a year each and the fourth, the Upper Susitna Valley, where we have lived since the spring of 1970—on a little lake ten miles by trail north of the town of Talkeetna.

If you're curious as to what it's like to live in the deep woods, and what the people are like who live there, you've come to the right place. It's been fascinating reliving those early days while writing about them now, and I want to bring the reader along through all of it, to the point of smelling the pine pitch when a green log is peeled or discovering with a shock that an enraged bull moose can roar like a bear and look just as horrific.

Most Americans would consider it punitive in and of itself to be living in a climate like Alaska's without electricity, plumbing, or thermostatic heat. But we didn't. Kerosene lamps, an outhouse, water hauled in buckets from a lake, a wood-burning stove, and near-total isolation (except for a handful of close friends, our extended family) were part and parcel of what we were after: the elemental life, subsisting largely from the land, a life resonant of the kind our ancestors had led for eons before the fall into history.

Beyond the generic privations mentioned, there were in our experience hardships of various kinds, difficulties supplemented, as it were, by engagements with bears, charging bull moose, and stormy seas. This book tells the tale of those tough, exciting, jubilant years and concludes with our determination after our cabin burned down in 1973 to rebuild and live out our lives here in the bush.

Back Lake, Alaska
Summer of 2003

I wish to speak a word for Nature, for absolute freedom and wildness, as contrasted with a freedom and culture merely civil—to regard man as an inhabitant, or a part and parcel of Nature, rather than a member of society.

THOREAU

I was aware that something happened to men when they were in the bush. As they shed their city habits and settled down to the hard physical work and simplicity of primitive living, they laughed more and took pleasure in little things.

SIGURD F. OLSON

To the Indian the material world is sentient and intelligent. . . . A mysterious and inexplicable power resides in inanimate things. . . . In the silence of a forest, the gloom of a deep ravine, resides a living mystery, indefinite, but redoubtable.

FRANCIS PARKMAN

1

Wilderness 101: Lake Nerka

Cool, clear water.

(August 1964–May 1965)

One of the first lessons I learned about outback Alaska was that I had to be ready to go it alone, to fall back upon whatever experience I had so far and hope my own ingenuity could work things out. It seemed I could start out with a company of marines and before I got to where I wanted to go I would be quite alone and strictly on my own.

It didn't take long to figure out that in wilderness living you can count on some kind of predicament, little or big, confronting you more often than you might like. Predicaments, in the Alaska bush, are not an endangered species. They are abundant and seem to prefer one-on-one encounters. You will fall into a "sweat," as predicaments are called in the bush up here, at least a few times a year, one or another of them occasionally, and usually unexpectedly, maturing into a matter of life or death, on which occasions you will inevitably find yourself on your own. And until very recently there was no little cell phone to slip out of your pocket, no 911 at your fingertips.

Wilderness is a school of hard knocks, however beautiful its campus. No one enjoys a special dispensation, no more than do the eagle, the wolf, or the butterfly. Self-reliance is prerequisite to a passing grade. The Big Eskimo in the Sky would have it that way, the "men to match my mountains" sort of thing, perhaps as part of what scientists call natural selection. If you funk out you flunk out. Graduates have proven themselves capable of playing the dangerous game of existence.

The wild land and the wild sea will be themselves, feeling no obligation to modify their behavior in deference to the well-being or survival of innocents entering their domains. You read often enough about some high-minded person out of the city or suburbs wanting to embrace wild nature and, untutored and unprepared, winding up dead. This is not to imply, as many believe, that nature is hostile, a ruthless mistress who must be subdued and controlled if humans are to thrive. It's simply that, for one thing, she doesn't recognize the grave distinction between life and death that haunts the minds of modern humans. She sees existence as an ongoing drama of eternal transformations of spiritual energy. She is author, director, actor, and spectator of all the spectacles. (Nobody really fails the course. They just play out their parts.)

I came early to understand that it's a mistake to paint your picture of nature in Disney pastels, to expect only sweetness and light at her hands. Even rabbits—"bunnies"—in their own circles can be as passionate and fierce as wolves and eagles. But as to hostility, remember it is we who, since the dawn of civilization, have waged war against her, "conquering nature," bending her to our will. The problem, if there is one, is with us modern civilized folk, not with nature. For hundreds of thousands of years before civilization, our kind—as fully realized *Homo sapiens sapiens*—revered nature as sacred and sought only to live on her terms, in keeping with the goodwill of the Great Spirit. We need to learn from our "primitive" forebears how to behave toward the earth, to come to see her again as sacred, and in so doing dispel our sense of alienation, our existential emptiness. Imposing our will on nature is a species of suicide, as is now becoming apparent.

But I get ahead of myself. I had yet to reach these conclusions when I enrolled in Wilderness 101 at Lake Nerka. Nor was it ever a matter of sitting down and thinking things through. Our learning was more osmosis than intellection. We "picked up on" the wilderness along the way and began growing into our real selves spontaneously through the course of unfolding events and unpremeditated *seeing,* which often enough came across as shocks of recognition.

In any event, as regards the propensity of wilderness to test our mettle in one-on-one situations, that's how it was the day in August of 1964 when I set out for Lake Nerka. I wound up in a predicament and on my own.

I had made arrangements with Dr. "Bud" Burgner of the University of Washington's Fisheries Research Institute (FRI) to be their winter man at their outpost on Nerka. The FRI's main headquarters and research center was on Lake Aleknagik, the first of the Wood/Tikchik State Park's chain of wilderness lakes and rivers north of Dillingham. Unlike the tidal-flats landscape of the Bristol Bay fishing grounds, which is virtually treeless tundra dotted with pothole ponds, the lakes region is densely forested and mountainous. There are no areas of the planet more pristinely beautiful and grand. Nerka is the second lake heading north. It is connected to Lake Aleknagik by the Agulowok River, a fast, turbulent river, which in late summer and fall looks rather like a large trout stream, shallow except for the main channel, and strewn with rocks and boulders. It's wonderfully inviting water for a sport fisherman after trophy trout but tricky to treacherous for someone running up it for the first time, even if the boat is equipped with a jet-propulsion outboard instead of a deeper-draft propeller.

There were no cottages with docks and people along its banks to offer assistance should something happen. The only human presence was a crude camp of plywood shacks run by Big John Pierson. He catered to sportsmen of means from around the world who hoped to land a record-breaking rainbow or arctic grayling. I had

heard that Big John, a famous character in Bristol Bay, enjoyed out-
fishing his clients and opened his camp for business only when he
needed money, which would be after one of his jaunts in Seattle,
where reputedly he could go through ten or twenty thousand dollars in a week or two. The summer I hit the Agulowok, and vice
versa, the camp was closed.

This was after my first season of commercial salmon fishing
with partner Les VanDevere on my little misfit boat, the *Port N
Storm*. I had successfully run *Port N Storm* up the Wood River
from Nushagak Bay to Lake Aleknagik and was feeling pretty
confident, even cocky, about running up rivers, neglecting to consider that at any season the Wood River was much deeper and
broader than the Agulowok.

I was to meet with the FRI guys at their Aleknagik headquarters and follow them up to Nerka. Then after they left for Washington State in a week or so I would await the arrival of my family
from upstate New York. In the meantime, the idea was for me to
learn about their lab and what my duties were to be as winter
man.

I anchored *Port N Storm* in a protected cove just down from
their buildings. It drew too much water for the Agulowok, so I
would take one of their twelve-foot fiberglass boats up, following the other four. Why they didn't think to put the sixth man in
my boat, just in case—considering I had never run the wild river
before—I can't say. Maybe he was buddies with one of the others,
and they wanted to travel together, or maybe they assumed that
since I was a Bristol Bay salmon fisherman I couldn't possibly get
into trouble on water, not knowing how much trouble I had gotten
into on water.

Be that as it may, the flotilla was bouncing along on the main
channel's rollers about halfway up the river when my outboard
started losing power. In the strong current I dropped back fast.
Then the engine quit altogether and the river grabbed the boat and
I was being taken back at its mercy, which was nil. The boat swung

broadside and looked to be heading toward a stretch of rapids, white water boiling over black rocks. The roar of the river crashing against the boulders was as unnerving to me at that moment as would be the roar of a charging grizzly bear.

My mind accelerated: I must have sucked some gravel up into the jet, having strayed too far from the deeper channel while distracted by the red line of spawning salmon moving up through the shallows. The other boats were nowhere in sight, gone around the bend. I couldn't reach the engine's intake by tilting it out of the water. To clear the jet I would have to go over the side into the rollicking water, which was likely to result in drowning.

The boat was picking up speed, making good time toward eternity. There was no anchor nestled in the bow, which I considered a serious oversight on their part, though I doubt it or its line could have held against the powerful current anyway. Then, at a bend just above the rapids, the river smashed the boat into a cut-bank (a bank the current had somewhat hollowed out) and I grabbed hold of a stout alder overhead, almost getting jerked out of the boat. I lost some flesh and the alder gained some blood, but I hung on and managed to drag the bowline to me with my foot and tied up to the alder. The boat swung around facing into the current. I glanced upstream. Not another boat in sight.

With the outboard tilted up, I got out of my boots and pants and went over the side. The water was up to my chest, strong as a bull and cold as hell's ninth icy pit, but I grasped the gunwale hard and edged back to the stern and managed to clear the jet. If I had lost my hold, the water's force would have swept me into the rocks and boulders, and that would have been all she wrote. Back in the boat, I pulled my pants and boots on and felt warmth returning. It was a clear, sunny day. The outboard, almost new, started right up. I untied from the alder and swung into the current, being very careful this time to nose into the water of deepest blue.

My Alaska adventure could have ended that day, as, really, it could have ended on any number of days and nights while commercial fishing. It will become apparent that this cat had more than nine lives to be put at risk.

When I left the river and entered the lake another thought troubled my mind. Nerka was a very big lake, stretching out before me into the distant haze. It was shaped something like a boomerang or bent arm, about seventy-five miles long from tip to tip and anywhere from a mile to three miles wide. The FRI station, I knew, was located near the center, at the "elbow." But what I didn't know was whether I would be able to spot it across the expanse of water. It could be tucked away in a cove, in which case I might sail right on by, not realizing I was now scooting down the lake's upper arm. I could go on searching until I ran out of gas and then just hope that they would find me, since I hadn't found them. But I saw a white spot ahead, which quickly became a boat. One of them must have noticed that there were only four boats on the water, deduced that I was not among them, and was now backtracking to find out what had happened to me, ex post facto.

He waved and I waved back. Then I opened the throttle and caught up with him, following in his wake, determined not to let him out of my sight. Which was good policy because the station was indeed inside a small bay and could easily have been missed. I would have found no one anywhere around the lake to give me directions, not even the Coast Guard or the Boy Scouts.

There were the four white boats, plus a couple of weathered-looking gray skiffs, beached in front of a complex of four or five log buildings. Behind them, the mountains rose steeply from forested slopes to the stubble of alder and willow and on up to bare rock ragged against the sky. This was a long ways, in distance and in time, from the gentle hills, cultivated fields, and closed-in skies of upper New York State, from which I had lately come. It had the feel of another world, vast and open, with a wild tang to the air itself. That now I would be living for almost a year in such a place, in primal wilderness, bolstered my heart, straightened my spine, and strengthened my legs as I stood at the tiller and headed in.

All but one of the buildings were prefabricated, Lincoln-log-type structures. The exception was an old-time weathered cabin that appeared to be in good shape. It fronted the approach, at the center of the complex. This was the mess hall and headquarters of the station. It had one big room and two medium-sized bedrooms. The main room featured a long table and a huge cast-iron oil stove for heating and cooking, plus a large, sophisticated-looking two-way radio system in the corner. The cabin, like most old-timers, was low-slung, with double-paned windows, and was insulated: It would hold heat in and keep cold out.

This would be our home for the next nine or ten months, and I felt good about it. The worn linoleum on the floor was an eyesore, but Carol and the kids would be secure, even comfortable here. That was especially important because Carol would be arriving with our newest daughter Beth in her arms, just three months old, whom I had yet to see and hold. I had been doing a lot of wondering and a little worrying about the anticipated hardships and perils of solitary wilderness life as regards the welfare of my wife and children. More than once I had been ready to chuck the whole idea because of those concerns, given my inexperience. The FRI station was very reassuring, an ideal setup for easing into this new life.

One afternoon when the FRI crew were off doing their fisheries work I enjoyed a bit of solitude in the cabin. I sat on the old couch by the window, the sun coming in warm on my lap. The still air harbored no distant sound of traffic, no annoying utilities clicking on and off, only the quiet rippling of water on the gravel beach outside. The immense silence of the land settled over me with a kind of hush, almost like an embrace, and the feeling came like a whisper that we were on the verge of something very good, something a million years had formed us for: that we were coming home. I was sure life in the woods would bring us even closer together as a family, working and playing together, not hurrying off on scattered tangents, as typically happens with families Outside. It would smooth away the rough spots in my marriage as Carol and I were released from the nervous stresses and strains germane to mainstream society. And it would afford my kids, removed from all the rabid voices and images assaulting consciousness back there, the chance to grow up without severe distortions of their human nature. Sitting there, I sensed how simple and slow life was in the silence at the core of existence, so different from the complexities and frenetic noisiness of the cities and suburbs. I felt the difference passing through me as a seeping away of tensions, an easing of the mind. I had read about this in the works of poets and novelists, and now I was feeling it. What siren song of worldly goods could compare with the sound of this silence?

The risks and dangers, the hardships? They were part of it. Essential to it really. The good life of wild nature had always been risky and a little rough around the edges. And security, which people seem so desperately to crave, what was it but an illusion, a will-o'-the wisp luring ever deeper into the quagmire of fear—subliminal fear, the unrecognized substrate of alienated existence, even among the people of the richest, most powerful nation in the world. The quest for security is itself the breeding ground of insecurity. Security be damned. Better to go boldly with the prompting of your own heart. Present fears are less than horrible imaginings. (I think Shakespeare wrote that.) Worry is a fool's game anyway. As a Taoist sage once remarked, we don't know enough to worry. Yes, yes . . . but nevertheless, and despite all this good philosophy, I did worry at times about taking my family into the wilderness, and I did want them to feel secure, to be able to commit to this new life without abiding fear, although I knew they never could *be* secure, except in the ultimate sense that every hair is numbered, like every grain of sand. Human beings either have this faith—which is much more than a system of beliefs and moral mandates—bone-deep faith in the beauty, truth, and goodness of the cosmos, or they live in fear. I was to be confronted with this stark reality shortly, right there on Lake Nerka.

The FRI gang were all good lads, college kids, a couple in

graduate school, studying to be fisheries biologists, all familiar American types to me, the English professor. They wore the usual jeans and plaid shirts, and all but Burgner and one other fellow sported full beards, their insignia of roughing it in the wilds. We got on well, and they explained how I was to measure and weigh each fish caught through the ice, take certain of the scales and also the entrails, preserving them in a solution and labeling each jar as to where and when the particular fish species was caught. I was also to keep a daily record of the weather, temperature highs and lows, barometric pressure, and so forth. It was all easy enough and as far as I was concerned a very good deal, keeping such records in exchange for the privilege of wintering in wilderness without undue risk and hardship for my family, on a trial basis, as it were.

It was moose season. Carol and the kids would be arriving in Dillingham in about a week. I wanted to bag a moose before they came. Not that we would need "winter meat," as natives and backwoodsmen call it. I had money for food. But I wanted to show Carol that if we moved into the woods permanently, when maybe we wouldn't have money, I could feed the family. In bush Alaska meals are built around fish and game, mainly moose meat.

The whole money thing—the indirect purchase of subsistence through numbers, abstractions, and the soul-numbing means of accumulating those numbers, wage slavery—I hated, it was such a travesty of human nature. I wanted the real thing. I wanted to live as nearly as possible directly out of the natural world, as our kind had lived for 99.9 percent of our time on earth. Hunting had always been a big part of it. In 1964 I didn't know about the population bomb or ecological disasters or endangered species. I didn't have the impression back then of humankind as a burgeoning locustlike horde consuming more and more of the earth and its wildlife. It seemed there was a lot of wild land and wild animals left and that a family could go back quite a ways into the old life.

Burgner gave me the okay to use one of the older skiffs for a couple of days for the hunt, an eighteen-foot river skiff with about six feet of the bow decked over, powered by a thirty-five-horsepower outboard. It wasn't an ideal rig for a lake as big as Nerka, which can get very rough, because a river skiff's bottom is flat—fine for flat, shallow water but torturous and risky in any kind of chop. But the weather had been mild, the lake placid, and I was raring to go. Yet not so raring that I would go unprepared for the sudden arrival of a predicament, most likely materializing in the form of a blow. I was green but not incapable of learning lessons. I stowed some provisions under the bow deck—extra clothing, a sleeping bag and pad, sandwiches, and a sack of smoked salmon a native pal had given me in Dillingham, along with my Winchester 30.06 with four-power tip-off scope and .22 handgun for small game.

I had in mind an episode that had occurred in 1963 on our first trip to Alaska. Steve and I wanted to explore Halibut Cove across Kachemak Bay from Homer as a possible place to live if and when we ever moved to Alaska. We got caught out in the middle of the bay in a small boat by a big wind and wound up stranded on a stretch of deserted coastline for three days until the storm lifted. My Boy Scout training—Be prepared!—had made the difference between miserably surviving and surviving in good shape, for I had brought along a twelve-gauge pump shotgun, blankets, a tarp, and some food, "just in case." I was learning and remembering.

But what threatened me on this hunting trip, as it turned out, was something other than a physical predicament—although there was a bit of that too, because within a couple of hours of my leaving the FRI station at dawn, cruising down the lake's upper arm scanning the shore for moose, the sky darkened and a wind came up, driving a hard rain right down the lake and into my face. The waves built up quickly and started white-capping. I was taking a pounding, the bow lifting and then belly-whopping down hard, dousing me with spray, even though I had throttled way down. I needed to find shelter from the storm. A mile or so farther down I spotted a break in the shoreline and eased over toward it, being careful not to broach to the oncoming waves. It was a small bay and the waves rode into it with me, but it curved around a point of land into a protected cove that was almost flat calm, just some ripples coming in. A pair of swans took off, honking and rising on powerful wings, whooshing overhead into the wind. I cut the engine and nosed into shore.

The wind bristled through the treetops and I could hear the waves breaking along the beach outside the bay, but right where I was it seemed very still and quiet. I slipped the Winchester's sling over a shoulder and stepped out onto the shore. Heart-shaped moose tracks pockmarked the sand and then I saw bear prints, big ones, the claw marks still showing. A grizzly, and fairly recently, or the rain would have muddled the tracks. I was glad to see the moose sign. I could be hunting right there while I waited for the blow to pass. The grizzly prints put me on special alert but didn't trouble me. I had a good rifle, loaded with 220-grain shells with Magnum stopping power, and I was a good shot and had a track record of remaining calm in a tight spot. In close quarters requiring fast action the scope would be a handicap, so I tipped it off to the side out of the way of the iron sights and continued my still hunt around the cove. If I had to spend the night, I'd anchor out in the middle, where brer bear would be unlikely to bother me.

When I got back to the skiff a couple of hours later dusk was approaching. The rain had let up but the sky was still roiling with dark clouds, the wind sweeping through the treetops. I climbed aboard and sat with the rifle across my lap, facing upwind. Dusk was a good time to wait for moose to come to the water to feed.

The scene before me was very beautiful. The leaves of the white birch had turned mostly golden, with some greens still showing. They glowed like sunbursts against the dark sky. The underbrush was a medley of russets, purples, reds of every shade, and here and there lit up splashes of lime. It was as though all through the summer the trees and bushes had been gathering in the sun and were now giving it back, so that even at dusk of a dark day they seemed bathed in sunlight. The wind tore through the trees in showers of gold, and the soft patter of falling leaves all around me was like the sound of rain on a roof.

While still-hunting along the shore (walking quietly instead of taking a stand), I was aware of all this beauty and thought I must be some kind of royalty whose way was being strewn with splendor. At one point I stopped and looked up at the leaves twirling and streaking down to the dark earth, as if eager to get to "their final resting place," as some would have it, a touch of sadness and regret in the phrase. But I sensed none of that, no sadness or regret, as I watched them. They had put on their most gorgeous colors for the occasion, and I thought that if this is dying they don't seem to mind. Dying, for them, seemed . . . jubilant. I wrote in my mind words I still remember: ". . . and in ecstasy the yellow leaves let loose from their summer moorings and sailed away into a deep but dazzling darkness." Then on the heels of that some lines from Zen came to me: If you don't believe, look at September, look at October, the yellow leaves falling, falling.

Just like us, some poets and mystics say: We come into this world trailing clouds of glory and go out in a blaze of glory (or used to, a very long time ago). But certainly this is true of the salmon, turning a rich red to die, their spawning as much a death as a birth, their dying so obviously a consummation giving rise to new life. The prevalent "horror of the shades" revulsion and fear about death among us is so strong we refuse to talk or even think about it. But this dismal view of a primary fact of existence is simply a product of our alienated mentality, not a reality of nature. The reality was everywhere apparent, all around me a thousand voices speaking perfectly loud. It was a pleasure to think that these voices prevailed for hundreds of square miles in all directions from where I stood. The tinny voices of true insanity were far away.

All that day heading down the lake I had felt myself the proud hunter, an Indian or Eskimo immersed in a world resonant with these voices. There were no other sounds competing, not a sign of civilization anywhere. All the lakes and rivers, forests and mountains, were purely themselves, immaculate, unadulterated. Formally speaking, this region was a "park," a land subdued for human uses like hiking and picnics. But "park" is just a word. This country didn't feel like any park. It was untamed and powerful. You couldn't look it in the eye and say "nice doggie." It was wolf, not dog.

Back in New York State when roving the hills hunting I always felt comfortably at home. Pastures, cornfields, wood lots, the line of a country road winding in the distance, farmhouses with lights coming on in the evening as I headed back down to my house and family—all familiar, bucolic, friendly, and human-hearted. But as I sat now gazing at the thrashing trees across the cove, the dusk deepening, the warm colors fading, I felt a kind of chill coming over me—not a physical chill, my body was warm enough, but a chill around the heart, a strange failing, a sinking away of courage. Something was frightening me. Not the possibility of a bear or things that go bump in the night. I was easy about that. No, a feeling of emptiness, almost of dread. A state of funk, subtle and amorphous, had come over me like some kind of nerve gas. I felt unaccountably blank, cut off and isolate, lonely and afraid. Everything I looked at, the windswept sky, the shimmering foliage, the brownish shallow water and leaning grasses, all such that I had assumed to be that mother to whose fond care mankind must return, stood before me now as a faceless meaningless presence. It meant nothing to me, I had no connection to it. It was out there as on the other side of a thick glass wall. A blankness of numb emptiness froze me motionless.

Something other was out there, some uncanny power, an alien entity. It offered no comfort. It offered nothing, no connection, no meaning. It was inscrutable and somehow terrifying despite its great beauty and the ordinary circumstances, simply a man moose hunting on a windy day . . . like in James's *The Turn of the Screw,* the specter of the redheaded man seen across the lovely lawn in broad daylight by the new governess watching her from the parapet, then turning away and walking off and disappearing, leaving the air charged with terror.

The oppressive vacuity stayed with me for hours, well into the night. I couldn't shrug it off and I couldn't think my way out of it. My thoughts, my understanding of nature and mankind's place in it, were as useless as toys by the bedside of a sick child. I didn't belong in wilderness. I was too far gone, too blighted by the diseased mentality of civilization. I was no longer at home in the natural world; it was other, forbidding. Whatever had I been thinking, to want to leave everything for this? Sheer wilderness would shrivel my soul. Daniel Boone had been found after months alone in the wilderness lying on his back in a sunny glade singing away at the top of his lungs, jubilantly at home. But my spiritual compass was broken and I was lost. I needed people and lights and talk around me protecting my skinny little ego world. I couldn't handle a naked encounter with . . . this inhuman thing. I wasn't strong enough, right enough, for it. —Was this the sort of thing, personified as Satan, that Jesus overcame when in the wilderness?

And then suddenly, coming from God knows where, I remembered something. It came to me in a rush, like a wind. Something like this had happened to D. H. Lawrence! To a genius, a man of profound spirituality and courage! Yes! In *Kangaroo,* the passage where he walks into the Australian bush on a moonlit night and senses a presence that makes the hair on his neck stand rigid with horror. The awesome spirit of the land. What the Aborigines, the Pygmies, all the Indians and Eskimos were aware of, with dread reverence. What shamans could enter in trance and return from with power to heal. Except for the great mystics and artists, civilized people had lost that direct connection, lost that awareness, their religions secondhand affairs merely pounding the pulpit of moral mandates. Their consciousness has been captured and tied to words, symbols, an abstract mental world. And wasn't there a character in Conrad's *Nostromo* who, isolated in the jungle too long, for like causes became demented and finally killed himself to escape the nullity?

With these thoughts rushing through my mind, reassuring me that great artists knew of, had even experienced, these metaphysical horrors, the awful feelings began to lift. I wasn't alone with this, wasn't the only alienated man in the world feeling his alienation, hitherto unsuspected, as awful, in some way shameful. I had come to some understanding. Maybe what these metaphysical horrors signified was that at least I wasn't dead, wasn't dead to the world of spirit, the Great Mystery, the *Mysterium Tremendum,* embodied in nature. Even if this contact was like a bum trip it *was* contact. Most modern people would have sensed nothing, experienced no tremors of alienation. Their sensibilities were closed off by what Blake called "single vision and Newton's sleep." Better to be shook with terror than to sense nothing. As they say in Tierra del Fuego, Fool who know he fool not altogether fool.

I was all right now, the horror gone like a broken fever. I had found out something important, glimpsed the depth of alienation in myself concealed by the veils of words I hadn't realized were veils. The words were good, pointing me in the right direction, but they needed to be proven upon the pulses of direct experience. A bum trip can be very instructive. This day I had been confronted by the threshold guardians and in some curious way had met their challenge and they had withdrawn. One day, I felt, we would meet on better terms, and I would become famous among the trees, a clear favorite. I meant to stay the course.

The enfolding darkness had now become a comfort, the wind in the trees and pattering leaves a personal pleasure. I reached for my pack and found the smoked salmon and sat there for a while munching on it—a good batch, not too sweet or salty. Then I stepped out of the skiff, pushed off from shore, and hopped back in. I drifted to about the middle of the cove and dropped the hook. I spread out the sleeping bag under the plywood deck and, feeling suddenly very tired, went to sleep listening to the leaves whispering.

The next morning broke fair. With a mild following breeze I cruised the opposite shoreline heading back but spotted only one cow, who stood watching me go by. My family was due into Dillingham in a couple of days. I would catch a ride in with Burgner the next day. In a way, I was glad I didn't get a moose, because now I could go a-hunting with my son Steve. It would be his first big-game hunt, and I'd let him do the shooting if we lucked into one.

I never spoke of the metaphysical horrors to anyone until years later. I was to learn many lessons of survival through those years and enjoy many adventures, but the realization of my spiritual alienation remained quietly in the back of my mind, in private. I would watch for its recurrence or, hopefully, its disappearance.

Dillingham in the early sixties was a cannery town, a fisherman's town. Salmon fishing was its reason for being and therefore, small as it was in size and population, it featured two bars, the Sea Inn and the Willow Tree, each one the real center of town. Alaskan fishermen, like fishermen everywhere, were tireless consumers of adult beverages. The bars did very well through the fishing season, better than most of the fishermen even in a good year, which in those days averaged one or two out of every five. In the good years they drank to celebrate their munificence and in the bad years to drown their sorrows. There were no bad years for the bars.

The main drag was a gravel road that ran through the town and out to the airfield. I didn't say airport. It was a big weedy field with a few runways and a small building with a row of plastic chairs shiny enough to suggest modernity. I stood outside restlessly waiting for the plane from Anchorage to come in with my family. It had been only four months since I had been with them day in and day out, but when I saw them one after the other emerging from the airplane it was as though we had been apart for years, and the sight of them, so familiar and dear, was like the day when all my dreams came true. First Steve, on the verge of turning fifteen. His eyes flew to me and his great big Alfred E. Newman smile lit up his face. Then Jon and Sally, together as usual, Jon just six and Sally pushing five. Jon's darker hair was mussed up and, sure enough, his tie was askew and a button missing from his cuff. That was the appearance he always made stepping down from the school bus at our drive, looking around from inside himself, taking his own counsel. Sally, with her round face, rosy cheeks, and blond hair, together with her wide blue eyes and dark eyebrows tilting up in an expression of pure innocence, looked like she was about to step into wonderland. Behind them, pausing on the top step, Carol, trim as a coed in a dress, stockings, and heels (still, after all the years, the pleasure I took in her nicely turned legs!), with the bundle in her arms that was baby Beth.

Jon and Sal ran up to me and I had my arms around them both, Jon almost managing a smile, Sally lifting up to kiss my cheek. Steve, so much the big brother, stood looking on beaming, his hand resting on Jon's shoulder. How was the trip? Did it all go smoothly? Beth slept most of the way?! And so on, the usual questions and answers, and everyone smiling. Then a kiss for Carol. I saw she had put on makeup, and I smiled to myself. Her familiar scent and the hint of perfume were keen in my nostrils and got the hormones firing off right on cue. So now, the brand-new little Durr child, so tiny, so light in my arms—and cute, at three months having passed out of the wrinkled old lady look of the newborn. We were a tight family. They all seemed to me so fine. I was always proud to be with them. I hear men and women today speak of the burden kids can be, and the expense, as if their imaginations were capable of entertaining other possibilities for their lives. But for me then it wasn't a matter of choosing, as though there were options. Family was to me like water to a fish, the medium in which I lived, quite unconscious of the fact. I never thought about it; it was simply life and there was no outside to it.

Jay Stovall, a seasoned bush pilot, would fly us from Dillingham directly to the FRI station on Nerka in his Cessna 180 on floats. He would also bring in a planeload of supplies, mostly food staples—flour, rice, sugar, canned vegetables, powdered milk, and the like. Steve and I would bag a moose; I was sure of that. And there would be plenty of fish and small game like spruce chickens, ptarmigan, ducks, and snowshoe hares. For a while yet we could pick fresh fruit like blueberries, salmon berries, the "watermelon" berries, and maybe raspberries. High-bush cranberries were plentiful and could be made into a vitamin-rich drink when crushed and the juice strained out; water and sugar must be added to get the right consistency and because otherwise the juice would be too tart. Healthy foods. The kids would grow up strong.

Moving in was simply a matter of stowing our things away. Pots and pans, cutlery, dishes, bedding, and so forth, were already on hand. There was even a rudimentary clothes washer powered by a gasoline generator. We couldn't have asked for a smoother transition from suburb to wilderness, and I knew it. What I didn't know was that things would be radically different when we moved into wilderness on our own.

Carol, with her woman's sense of practicalities and mother's concern for safety, saw that the station passed muster on these counts (though she harbored doubts about such things as bears and cantankerous moose in the rut, not to mention wolves, wolverines, and lynx; she would have to keep close watch on Jonny and Sally). She had trusted her "Great White Leader"—the somewhat sarcastic title she sometimes applied to me—and so far it looked good. She was here, her husband and children with her, the setup fine. She was ready to join in the adventure. I often found myself marveling at the spirit of adventure investing the slight frame of "my little woman." She had been born and raised in a quiet, staid neighborhood in Queens by conservative middle-class parents whose most daring adventure had been to move into their present quarters from a house three blocks away. Her mother barely escaped a nervous breakdown, the move had been so traumatic for her. But Carol just kept getting stronger as she entered deeper into bush life.

On his last trip in, after handing the boxes of food out to Steve and me, Stovall stood on the pontoon by the open door of the plane.

"Spotted a moose coming in," he said. "Looked like a pretty good-sized bull. Standing in an open glade."

"We're in the market," I said quickly. "Where's he at, Jay?"

Steve and I in hip boots held on to the pontoons, looking up at Jay.

"He's up on a little plateau like, on that first big mountain, just past the second point of land going down. There's a small cove, and he's right up above on the open plateau." He paused. "He's not a moose I'd go after." Jay was a little portly, and pilots generally were averse to grunt work. "Too goddamn much work," he said, grinning. "But he's there if you want him that bad."

I glanced at Steve, and smiled at the excitement in his eyes. "We're on our way," I said to Jay. He nodded, grinning. *Chechakos!* (Greenhorns.) "Good luck," he said, then turned and climbed into the plane. We gave him a good shove out on the pontoons. He started the engine and faced into the wind, gunning it. He lifted off fast because of the good headwind.

Within half an hour Steve and I were ready. Carol had heard the talk about how mean-tempered the bulls could get during the mating season and cautioned us to be careful. If we weren't back by nightfall she would call Jay to bring up the marines. Jon and Sal stood by watching everything, picking up on the excitement. Their father and brother looked sort of heroic stepping into the skiff with their big guns, going after a *moose.*

"Okay, okay," I replied to Carol. She stood on the beach with wind blowing her hair, holding on to Jon and Sal, Beth sleeping snug in our big bed. It was getting late in the day. She didn't like seeing us heading out.

One pull on the cord started the outboard and we roared off full throttle. We didn't want that bull to amble away.

In about ten minutes we passed the two points, found the cove, and nosed in. There was only enough light left, if we nailed him, to gut him and get back to the station before dark, so we had taken just our rifles and hunting knives. We'd go back the next morning with extra knives, sharpening stone, hacksaw, and rope to do the skinning and butchering, and bring pack-boards for carrying the quarters down to the boat.

We didn't give a thought to the hard labor that would be involved. We were both in good shape and eager for the hunt. We weren't worried about sweat and strain and tough going. In a way, that's what we were there for: to do as men anciently had done and to prove capable of doing it. I wouldn't have wanted a guide and packers even if they had been available. This wasn't a safari to chalk up a kill on our scorecard. This was a family affair, a subsistence hunt for winter meat—and a test of our abilities.

The climb up was very hard going, not only steep but through dense alders and patches of devil's club, both formidable opponents of easy going. Alders are gnarled, stout as a man's forearm, and grow in every direction but straight up. We had to duck under some branches, step over others, and in places bull our way through, getting scraped or knocked by a branch. Devil's club are accurately named. Like alder, they grow and twist in every direction, making it tricky to sneak through a patch of them. And sneak you must, because if you were foolish or ignorant enough to try to wade right through, two things would befall you. First, you would be pricked through your clothing by the needle-sharp thorns covering every inch of the big plant, even the one- or two-foot leaves. Second—and here's where "club" applies—the stalks are stiff but springy, and should you step on one in passing, when released it will snap back up and club you, driving home dozens of the thorns.

As if all these features weren't devilish enough, the thorns carry with them some sort of toxin, so that even after you've plucked them out of your flesh each wound will remain red, swollen, and painful for days.

Alaskans show great respect for devil's club and if possible give them wide berth. Steve and I did the best, most respectful job we could maneuvering through them when we couldn't go around them, but for several days after this hunt we picked out embedded thorns and tended infected wounds. You seldom encounter such difficulties when passing down the aisle of a supermarket to select your steaks and roasts, and understandably most people prefer it that way. Which is fortunate because otherwise there would be no wild woods left. But me, I'll take the alder and devil's club every time and the smell of the earth under the light rain and the rightness of exerting my power to garner our dinner wild and free on the hoof and in my mind knowing that this was primal bedrock truth. Truth is one way of naming what we crave.

Breathing hard, we reached the leveling-off place on the mountain. After moving through some woods as quietly as possible we stood at the edge of a meadow or glade about the size of a football field. It was empty. But the bull could be nearby among the trees, in the thick brush. Despite their size moose can disappear into their habitat like phantoms. We moved slowly along the edge of the glade toward the trees at its far end, the tundra spongy underfoot, the air fragrant with it. It had been drizzling, so the damp tundra made no sound. Near the fringe of trees we stopped and listened, scanning the brush. Nothing.

But this surely was the general area where Jay had spotted the bull. He could be close. Was he downwind and turned toward us, feeling a little (or a lot) cantankerous about our intrusion, our human scent aggravating his nostrils? We went on through the trees and there was another glade before us but still no moose in evidence. Rifles at the ready, we stepped cautiously out into the open. Steve was several yards to the left and a little ahead of me.

Suddenly, near the trees and brush at the far end of the glade, he dropped to his knee, staring ahead intently. I did the same, though I saw nothing. Steve kept glancing over at me, and I knew he had seen something. What else but the bull? I stayed frozen in place and watched him, not daring to speak. I was sure this would be a close encounter.

Here Steve describes what was unfolding before his young eyes:

I heard a branch snap and went down on a knee instinctively. And then the brush was moving and within thirty yards of me and all at once the huge head of a bull moose emerged, antlers wet and glistening. It seemed my breathing and the thumping of my heart must be loud enough to spook him. But he appeared totally unaware of the two of us crouched in the open so close to him and I was thinking even Mr. Magoo would have spotted us. Then I heard a sound several yards ahead of him and glimpsed the head of a cow through the brush. Aha! This bull had something on his mind other than the possibility of hunters. We had caught him way off guard.

I would have had a decent neck shot just then, but I hesitated. I didn't want to blow it. I'd wait until he moved out a bit and showed his flank. I glanced over at Dad. He was staring in the direction of the cow but seeing neither her nor the bull following her and I was wishing I could tell him what was happening so all the hard decisions wouldn't be up to me. The bull started up a small knoll. If he went over the top he'd be gone, but most of him was still hidden by the brush. I wished I didn't have to make up my mind whether to risk a shot or not. He was moving really slow and my heart was pounding really hard. I almost wanted him to hear it and bolt and end the suspense.

I was on the verge of making a run at him when he turned slowly toward the clearing. Either luck was with me or fate was against him. He was still in the brush but moving toward an opening. Another few feet! "He's gonna cross!" my voice said in my head and I flicked off the safety. Then he stepped out into the open. He was huge, powerful-looking, bigger than I'd ever imagined. I admired him for a second even as I lined up on him. I was glad I hadn't tried for the neck because the barrel of my rifle looked like it had the palsy. I held on his flank and squeezed the trigger and BAM! the silence was shattered and he went right down. I'll never forget watching him fall. Like in slow motion his front legs buckled and he seemed to look in my direction, searching for what had hit him so hard. Steam rolled out of his nostrils and he lay still.

One other thing that stays with me about this hunt was something I felt on the boat ride back after we'd gutted the moose (which Dad will describe following this). As the skiff slapped its way along the tops of the waves, sending plumes of spray into the cold night air, I knew something in me had changed. It wasn't just because of the moose. It was these dark mountains looking down on us. It was this wild lake beneath us. Just two weeks ago I'd been engaged in a deadly serious discussion with a few of my high school buddies back in Morrisville, New York, concerning the pressing issue of whether brown or black shoes would be "in" this year.

When I heard Steve shoot I was at a loss for an instant, worried that he was at a loss too and shooting blind, since I hadn't seen anything. Maybe a wounded animal on our hands, and the light fading. Then he yelled, "I got him! I got him!" He sprang to his feet and started running. I followed and when I reached him he was looking down at a very fine bull with a perfect rack. Excitedly, he told me everything that had happened. A flush of pride went through me. He had stayed cool in a hot situation, made all the right decisions on his own, and brought home the bacon. I was tempted to dip my finger in the blood and stripe his forehead and cheeks, as I'd read natives used to do to honor a young man's first big-game kill, but settled for a congratulatory handshake and some snapshots. People of our time don't have the rituals anymore that would give expression to the sacramental nature of existence, and that is a great deficit in modern life.

Then, since a moose is more than the shooting, we set about the job of gutting the thousand-pound animal. This must be done and the chest cavity opened to the cooling air without too much delay, especially during the rut, or some of the meat might spoil. It would be hard, bloody work. But first we stood another minute or so looking down at him, feeling the strangeness of being so close to him, able to touch him, this awesome creature of the wild. I thought of how the Indians honored their downed game and thanked it for giving its life for their lives—and how horrified they'd be by a modern stockyard and slaughterhouse, how it would be to them an unthinkable sacrilege to treat animals that way, as mere meat, commodities, machine-slaughtered without respect. My family would know better. Steve knew better right now, on the eve of his fifteenth birthday. This was something important he wouldn't be taught in school.

It took Steve and me a couple of hours to do the job on his moose. For the last hour or so it was quite dark, so the one of us holding the flashlight could contribute only one hand to the effort. We were both bloody and wet, some of the blood being our own, as we had cut our hands a few times working by flashlight deep inside the chest cavity, up to our wrists in warm, sticky blood. The innards of a big bull moose form a pile about the size of an armchair, and because we had punctured the stomach and intestines in the bad light, enough fresh-kill odor was being wafted into the airways to alert the nostrils of any predator downwind. I was hoping there wasn't a bear sniffing the air in that direction.

It took a good portion of the strength we had left to push the mass of guts away from the carcass. We found the huge liver and heart, cut out the tongue, and put them in a plastic bag but decided to leave them until next day because we were too tired to tote anything but ourselves and our rifles down through the devil's club and alder to the boat.

Carol, who had begun to worry when we didn't show up by dark, was aghast at sight of her sanguine hunters, and Jon and

Sally stood back away from all the blood and our left hands wrapped in bandannas. We got out of our bloody clothes and laid them outside on the gravel beach for their first rinsing, since the drizzle had turned to rain. I was telling them how it had been, how Steve had handled the whole thing just right. Carol's eyes were shining with the kind of mute pride that anciently must have filled women's hearts when their men returned successful from the hunt. The primordial past is still present in us, underneath all the modern shit and shinola.

Then we washed up, ate, and went right to bed and directly to sleep. My last thoughts were that we had gotten our winter meat and that the fall temperatures were probably about right to age it for a week or two, after which it would start freezing. Perfect. I slept the sleep of the just, with both legs well stretched out. I had got some satisfaction.

A wind came up through the night. When I looked out at first light six-foot waves were white-capping into the bay and a hard rain was pelting the roof. I pulled the covers up and went back to sleep. The only thing you can do about weather is go with it, which is one of the reasons why I've always liked weather, any kind of weather, better than having to make up my mind about anything. Weather and I are like a couple dancing together, and I feel no discomfort playing the feminine part. A little passivity in the dance of life is good for men as well as for women.

The wind and driving rain kept up all day, and that was that. I'm not sure about Steve's young body, but I know mine was happy to sit around warm and dry waiting on the weather. It was cool outside, almost down to freezing, so I wasn't worried about the meat quickly spoiling, and the hide with its thick coat of hollow hairs would shed most of the rain. So I wasn't much concerned about the meat. Except for the possibility of a bear.

The possibility proved an actuality the next day when the wind and rain had stopped and we went after our meat. We reached the spot and were shocked to find that the moose was gone. But we were several yards off the mark. When we looked closer we saw patches of hide sticking out among clumps of tundra. Most of the carcass was covered with torn-up tundra. The work of a bear, no mistaking it. That's what they do after they've eaten their fill, intending to return for seconds when hungry again. The heart and liver were gone. I'd read a lot about moose and bears and Alaska, and another thing I knew about this situation was that the bear was probably close by in the brush watching over his cache of meat. Which was really, as far as we were concerned, our cache. Prudence would have advised a hasty retreat, but as Blake observed, Prudence is a rich, ugly old maid courted by incapacity. We felt we had capacity and determined to ignore the old hag. Steve would stand watch, rifle in hand, while I started skinning. If brer bear came for our meat he wouldn't live to regret it.

But there were a couple of things I didn't know then which I do now. An aroused bear could cover the distance from the brush to us with the speed of a charging lion, and even if Steve got off a fatal shot the bear could complete his mission and kill us both before he died. Years afterward I read a true account about three experienced Alaskans on a hunt who had just beached their boat when a grizzly charged. They had barely enough time for all three of them to get off accurate shots with high-powered rifles. They killed the bear, but not before the bear killed all three of them. Had I known these things at the time I might have found Prudence more attractive than Blake had portrayed her. I suppose we had beginner's luck and the bear wasn't in the bushes watching us with mounting rage. Or maybe the fact that we were actually taking his moose so consternated him he wound up intimidated, thinking we must be two horrendous hombres with special dispensation from the powers that be to keep a grizzly from a kill, as wolverines, for instance, have been known to drive wolves off a kill.

We took turns at first standing guard and skinning, but the bull was on his side and had to be rolled over to get at the rest of the hide. With our rifles close by we leaned into it but couldn't do it.

The antlers dug in and frustrated our efforts. So, off with his head! And that took two of us to accomplish, and so did the quartering. One of us held a hind leg out of the way while the other cut into the haunch trying to find the ball joint. So for most of the operation no one was standing guard. We weren't throwing caution to the winds; we were mindful of the bear, but there simply was no way one man could have done the job. (In the years since then I've cleaned out a few moose by myself with the help of a come-along, ropes, and some nearby trees.)

So we went about our business, huffing and puffing and taking our chances. I had long ago accepted the likelihood that wilderness would be dangerous. But life offers more kinds of death than by an angry bear defending what he considers his lucky bonanza. That was part of the natural scheme of things. Such a death would be, in a way, honorable—certainly preferable to measuring your life out in coffee spoons. This had something to do with our turning down the cautionary advice of dame Prudence.

A hindquarter of a bull will weigh in at better than a hundred pounds. We tied one onto a pack frame, and Steve helped me hoist it onto my back. I was a mature man still in his prime, with a lot more bulk of muscle than my fifteen-year-old son, so I carried the hindquarters down and he the front legs, which were considerably lighter. We made three round-trips, carrying our rifles each time. While I considered a deadly encounter with a bear an acceptable possibility of wilderness life, I had no intention of serving the two of us up gratis. That was never part of the deal among animals in the wild. You have to earn your dinner. Brer bear would have to take his chances with us, as we with him.

It was a balancing act going down with the loads on our backs, stooping under or leaning around the alder branches, the weight of the quarters wanting to carry us all the way in whatever direction we stooped or leaned. At the bottom of the descent each time we slipped out of harness and collapsed on the beach, breathing hard. But we had the boat loaded and it was growing dark. The hide and antlers would have to wait until the next day. We were very tired but felt very good. We had the meat and the bear didn't. The heart and liver he was welcome to, especially since he had been such a nice bear.

Carol laughed when we walked in the door. Heavy-eyed, slack-mouthed, and stoop-shouldered, we looked like a couple of cata-tonics about to lapse into a coma. Too tired to hang the meat, we left it in the boat covered with a tarp. In the morning we'd hang the quarters in the shed and go back for the hide and antlers. For now, we cleaned up, ate, and rested.

Steve looked at Jon and Sal standing there bright with interest, Jon with that little frown of absorbed concentration he often wore, Sal with eyebrows raised in a look of innocence so pure you could see blue sky in her eyes.

Steve fixed his gaze on them and in a serious, slightly ominous tone said, "There was a bear . . ."

He made me think of Coleridge's Ancient Mariner capturing the attention of the wedding guests. "There was a ship . . ." quoth he. No way could the wedding guests walk on by and join the fes-tivities. And no way could Jon and Sal let Steve stop there. They wanted the whole tale, and in detail. Steve was glad to oblige. Dur-ing the telling, Carol let out a little "Ooo" once in a while but sat listening, some concern showing. She knew of course that bears lived in Alaska, but to have to do with one so soon . . . what did that portend? The kids' eyes never left Steve's face through the whole story. They were there on the mountain, watching the bushes, holding their breaths. And the story of the hunt and the bear was told, as anciently such stories had always been told in family circles. TV could have nothing comparable to offer.

Before we went to bed, early, Jon made us promise to take him along next day. He wanted to be in on it, see for himself and help. He would carry the ax and saw. He was a skinny kid with spindly legs but stout determination.

"Ooo," said Carol, looking at him. "I don't know."

"It'll be okay," I said. "If the bear didn't challenge us today for the meat he won't tomorrow for the hide. Not out of spite either. A nice bear." I smiled reassuringly, the Great White Leader.

Bears would be a part of our life if and when we moved into the Alaska bush, and I wanted to head off any paranoia about them. That there were bears and wolves and moose and all the other wild animals in Alaska was a big reason for wanting to be there. What a sorry existence it would be to spend your whole life having to do only with hordes of hominids in a context of concrete, steel, glass, and for some, little bits of lawn, a life void of wild animals and devil's club and alder. Talk about deprivation!

As it happened, the most grueling pack down was with the hide. Few Alaskans bother with moose hide, but I wanted to do like the Indians and not waste any part of the animal. I figured that in the cold months ahead that big hairy skin laid out on the floor of the cabin would make a warm playground for baby Beth, which indeed it did even though it buckled as it dried and the hollow hairs broke off and sometimes wound up in inappropriate places like a stew.

I put Jon between Steve and me on the climb up. Those spindly legs were powered by his excitement to be in on it. He put his head down and scrambled up the steep ascent, slipping through the alder and devil's club easier and faster than we could. We didn't have to wait on him at any time. I was sure it was good for him to be there on this important mission. The bear thing was an extra excitement. He wasn't worried about the bear. He was with his father and big brother.

When we reached the site of the kill, Steve, who was ahead, pulled up short, staring down at the hide. He turned to me.

"Didn't we leave it hair side up?"

"Yes, hair side."

And then I saw why he had asked. It was skin side up—and there were several puncture holes in it that hadn't been there before. Whoa. Did that signify angry bear? And to be able to bite through a thick, tough moose hide! Obviously a bear could get a man's head in its jaws and pop it like a grape. Was this his way of signing off and letting us know what might have been had he not been such a nice bear? Well . . . not outside Disney.

Bears, grizzly bears particularly, are inscrutable, unpredictable. We stood with our safeties off our rifles and watched the brush. Out of the corner of my eye I saw Jon staring at the holes in the hide, trying to figure it out. Then he looked at Steve and me standing there watching the brush, rifles at the ready. If his boy's attention had wandered about before, now it was focused. We stood waiting for several minutes but then relaxed. Nice bear: "No hard feelings. You're welcome to the moose." Or whatever. The fact was he left us alone.

The hide was big and green and wet with rain. It weighed a ton. Probably too much for any one man. How to get it down to the boat? Back in New York deer hunters sometimes carried a deer out hanging from a pole between two men, which really wasn't a good tactic because the weight of the deer swinging turned walking into staggering. So we cut down and trimmed two small spruce trees for poles, placed the folded hide on them, and tied it down. We'd have to make another trip for the antlers, which also were heavy and awkward to tote through the alder and devil's club. We lifted the poles to our shoulders and started off with Jon in front so we could keep an eye on him. But then there were the alders, hard enough for one unencumbered man to navigate, impossible for two with a load in tandem. We had descended only a few yards when an alder tripped Steve and he went down, a pole bruising his right shoulder pretty bad.

"Okay," I said. "I can take it. If we can get the pack-board up on my back, I can take it." Steve looked a little doubtful. "It's the best bet," I said. "Hell, it's all downhill. Gravity's on my side. If mothers can lift cars off their kids I can get this hide down to the boat. This is the last big push. Steve, you take the rifles, and Jonny, you hang on to the ax and saw."

A father and his two sons working together. That was good; it was what I wanted for the family. Not living in separate worlds passing one another in orbit, but up close and together in the business of making a life.

I made it down to the boat on trembling legs and squirting adrenaline, and dropped down and lay back, still in harness, blown out and breathless. Steve helped me out of the shoulder straps. We loaded the hide into the boat and headed back, bouncing through the chop with the wind and spray in our faces. It was actually pretty cold, but we didn't mind. We felt good, strong for this life. The hunt was the first feather in the family cap.

I was always the first one out of bed in the morning. I would turn up the heat in the oil stove and start the coffee and bacon, then launch into my rendition of an old cowboy song, with lyrics revised to fit Alaska. I sang it every morning, good and loud, and the kids loved it. It was corny but it brought them out of bed smiling. It expressed the spirit of our adventure. It went like this:

When it's breakfast time in Alaska
And the wind [or ice, depending] is on the lake
How I long to be in Alaska
For myself and family's sake.

You can smell the bacon frying
As it's sizzling in the pan,
Hear the breakfast horn ["Get out of bed!"]
In the early morn,
Drinking coffee from a can.

Just a-hunting, fishing, trapping,
Riding snowshoes all day long,
Just a-hunting, fishing, trapping,
And we sing a happy song.

Once you try it
You'll say, Buy it!
And you'd work for any wage,
Just to be again
Where it's free again,
When the wind [ice] is on the lake.

By the end of the song they'd all be standing by the stove, Carol and Steve too, Beth in her mother's arms. At bedtime almost every night I sang them folk songs, accompanying myself on my old Martin guitar. There were always requests called out from the bedroom. When the requests stopped coming I knew they were asleep, and I'd join Carol and Steve at the long table. They might both be reading, or Carol might be sewing. At one point they got into cribbage with an intensity of concentration that evidenced the absence of distractions of the more exciting variety.

The light from the kerosene lamps was soft. We grouped a few of them together for any kind of close work or reading. I was on a sabbatical from Syracuse University and had been awarded a Guggenheim grant to write a book, so most nights I would be reading or writing. These were quiet hours. We were a quiet family. This low-keyed life seemed to suit us—as it had suited our forebears all the way back to the beginnings of time. We all slept well.

Outside, the trees were bare now, the underbrush sere and gray, with spatters of red from the high-bush cranberries. These berries never froze, and some of them clung to the branch right through the winter, wearing white caps. The days were shortening, the nights lengthening, the temperatures going down. All of which made the cabin cozier than ever. In that life, immersed in the elements, being warm and dry wasn't something beneath notice, taken for granted, as was the case back in that other mode of life we had left behind. When the wind blew hard, driving rain and, later, snow against the cabin, we felt, as Emerson had put it so well, "enclosed in the tumultuous privacy of storm."

Steve and I had the weather detail and ice fishing to attend to every day. That sent us outdoors regardless of what the weather was doing. And then too we went off on a lot of hunting and exploring excursions, more often than not with Jon tagging along on those tireless legs of his. The days blended one into the other, and we were never restless or bored. Steve and I believed we could spend the rest of our lives exploring into new territories and never tire of it, the land was so marvelous. Friends and relatives wrote and always wanted to know: But what do you do with yourselves? Don't you get bored to death with nothing to do? (No new movies or even TV, no mall shopping trips, no parties, not even the nine-to-five regimen . . .)

Besides the housework usual for a woman in those days, Carol put a lot of time into getting Steve and Jon through their correspondence-school lessons. I helped with the English studies. Jon was doing well, but Steve tended to be truant, which made Carol bristle at times. Then of course there was caring for Beth, still a very small bundle, who was beginning to scoot around pretty well, Carol after her. And the Saturday baths in the big galvanized washtub—good exercise pumping all that water by hand and filling and emptying the tub with buckets. Later, when the snows and deep cold came and Steve and I were bringing back snowshoe hares for the pot, she enjoyed sitting by the lamps and cutting and sewing liners for boots and mittens out of the hides we home-tanned (lye soap and lots of elbow grease). She liked working with her hands like that, being quiet and lost in her own thoughts. Jon and Sal had begun to complain of cold feet so she fashioned rabbit-skin booties for inside their mukluks, and they worked: no more cold feet. I could tell that Carol got more satisfaction out of having made those booties for Jon and Sal than she could ever have purchased from a catalog.

Spruce chickens through the fall were on our menu. Fattened on berries, the birds' breasts, tender and tasty, could be prepared in all the ways chicken can. In the winter they fed mainly on spruce needles and weren't nearly such good eating. These birds were easy to harvest once you put them up. Back in New York, the ruffed grouse, or partridge, would fly off like a rocket and were hard to hit even with a shotgun. But these northern cousins of the grouse, being ignorant of man and his thunder stick, just flew up to the branches of nearby trees, no doubt thinking themselves above harm. That's why they're called "fool hens" up here. We took them with .22s.

We were also able to catch all the fish we cared to eat, some through the ice for the FRI data, but before the lake froze over we discovered a munificent fishing hole. Around the bend from the station about a mile was a fiord named Amokok Arm. At its far end the arm was enclosed by rock cliffs coming straight down into deep water, but a short ways into the arm a creek descended through a draw and pushed into the lake. Very large arctic char lay off its mouth waiting for tidbits to come their way, and since they, like the spruce chickens, were unsophisticated about man's artificial devices they snapped at our lures without hesitation.

We'd stand on shore next to the creek and flip a spoon into the current and let out line as it was taken out and down. Almost the instant we closed the bail of the reel on our spinning rods and the line tightened and the lure started its wiggle we'd feel the weight and the dogged struggle of a big char. Once in a while it would be a two- or three-pound rainbow, and that would get us whooping as it fought hard, hurling itself flipping and flailing out of the water, showing its perfection of form—good fish with small heads and broad, deep bodies. We'd hand the bent and quivering rod to Jonny then and got a kick out of the serious concentration on his face as he fought to reel the rainbow in. These fish were excellent eating, fresh caught and cooked that very night. We put together a rig out of odds and ends and smoked some of the fish when we had more than we could eat fresh.

An abundance of fish and game were laid at our feet. You

would need a special endowment of stupidity and incompetence to go hungry in that country. I can't imagine why the Puritans had to be rescued from starvation by the Indians. America at that time, before there were enough white men to kill or pollute everything, teemed with fish and game.

The big treat every night was an hour's allotment of music over the two-way radio—"allotment" because the radio ran off deep-cycle batteries, recharged with a rather cranky small generator, and we had to conserve power for our nightly check-in with Jay or Katie Stovall in Dillingham. The music was broadcast all the way from Anchorage and the reception wasn't hi-fi, but we all listened in, sitting around the long table soaking it up like camels at an oasis. And that was something else about life in the silent places we were learning: Little things—little by the standards of city and suburb—became big. Small was beautiful, less was more, and lean was better than fat. Lots of silence and emptiness were the proper setting for the caw of a raven or the sound of wind—or music from Anchorage. You lose "the degrading thirst after outrageous stimulation" (Wordsworth) afflicting people back there in the gilded cage, thereby becoming rich by measure of how much you don't need or want. Fat cats tend to have hungry hearts, else they wouldn't have gotten fat.

The coming on of winter was exciting. I had read so much about the north country, "the land of ice and snow"—of temperatures falling through the bottoms of thermometers, snowstorms blotting out the lives of careless travelers, and cabins snowbound by ten-foot drifts—every hint of the Coldman's coming loomed large with excitement and a little apprehension: His breath was like a frigid mist rolling down from the mountains, their tops at first dusted with snow ("termination dust"), and with the days passing, the white line steadily reaching farther down and into the trees, snow settling finally on the yellow grasses and barren bushes, ice forming in every nook and cranny along the shore until by November the lake had frozen over, the snowstorms had turned the world white, and the Coldman stood astride the land like a colossus.

The varying, or snowshoe, hare and the ptarmigan had turned white as snow also and were invisible to the unpracticed eye at ten paces. All fauna had donned their winter coats of fur or feathers, the bears snug in their dens, the moose in their thick hides of hair, and we in our cabin. The cold deepened as the days shortened, at times dropping to thirty or forty below through the night and "rising" to maybe ten or twenty below by midday. First light at about nine-thirty, lamps lit about three-thirty. As the Coldman tightened his grip, the lake moaned and rumbled, fault lines streaked from shore to shore, and trees popped as the ice expanded in their veins until, as Steve remarked, it sounded like batting practice at Yankee Stadium.

Lying under our down quilts at night we listened and knew that the lake and all the land was alive. That people could have regarded the earth as a dead thing, a mere lump of "resources" to be extracted, a thing void not only of spirit but of life itself, testifies to their blindness and goes a long way toward explaining the destruction of the planet.

Stovall had made a last flight in just before freeze-up, bringing mail and various goodies from the folks back home. He would need at least six inches of ice before he could land again on skis, which would likely be about the end of November. In the interim we'd be isolated with no way out and no one able to get in should something happen. A helicopter? Maybe. We needed to be careful and watch our step.

September had been unexpectedly mild, with lots of rain, and much of the moose meat had spoiled, even though we ate moose almost every day and jerked what we could. (I heard later that a joke among my colleagues whom I wrote to occasionally was that when a student asked about me they replied, "Oh, Professor Durr? He's up in Alaska jerking moose." Which left the students with no further questions.)

For jerky the meat had to be free of fat and gristle. We sliced the top round into strips about a foot long, an inch wide, and a quarter inch thick, brushed on some soy sauce, sprinkled it with oregano, black pepper, and garlic, and strung the strips up to dry over the stove, being careful not to let them fold on themselves or touch one another. Jon and Sally were in charge of the oregano, pepper, and garlic shakers and were very diligent. More fun even than coloring or watching Mom and Steve at cribbage, and it was clear they liked the idea of being in on it and helping out. It was a family project. When the strips had thoroughly dried and shrunk to the point where we could snap them in two, they were ready and would keep almost indefinitely. Jerky had been a staple of the Indians' winter diet. It was a lightweight, compacted protein with a taste, smell, and texture we became addicted to, often munching on it at night. I always carried some with me on hunting trips, for emergencies (and for munchies). Jerky has the flavor of Zen.

Wilderness in winter has its own kind of beauty, every bit as grand as at any other time of year. Even the cold itself was in its own way a pleasure and lifted your spirits (so long as you dressed right for it). I wanted to get Carol out into it more, get her out of the cabin and her usual daily rounds for an hour or so every day. Just walking would be fine, but I hit upon the idea of a rabbit-snare line. That would add additional motive to the walk and bring her into closer contact with the woods and the trapping game. She liked the idea and every morning after breakfast bundled up and headed for the snare line.

We went together the first morning so I could point out likely rabbit cover and the runs the rabbits used. I set the first few snares, showing her how, then let her try. She was into it, and I think she enjoyed getting away from the cabin, off by herself for the brief while almost every day. There weren't that many rabbits in the immediate area, so we didn't have to check the snares every day if she was involved with something else, or Steve or I could do it. She never expected to catch anything but one morning she did.

Suddenly she was staring down at a frozen bundle of white fur. She had mixed feelings about that, but when she got back she put her bravest wilderness-woman face on it, holding the rabbit up and smiling for the camera.

As the snows deepened and snowshoes were needed she gave it a try and gave us some laughs watching her get tangled up and go down face first into the snow. She did that a few times and then we just pulled the snares. Every now and then afterward she got into the snowshoes and before long was able to walk on them without too much belly-whopping. She considered, rightly enough, that being able to use snowshoes might one day be important. Carol became the best wilderness woman I have ever known.

We hoped to make a rabbit-skin robe or blanket, such as natives had used, from the hides Steve and I brought back from our hunts. By all accounts those robes were lighter than a good wool blanket and ten times warmer. A man could wrap himself in one of those at subzero temperatures and be warm as . . . toast. They weren't hard to make. After home tanning, natives circular-cut each hide into strips about an inch wide. They sewed them end to end to whatever length and width they wanted, then twisted each length hair side up and wove them into a blanket. We never accumulated enough hides—about a hundred are needed—but besides mitten and boot liners Carol made Steve and me hats with the fur. They were crude, Robinson Crusoe affairs, but they did work. It's well known that native cold-weather clothing is vastly superior to the white man's, both warmer and lighter, which was why European explorers quickly adopted the Eskimos' gear. We had best quickly adopt the natives' head space as well—the one they had before we dispossessed them—so that maybe this pleasant planet will remain a place where life can be enjoyed.

For Thanksgiving we had no turkey but we did have two guests: Albert Prince (unavoidably known as Prince Albert) and Homer Carney. They were up from Dillingham to do a little trapping. Homer was a white guy who had drifted into Alaska and found the freedoms of frontier life congenial. He married a native girl and was more or less hanging out, dreaming about scaling great heights but really just going with gravity. Albert was a native, a strong, good-natured young man at home in the woods. They had put up a camp down the lake a few miles and had hitched up the dogs to come by to visit. Albert and I had known each other in Dillingham.

In the bush, visits usually meant one or two nights' stay over. Well, we had no turkey, but we now had five hunters, counting Big Jon. We figured about a dozen spruce chickens should add up to one turkey. So off we went, in holiday spirits, the five of us spread out to cover more ground (I kept Jon by me), one snowshoe foot after another, muscles feeling good, shushing through the perfect white woods, inhaling the clean air, hunting our dinner. It took us half a day to come back with eleven birds. Close enough. We stuffed each one of the birds and baked them golden brown. The dinner was swell, and we enjoyed having company for a couple of days. A week or so later temperatures were hitting forty below and Albert and Homer were hitting the trail back to Dillingham, where accommodations were a good deal warmer than their tent.

Christmas was also partly a homemade affair. To be sure, the folks back home sent us all kinds of goodies and gifts via Stovall Air Service, and there was no need to hunt our Christmas dinner, because Jay and Katie presented us with a turkey, apologizing for not having thought to do the same at Thanksgiving (we had assumed the ice just wasn't thick enough at the time for Jay to land—and anyway we liked the idea of getting our dinner right from the woods).

The tree and its decorations were up to us. Steve, Jon, Sally, and I went out and found a nicely shaped spruce and set it in a corner, where it reached from floor to ceiling. Evenings through the week before Christmas we sat around the big table making construction-paper chains, sewing popcorn into long strings punctuated by the reds of cranberries, and crumpling candy wrappers and wrapping paper into balls. Carol baked gingerbread men to hang on the branches and somehow we had candy canes. Even a few weasel tails made the scene, *ermine* decorating our majestic tree as previously ermine had adorned the robes of kings and queens.

We didn't skimp or rush. It was easy sitting around the table making the decorations and talking. As a result, our tree was fully decorated and especially in the lamplight seemed splendid and a little mysterious. Glowing and glittering and filling the cabin with the scent of evergreen it seemed to me redolent of the numinous world humans used to live in but at best can catch only glimpses of now.

By Thanksgiving in the north country all the fur would be prime. Trapping had always been part of the lifestyle of indigenous peoples, and in the early sixties it was still an accepted means of support for the backwoodsman and his family. The trapper's life in fact was often romanticized in books and films, very much as was the pioneer's or cowboy's. Just as we didn't hear anything about the pioneers' theft of Indian lands or massacres of Indian villages (it was always the other way round in the popular media) so also did we hear nothing of the unavoidable cruelties of the trapper's trade, most people not even realizing that the animals were sentient beings. The focus was always on the trapper's hardihood and skill in face of wild and dangerous nature. Of course, much of that was true enough. Running a trapline in the north woods was very different from driving downtown to the office, but just as most pioneers in the real world had been indifferent or hostile to the wilderness they were "conquering" (any lands not settled, plowed, mined, or cut down were considered wastelands in need of developmental redemption), so most trappers were after the bucks, not intimacy with nature, and would have preferred pursuing their vocation in their backyards—though again, with many exceptions. Many trappers were answering the call of the wild and quietly loved the woods.

The point is that we, in the sixties, were unaware of the global picture, of the ecological disasters and looming crises. Like most Americans at the time we were living in an innocence born of ignorance. The Indians and Eskimos were our heroes and role models and they hunted and trapped, and so therefore did we. I had planned on a combination of commercial salmon fishing in the summer and trapping in the winter to supply the cash we'd need to make it in the woods. So at Nerka Steve tended a small trapline. For a greenhorn he did very well, catching several foxes, mink, weasel, and one wolverine.

We put in many hours in the evenings skinning them out by the lanterns. You can case-skin a hare with head and paws removed almost as easily as slipping out of a tight-fitting glove, but the others require slow and careful work, because you want the entire hide—feet, toes, claws, head, ears, eyes, nose, and mouth—without any fat or flesh clinging to the skin and without any tears or cuts.

With the wolverine, there's a little story. The wolverine, despite its relatively small size compared with a bear, had the reputation of being one of the most powerful and ferocious beasts in the north woods, fearing nothing, ready to go for the jugular of anything, including trappers and hunters. As mentioned, a lot of our first moose had spoiled, and by December we were in the market again. Steve came across fresh moose tracks one morning on his trapline and hurried back to get me and our big guns (he carried a .22 handgun on the trapline). We followed the tracks and lucked into a small bull feeding on some willows. Steve popped him with a single shot.

People who object to hunting regardless of circumstances or the abundance of game and paucity of hunters in an area such as Lake Nerka fail to face the fact that everything that lives has to kill to stay alive. Humans from prehistoric times have always included some meat in their diet. You either do the killing and butchering yourself and thereby learn what it's all about, this business of staying alive, or you let someone else do it for you behind the scenes and pretend it isn't so. The tenderhearted lady who throws her hands up in horror at our taking a moose or spruce chicken carefully addresses the quality and price of the steaks, chops, and chicken so neatly encased in plastic that she will serve up at dinnertime. It never crosses her mind that she is eating a killed animal, and she is apt to be thoroughly ignorant of what the animal endured in the process of becoming those attractively packaged steaks, chops, and chicken: its unnatural and often tortured existence up to and including its slaughter. The wild moose or spruce chicken, on the other hand, enjoys its natural life up until the instant the bullet—or the bear or fox—ends it.

Trophy hunting is another matter, mounting the antlers or head on your study wall as evidence of your prowess and manhood and, as has often been the case, not bothering to harvest the meat. That's illegal now in the United States, though you still hear of a case now and then. I regard trophy hunting with something of the loathing I feel for the buffalo hunters who took only the tongue and hide, leaving the carcass to rot. It ain't easy to swallow, it sticks in the throat.

Now about the wolverine. After taking care of the downed moose and packing the meat back, Steve and I set traps all around the gut pile, sure it would attract some predators. We worked very carefully to conceal the traps under a dust of snow and to avoid leaving any human scent by wearing freshly washed woolen gloves. The site was like a minefield.

Steve and his dedicated sidekick Jon strapped on their snowshoes next morning after breakfast and with great expectations hurried to the spot. They crossed fox, weasel, and mink tracks along the approach. Their excitement stepped up their pace. Jon made good time, keeping up by following behind Steve and taking advantage of his "float" (the print of depressed snow made by snowshoes). But when they got there they saw the fox tracks circling the area, staying well clear of the minefield. But how could that be? The sets had been by the book. What had tipped them off? Ah . . . smart as a fox, eh? Simple as that. A pair of mink and weasel tracks went right to the gut pile without springing a single trap. No doubt they had walked off with full bellies. Either they had avoided the traps or had been too light to trip them, possibly because the triggers had frozen in slightly. Steve decided to leave the area undisturbed.

"Good thinking," I said when they got back and described what they had seen. "Now there's fresh mink and weasel scent mixed in with the gut smell. That'll help mask any human stink we left, which would be fading by now anyway." I visualized the scene of the night before, the foxes wary, circling, keeping their distance, maybe wised up by some of Steve's prior sets that had accounted for a few of their brethren, but then maybe watching the mink and weasel move right in to chow down, which got them to thinking, "Well, look at that. Those little bastards are loading up. Maybe it's okay. I'll come back tomorrow night and unless there's some sucker caught in a trap, I'm going in."

"I bet they come back a little hungrier and a lot bolder tonight," I said sagely, reciting the trapping lore I'd gotten from books, enjoying playing the old-timer for my boys. I even laced my speech with a little standard sourdough lingo. "Reckon they spent the day a-thinking about that there pile a tasty guts and them spunky mink and weasel helping themselves to it. Almost sartin-sure they'll be back, and we're ready for 'em, boys. By gum!"

I took a couple of Steve's fox hides down and draped them around Carol's shoulders. We kidded around a lot, in between our more serious role-playing as wilderness adventurers. There was just us, the family circle, and the great surround of wilderness, and the vigorous simplicity of our lives tended to obviate stress and leave us light of heart. I arranged the soft fur around her face and switched to Injun lingo.

"Soon lady be heap much warm in fox parkie."

She struck a glamour pose with the luxurious fur framing her smile, and I saw how pretty she was, quite fit to adorn the cover of some high-toned and elegant fashion magazine.

It had yet to dawn on me that the fur of trapped animals did not go to keep the indigenous flesh of Eskimos and Indians warm but to decorate the egos of affluent women for whom fur was more a matter of conspicuous consumption than a garment gratefully keeping them from the cold. When it did dawn on me years later, along with my growing doubts about the cruelty of the trap, my days on the trapline abruptly ended, even though our need for some cash hadn't.

The shock of recognition came one day when I went out with Steve on his round of traps. He had caught a fox. Behind the initial rush of excitement at the catch came a sudden twinge of misgiving as I looked at that beautiful creature pulling back with its paw locked in the steel jaws of the trap and staring up at us with vivid, frightened eyes. That sight, fixed in the back of my mind like a time capsule, eventually came to supersede and cancel out all the lore and romance of trapping I had accepted as simply part of life in the great north woods. The disenchantment didn't take effect all at once, but it started with that one fox. (Amazing, the power of long-standing cultural stereotypes to blind us to actualities, even to our own deeper feelings and intuitions.)

A live wolverine, however, makes an impression quite different from that of a timid fox, especially to young minds filled with stories about its demonic ferocity.

On the third morning when they reached the traps, Steve, who was in front, stopped suddenly and took in a sharp breath. "Wolverine!" he whispered. "And he's caught by just a toe or two."

Here's Jon's reaction to this startling and momentous information:

I had never seen one, but "wolverine" sure didn't sound like something warm and cuddly. And then I saw it. To my six-year-old eyes, the furious ball of fur with six-inch fangs and claws lunging against the trap chain, wanting to get at us and tear out our

throats, looked like the cartoon Tazmanian Devil with a bad case
of rabies. The sun glinted off its pearly white fangs, and I was sure
those daggers were about to perforate my young body. In my
mind's eye I saw it in its dark lair licking its chops and sharpening
its claws on the bones of little boys. I wanted to run but couldn't
move. Steve was firing the .22 but having a terrible time hitting the
thing and I was hoping he wasn't as scared as me and that his
marksmanship would improve instantaneously.

Steve's .22 was a single shot, so "rapid firing" meant as fast as he
could shoot, eject, reload, and shoot again—at a target that was
lunging and bounding from side to side, held back by only two
toes, which it would be glad to sacrifice for the joy of tearing those
two bastards to pieces. Steve's nerves held steady enough to permit
his cold fingers to insert the tiny bullet into the tiny hole of the barrel and to do it repeatedly even though his shots were having no apparent effect. Actually, most of the bullets were connecting, we
found out later. Steve also carried on his hip a Ruger .44 Magnum
handgun. He didn't want to use it because a .44 makes a big hole,
but he was ready to use it if necessary. But even a wolverine can
absorb only so much lead. Finally it lay still, stretched out at the
end of the chain. A trickle of blood from its mouth soaked into the
snow. The silence settled back down. Steve approached, .44 in
hand, and saw the beautiful rosewood diamond pattern of its
long-haired fur. But Jon hung back, staying put. Nothing like this
had ever happened back on the farm. This world was different.
There could be no fidgety, bored little boys in this world.

Well, it was a major catch, a very valuable fur, and insofar as
we were liable to the notion that wilderness was a testing ground,
that wolverine pelt seemed like a badge of merit, especially to the
two boys, given their belief in the predator's ferocity. They had experienced something of the life and death drama continually being
played out in the peaceful forest and had stepped up another rung
on the reality ladder to manhood. In 1968 when we moved to

Alaska for good we used the pelt for the ruffs of our parkas, for which use it has always been prized by the natives because the fur doesn't frost up from your breath in severe cold. The sealskin of the parkas was store-bought, very fine and serviceable, to be sure, but the ruffs were more than that. They weren't gotten with money. They were storied and personal and meant something special.

And that kind of difference held true for the meat we brought back from the hunt, even though I had money to buy food. On one of our wider-ranging explorations Steve and I found the happy hunting ground for snowshoe hares, whose distribution typically isn't uniform but patchy. It was a point of land a few miles across the frozen lake. For us, such a find was more exciting than discovering gold: to step up off the lake into a patch of dense willow and see the snow crisscrossed by the big "Y" prints of a lot of rabbits!

That was the thing about exploring, moving into new territories; you never knew what you'd come upon, not only in terms of game, although that was always a point of special interest, but as regards the terrain itself. The look and feel of the land was a subtle enchantment luring us on, deeper into it—around that next bend, into that thick cluster of dark spruce with the feel of a sacred grove, or across an open valley with only some brush and dead grass showing here and there above the immaculate snow, spare as a Zen garden. There were always some tracks to read—the neat line of delicate prints stitching the snow that meant fox, the deep indentations of heart-shaped moose hooves and maybe the moose itself moving away in its swaying trot, or a flock of ptarmigan exploding into the blue sky.

One day around Amokok Arm we came upon a huge flock of ptarmigan, hundreds of them. They were invisible at first along the beach, but when they started moving out ahead of us it seemed the whole beach had come to life. Then they rose in waves and it looked as though the snow was being blown back into the sky in giant flakes. "Dead of winter" is a misnomer. The land was alive right down to the tiny prints of the field mouse. The bears might be sleeping (and even so, you knew they were there, they were present), but all the other creatures were wide awake.

In that rabbit country we found across the lake Steve and I would hunt all day, spurred on by all the tracks and the fascinating new terrain. The hares were so thick there we spotted one just about every ten or fifteen minutes. Most were sitting motionless beside a snow-covered blowdown, invisible but for the black dot of an eye and the black tips of their upright ears. We quickly became practiced at picking them out from among the mounds of snow and bits of black branches. Back east with the cottontails we always carried a shotgun because the only time we saw one it was going flat out at top speed, which is very fast. But the snowshoes just sat motionless, beguiled into security by their near-perfect camouflage. We carried .22s and aimed for the head, which was best for them and for us, sudden death and no spoiled meat or hide. If we happened to push one out it usually bounded off a short ways and sat again, behavior very detrimental to their longevity.

On these hunts when the short-lived winter sun was lowering in the sky, tinting the baby-blue with metallic pink, we started back across the lake bringing home the bacon and maybe a dozen more hides toward the robe. The lake stretched away white and void into the distance, the only sound our footsteps in the snow sparkling and glittering before us like a field of diamonds and opals. The walking was its own thing, not at all tedious. The weight on our backs felt right, legs doing what they were made to do and liking it the way a dog likes running, breath coming easy, enjoying the sweet-tasting air, the crunch of our boots so subtle a pleasure it hardly reached consciousness.

Back at the cabin we hung the hares outside, frozen solid, and went into the warmth and kerosene light and told about the hunt. Waves of relaxation passed through our bodies, the legs especially, tired now and happy to be resting. I didn't used to feel this good when I returned from a day on campus exercising my mind but not my body and needing an old-fashioned or two to unwind. Doing the natural thing is the ticket. We were made for walking in the open air. The root meaning of sin is to miss the mark. The mark is nature. Hit that mark and you will be all right. You'll feel good.

No doubt it was my taking the Indian and Eskimo cultures as my paradigm that led me to do something I now regard as stupid. I gave Steve, at fifteen, the okay to go off by himself to hunt the grizzly bear. Young Indians and Eskimos did things like that as part of their rite of passage into manhood. But they hadn't grown up in a city or suburb and were to the manner born, learning the ways of wild nature from their earliest years. Circumstances alter cases. Steve didn't have those advantages, and knowing what I do now about *Ursus horribilis* I wouldn't let him go, certainly not alone. I can only be thankful that on those solitary hunts on Church Mountain he didn't run afoul of his dangerous quarry.

One evening before freeze-up Steve and I were on the lake heading back to the cabin when we saw a skiff coming toward us. This was the first time we had run into anyone on the lake. We wondered who it was, and kept our eyes on it. Dusk was deepening but as the skiff drew near and passed about ten yards off we made out two figures, one in the bow and the other handling the outboard in the stern. Between them was a mound of brown fur that even in the half-light we could tell was a bear hide. The two men looked over at us and nodded. We did the same. And then they went on by. Only a glimpse really, but there was no mistaking it. These were two natives, short and broad-bodied, wide cheekbones, and there was that about them as they passed slowly and deliberately down the lake that conveyed a sense of seasoned hunters. These were the kind of men who should rightly stalk the grizzly bear, not my fifteen-year-old son from the New York countryside.

Nevertheless, I did have a lot of confidence in Steve's judgment and abilities, and it was a principle with Carol and me not to clip our kids' wings with too much caution but to let their spirits expand according to their own propensities, even if some risk was involved. Carol, of course, was much more conservative about this than I. Fortunately, in this instance, Steve had been able to spread his wings without getting them clipped by jaws or claws.

Actually we had a lot of luck that way. First, the bear that had laid claim to our moose hadn't argued his case. Second, Steve didn't stumble onto a bear on Church Mountain. And there were a third and fourth instance.

The third occurred in late autumn just after the first light snow. Steve and I had been exploring around the bend from the cabin, up Amokok Arm, and were on our way back when we saw giant bear tracks coming out of the brush and turning toward the cabin. The tracks overlapped our footprints, as though following them back right to the cabin, where Carol, Jon, Sally, and Beth were going about their unsuspecting business. Bears do break into cabins, looking for . . . something to eat.

Adrenaline flushed through our bodies in a quick anguish of fear. (That awful feeling returns to me to this day in dreams of mountainous bears getting into the cabin.) We broke into a run. We had our rifles with us (at that time Steve still wanted to bag a bear). The bear was walking, we were running. It wasn't far to the cabin. We'd catch up to him in time—unless the tracks had been laid down while we had been heading up the arm! But just around the point, where he was likely to get a whiff of the spoiling moose meat, the tracks veered off back into the brush. We passed that spot with our safeties off and kept up the fast pace in case he had zigzagged back down.

We were red-faced and breathless when we burst through the door, startling Carol and the kids, who looked at us with big eyes. I said it was okay, that we had just climbed a steep hill following some rabbit tracks. (Carol didn't connect to the fact that you don't go after rabbits with a 30.06.) I didn't mention the bear. Paranoia about bears was to be avoided as much as possible. Then Carol said she'd been a little nervous a while back because Shad, our Labrador retriever, had started barking and growling in an agitated way while looking down the beach in the direction we had just come. She guessed he probably had heard us, and that was a relief.

"Yes," I quickly agreed, "that must have been it." I reached down to pat Shad's head. We'd had him since he was a pup. "A dog is a good early warning system in an isolated spot like this." It was true. Bears are shy of dogs and usually try to stay clear of them. I was thinking it had probably been Shad's furious barking that had turned the bear away from the cabin.

Carol always contended that Shad had two personalities, a city one and a woods one. City Shad was all grins and wagging tail with people, but woods Shad was wary and on watch. When Steve, Jon, and I were off hunting or whatever, Shad assumed the role of male protector. One day when we were away hunting, a lone Indian appeared out of nowhere and knocked on the door. Shad got slowly to his feet, Carol related, and staring hard at the door let out a growl so ominous Godzilla would have had second thoughts. Carol opened the door hesitantly, and Shad was right there at her side, bristling and low-growling, totally demonized. The Indian froze on the spot. He wondered did the lady have a little tobacco to spare? Carol wasn't about to ask him in. "Just a minute," she said. She told Shad to stay. Which he did, locking the stranger in place. Carol came back with a tin of tobacco (we had begun rolling our own). The Indian, who was probably a kind and gentle soul, thanked her and started stepping back, eyes on Shad, whose eyes were on him.

But the day after the bear scare, nevertheless, under the guise of the Great White Leader being supercareful to anticipate any and every eventuality no matter how remote, I persuaded Carol to learn the use of the twelve-gauge pump shotgun, explaining casually that it would be a good idea for her to know how to shoot it in case some varmint or other came after our meat stash, adding that, loaded with buckshot, it was powerful enough at close range to stop even a bear or small dinosaur from coming in through a window. Which it was, at least as regards the bear, and I wasn't worried about the dinosaur.

Carol's eyes were fixed on me a little suspiciously, but she went along with the idea. I had her hold the gun at her side and blow up some rusted five-gallon cans at about six to ten paces. You don't have to aim a shotgun at that range, of course; you just point and shoot. And yes, even Mr. Magoo could hit a target as big as a bear that close. All she had to do was keep her cool and not freak out. I believed she could handle the situation.

The fourth scenario of the *chechakos* and the bears is probably, to me now, the most embarrassing because it is the most foolhardy. Any encounter with a bear is potentially hazardous, but all agree that the one configuration guaranteeing the greatest hazard is a sow with one or two cubs. Like mothers universally, mama bear is extremely protective of her offspring and will fight to the death—your death most likely—on their behalf. As has been noted, bears generally are unpredictable. When encountered, they may charge or bolt or simply ignore you, depending partly on the circumstances (they react badly very often if surprised at close range) and partly, it would seem, on their mood. Some friends of mine tell of a bear they saw at a distance on a beach who kept coming at them for no apparent reason. In a bad mood? A thorn in his nose? A wild hair across his ass? There's no telling. But if you accidentally (who would do it on purpose? . . . except maybe a *chechako*) get between a sow and her cubs, mama's response is perfectly predictable. She will charge.

The only factor that saved Steve and me from a violent and possibly deadly episode, the fourth of this Nerka series, was that we happened not to position ourselves between the sow and her two cubs. We can take no credit for having emerged unscathed. On the contrary, we were asking for it. By all the laws of nature, our behavior gave mama license to kill. Our only excuse was that at first we weren't sure it was a sow and cubs inasmuch as the cubs were almost fully grown. But that's no excuse at all: To go charging up a mountainside after not one, not two, but three grizzly bears is folly enough even if they hadn't been a sow and two cubs.

What happened was this: In the spring I was taking the whole family on a pleasure cruise down the lake, moving along slowly fairly close to shore. It was a lovely day, the sky blue and the sun once again warm. Steve still had bear on his mind and was scanning the hillside as we moved along. "I'm never going to see a bear," he said, and in the next breath, "There's a bear!" I jerked my head around to where he was pointing up the steep hill and caught a glimpse of bundles of rippling blond fur. It wasn't enough that we had spotted them and could sit there in the boat offshore and gleefully—and safely—observe them. No, no. We— or at least Steve and I—had to have a closer look, with Steve thinking this might be his chance to bag a bear and with me obviously not thinking at all.

I pulled into shore, we grabbed our rifles (even on a pleasure cruise we brought the rifles, in case we stopped to explore some spot), and started up the hillside. The thick alder made things even more exciting because if the bears held their ground, feeding probably, we wouldn't be able to see them until we were right on top of them. As mentioned, they hate surprises.

"Can you see them?" I asked Steve in a stage whisper.

"No," he replied, "but I think they're still there because I don't hear anything."

Hmm . . .

We pushed on, Hawkeye and Chingachgook, and then we did hear something, something neither of us had ever heard before but which was instantly intelligible to our primeval reptilian brain: the warning cough of an aroused bear. That bear knew exactly where, if not what, we were—just several yards below her and her precious progeny. Common sense immediately resumed the throne of my mind, yet didn't entirely dislodge the bravado that had usurped its place, for I said, once more in a stage whisper, "I wonder if it's too late to say we're sorry."

We stood at the ready, safeties off, expecting a freight train of mammalian wrath to burst through the alder at any moment. But as I mentioned, our foolish impetuosity hadn't been unfortunate enough to place us between the sow and her cubs. They were right there by her side, and since whatever we were was no longer advancing but had stopped dead in its tracks at her cough, she decided to leave well enough alone, and we caught a glimpse of blond rumps crossing a patch of snow and going over the crest. Steve recalls that they flushed some ptarmigan and one of the playful cubs took a swipe at a bird and tumbled over a snowbank, and the tension of potential disaster was relieved by a touch of comedy.

Had we somehow gotten between the sow and her cubs the odds are you wouldn't be reading this. We went back down the hill faster than we had gone up it. When we reached the boat, Carol, who was endowed with the same kind of instincts as mama bear, was fuming. She glared at me, all the usual softness gone from her eyes. "What is *wrong* with you?" I was at a loss for words, though it should have been easy to come up with "ignorant *chechako*" or just plain "fool."

Carol, with Beth, had a midwinter break from Nerka when she flew out with Jay for a week in Dillingham with the Stovalls, who in typical Alaskan fashion of hospitality wined and dined her. I suspect that Carol welcomed the visit more as an opportunity to sound out Katie Stovall about life on the last frontier from the woman's point of view than as a chance to get away from the cabin and soak up some civilized amenities. She always preferred being with her family and truly enjoyed our quiet life at the lake (except for the bears). Katie was Alaskan born and bred. She lived the life, tending her own salmon-fishing site alone through the summer season, with years of bush subsistence behind her. I think

Carol returned from her visit reassured about Alaskan life, because she had found her hostess stout of heart and robust of spirit, traits rarely discovered among middle-aged women of Middle America. Carol must have figured that were frontier life radically insecure or hard Katie would have come across as at least a little anxious or frazzled. —I should mention that while in Dillingham with the Stovalls Carol took the opportunity to bring Beth up to snuff with her baby shots.

At Easter time a man named Sherb Smith flew into the cove and invited us all down to the village of Aleknagik for a visit and dinner. He and most of the village were Seventh-Day Adventists, very sober, frugal folks who had managed by hook or by crook (a lot of the latter, according to some natives) to turn wilderness into a comfortable and prosperous living, with white frame houses, a meeting hall, straight streets, new cars, trucks, and airplanes, and fat bank accounts. They had managed to own or control all the best fishing sites, which meant big bucks. They also managed, being strict vegetarians but patriots of American culture, to turn cooked vegetable matter into the semblance of hamburgers and turkey, drumsticks and all.

These folks were physically healthy and materially secure and no doubt felt themselves to be righteous in the eyes of the Lord. But as far as we could tell, though they leveled a lot of indulgent smiles at us, they appeared rather sallow and seemed bereft of that certain fire and robustness of spirit so evident in the wild and wooly Stovalls and other Alaskans we had met—notably Gene Pope, the reprobate of Lake Iliamna featured in *Down in Bristol Bay*. Their equanimity seemed a little gray around the edges, and I couldn't help thinking of that movie, *The Body Snatchers*, wherein pods from another planet take over the bodies of earthlings, retaining their looks, dress, and apparent identities but dispossessing those bodies of all emotion, spontaneity, and spirit, installing in their stead a kind of flat-lined rationality. To Zen eyes, these "grass eaters" (as they were called by the Eskimo meat eaters) were stone Buddhas.

Regarding "civilized amenities," people back home in their letters often sidled up to the question of the outhouse: Wasn't it . . . inconvenient . . . and a little awful? As though indoor plumbing had always been a feature of human existence and not merely a recent innovation, as if contentment, or a measure of happiness itself, depended upon the flush toilet, as if our ancestors for a million years and even the rich of yesteryear, bereft of the flush toilet, had lived in a condition of deprivation hardly superior to the beasts of the field, the birds of the air, or the fishes in water. And yet even today there are some poor wretches lacking the computer, the automatic ice-cube maker, and the digital whatever!

A little willing suspension of disbelief is called for here, because I swear the outhouse didn't faze us at all. It wasn't a disconsolation to be endured. It was in fact more asset than deficit: the bracing morning walk, greeting the day in person, the complete privacy (no worry about noise), and should there be a bit of a sub-zero nip in the air and consequent chill in the flesh, so much more welcome the warmth of the cabin upon returning. All things are known by their contraries, as Blake taught. The pleasure of heat can easily be taken for granted and obviated if all you do is move from your heated bedroom to your heated living room to your heated bathroom to your heated car. That's whiteout. To know the pleasure of heat you've got to experience the pleasure of cold. "Pleasure of cold"? Yes indeed. The touch of the Coldman can be exhilarating, stimulating the bloom of winter roses in your cheeks and putting spring into your step.

Ah, but what about the outhouse seat at ten or forty below? Here rudimentary technology comes inexpensively to the rescue: You carve a seat out of Styrofoam and voilà! instant heat upon contact. No electricity required. Replacements readily available. All right, but what about the mosquitoes in the summer? Screening and a mosquito coil. Okay, but now the nitty-gritty: Everyone knows outhouses stink. Only if you're a shiftless skunk. Cabins with outhouses invariably heat with wood. A ladle of ashes after every outhouse use, plus the circulating fresh air if you built it right, takes care of odor. Works better than the chemical the FRI used and better than a flush toilet in a bathroom without ventilation. And there's never any difficulties with the plumbing. The secret of success with outhouses as with a lot of other things is getting Madison Avenue out of your head and seeing for yourself.

Also lacking a shower, which until recently kings and queens lacked, we sponge-bathed in a big galvanized tub, as did all the other brave pioneers of the American frontier, if lucky enough to have one. Did George Washington, the richest slave owner in the United States, own a shower? What price Convenience? (In America, Convenience is always capitalized, like God.) But what does it profit a man to gain a shower and lose a wilderness? Anyway, the sauna fills the bill. Prized by natives—and by us—a sauna cleanses more thoroughly, from the inside out, and bestows benefits upon body and mind a shower can only envy. Over the past thirty years or more, I've seen brighter days and done better things because of the sauna.

By February of that year on Lake Nerka the days were lengthening, the sun was gaining strength, and the Coldman was loosening his hold on the land: slowly but steadily weakening. Nevertheless, it would be a few months before the actual spring breakup when the snow would melt, the lake ice turn to water, the first green shoots of fireweed and fiddlehead ferns push up through the layers of dead leaves, and the Coldman would be exiled to his polar ice palace, brooding until the brief northern summer's pretense had played itself out, the woods once more turned golden, and he returned to claim his kingdom.

Breakup was slow that year. Despite the long days and strong sun, patches of snow lingered in the woods well into May. It was time for us to leave the lake. We felt a periphery of regret, but the focus of our attention was on what lay ahead. Plans were a little uncertain, but it looked like Steve and I would be fishing with

Gene Pope on the old Otter for the season of '65. The big run of salmon was expected on the Naknek side. Pope wrote that he might be able to arrange for Carol and the kids to stay in a cabin in the town of Naknek. If it worked out, in between fishing periods Steve and I could be with the family. At the end of the fishing season of '65, which was expected to be a good one for the fisherman, we would return to New York and my professorship (I had just been promoted to full professor) to mull over our Nerka experience. I planned on heading back to Bristol Bay the following spring, this time to fish my own funky boat *Port N Storm,* the idea being to see if I could make it fishing on my own. I would have to prove up as a commercial fisherman in no uncertain terms before we could seriously consider leaving civilization for wilderness life.

We were to meet Gene in Dillingham on or about the twentieth of June. The ice was finally gone from our cove by the fourteenth. We contacted Jay and he flew in to haul a load of our stuff into Dillingham. On the fifteenth we packed the rest of our things into the skiff and started down the lake toward the Agulowok River, but a sudden squall came up, whipping the water into a froth, and we had to turn back. The next day broke fair and calm and we took off again. The Agulowok was now at flood stage from the spring runoff. All the rocks and boulders of the previous autumn were covered by a foot or two of fast-flowing water. The river had become a kind of expressway down to Lake Aleknagik. It was an exciting ride. For the kids, bundled in their life vests and innocence, it was sheer thrill. But I was somewhat tense—enjoying the wild ride but watching the water ahead very closely, playing the rollers carefully, constantly working the throttle to maintain control.

At Aleknagik we stowed our gear on the old *Port N Storm* and after some difficulties with the engine and thanks to a little help from the FRI guys we got her running and shipshape. I shook hands with Bud Burgner and his fisheries biologists from the year before and then we set out on a little pleasure cruise to the upper reaches of the big lake, where I knew there were no human dwellers. We had a few days before Gene Pope was due into Dillingham with the Otter. The weather held fair, sunny and warm. Once we got up past where the Agulowok poured into the lake we saw no signs of human habitation, past or present. Flocks of ducks and geese rose before us, loons called, and we saw a couple of black bears and a moose (on separate occasions) and not another person for the whole three days.

Here's a snapshot suggesting the tenor of our vacation time on Aleknagik. Carol, who loved to swim, was beguiled by the blue skies, hot sun, and crystal water into thinking that a refreshing dip was called for. We were anchored in a shallow cove, and the sunny bottom made the water seem warmly inviting. She slipped into a halter and shorts and, calling me chicken because I had declined to follow suit, dove over the side into what I knew but had refrained from mentioning would be ice water. Like one of those fast-reverse motion pictures, she appeared to pop back out with as much alacrity as she had gone in, eyes and mouth wide open and gasping from the shock of it, which left Steve and me gasping for breath from laughing. Jon, Sally, and Beth stood at the gunwale happy about the whole thing.

Nerka had been a great introductory course, a wonderful time for us all, and we had learned a lot, but it was really a setup. Too easy, too many cushions between us and the hard facts of settling into wilderness. The real thing awaited us if and when we made our move. The Big Eskimo in the Sky smiled knowingly, and the Coldman snickered.

2

Picnic at the Walrus Islands

Bob and Carol outside the dome.

(August 1965)

I and the whole family were seated—ensconced—in a reassuringly standard booth in the Green Café in downtown Dillingham. I was indulging in an orgy of Americana: vinyl booth, hamburger and fries, vanilla milkshake, the whole straight course, and in the background the certitude of a warm, safe bed later on.

Steve and I had just gotten back from the Naknek side after the fishing season of '65, the season of the Big Run, when the canneries had to set a limit of two thousand fish per boat per fishing period because they couldn't process any more than that, the season when a night's sleep was a luxury we mostly couldn't afford, when muscles that wanted to mutiny were lashed back into service because the nets were *smoking* and the fever was upon us and we didn't care that we were bumping bottom with a stern load of fish and just might sink.

From Nerka, Carol and the kids had parked for a couple of weeks in Dillingham after Steve and I joined up with Pope and Teresa Prince (Albert's sister) on the *Otter*. The Dillingham Hotel was not the Hilton—toilet down the hall, no lock on the door, twenty bucks a night. But Katie Stovall found them a nice apartment, rented on a weekly basis until the arrangements had been made for the little cabin at Naknek, on the bluff overlooking the river. It was neat and clean though without water, which a neighbor supplied for fifteen dollars a month. The place belonged to Johnny Nielson, Gene's old friend from the Iliamna country. Carol disliked the shabby town and all the drunken fishermen staggering around, but at least she and the kids saw me and Steve at those times when the fishing was closed to allow enough fish to escape the nets to ensure future harvests. Stovall had flown them over, and Jay Hammond (later to become governor) drove them and their stuff to the cabin. He had a house nearby and kind of looked after them. Now the whole family was back in Dillingham, soon to depart for New York.

In the Green Café Carol and I were in reaction to all the stress, strain, and uncertainties of the fishing season just past. We were hunkered down safe and easy in the bunker of bourgeois beatitudes, having had all we could handle of life on the last frontier for the time being. We needed a break. I felt the tensions that had built up in me over the summer oozing out onto the linoleum floor.

The whole business of commercial fishing, especially in a peak year like this last, was more trying than I ever had imagined. Nothing I had read nor any of the movies I'd seen about men who go down to the sea in ships could have prepared me for the demands of it—and the dangers. Maybe to the Outside professionals it was just a job, more or less well paying, but to me it had been a series of crises, a sequence of intensely dramatic episodes, a time that had tried my soul (as they used to put it in Tierra del Fuego). In my own mind I had been on trial, myself defendant, prosecutor, judge, and jury. The verdict seemed to be "Acquitted." I had done all right as a fisherman, hadn't freaked out any of the many times I might have. I saw proving up as a fisherman as my rite of passage back to the good life.

Nevertheless, it was pleasant, now that it was all over for the year, to be sitting in a regulation café there in Dillingham, without a tide book bulging in my back pocket, indifferent to the velocity of the wind, halfway believing that I was where I really belonged. This relapse would be a passing thing, I knew, but I didn't want it to pass too soon.

"Professor!"

Uh oh. That was Pope's voice. No mistaking it, or the implications of its particular intonation. He had something in mind for me. I was no doubt about to be hijacked into accompanying him on another *Adventure!* Even before his face hove into view I was sure it would be wearing his sincere and serious look.

The mountains were never high enough for Pope, their slopes never slippery enough, their chasms never treacherous enough. If a predicament didn't spontaneously arise to confront us, he would so conduct our affairs as to ensure that one soon would. (More fun that way.) But of course he never presented his plan in that frame of reference. This time the challenge he had in mind would be disguised in the language of "family outing" and "pleasure cruise": a beachcombing *picnic.* As if there ever had been or could be an activity taking place in Alaska's wilds that could legitimately be called a picnic.

Pope's voice was like a knell. No need to send to know for whom the bell tolled. It tolled for me.

Carol and I twisted around, and here came Pope and another guy down the aisle. If you were to judge by Pope's walk you'd think he was rolling down the deck of a boat out on the bounding main: elbows cocked a little and swinging a little, legs a little far apart, for balance, one shoulder hitched a little higher than the other, both shoulders rocking from side to side, and above all that the tight-lipped smile, as though he were holding back a laugh, and his grinning eyes fixed on me. I felt Carol stiffen next to me. She had met Gene briefly at the hotel before we'd left for the Naknek side. She wasn't at all sure about my partner, the wild man Gene Pope. It was instinct in her, reinforced by what she had heard about him over the summer. A woman and a mother, she was mindful of security, certainly of safety, and she was sure this man represented neither.

"Professor!" said Pope. "And the whole Durr family!" He smiled broadly, greeting Carol with exaggerated deference, almost bowing. He was awkward around respectable white women. I think respectability awakened in him that syndrome of convoluted feelings that had driven him out of Middle America in the first place. Respectability wasn't his thing, though he was willing to pay it lip service. He stood there, thumbs hooked in pockets, elbows out, looking and probably feeling somewhat out of place in such an all-American familial scene. After all, the Green Café wasn't even a bar. The other guy standing behind him wore the peaked white cap of the Bristol Bay fisherman, his face suitably tanned and lean, the bulk of his bare arms also testifying fisherman. He had a pleasant, self-contained, and relaxed air about him.

"I got someone here I want you to meet," Pope said to me. He beamed at the fellow. "This here is Jim Brewer. He's a teacher too! At Nondalton."

Pope was obviously pleased to be introducing Jim Brewer, a schoolteacher, as his friend and neighbor over in the Iliamna country. I figured right away that he had Carol in mind. It was instinct with him too to sense that Carol was leery of him. She wouldn't be the first respectable woman to look at him askance, as at some kind of threat. Jim Brewer was a schoolteacher and a family man, a sober and solid citizen, at least in comparison with Pope and some others I could name. Pope wanted some of that respectability to rub off on him, to soften Carol's hard view of him. He knew that I was thinking of coming to Alaska to live in the woods, and where better than near his place on Lake Iliamna, near a friend and partner, a *paisano!* Carol might need some convincing. More immediately at hand, he wanted the Durr family to come along with him and Teresa in joining up with Brewer and his partner, also named Gene, for a swell party trip out to the Walrus Islands, and he suspected that even in this Carol would be the hard sell. He was pretty sure she had veto power.

So there we were, to all appearances just friends chatting about pleasant things. No one would have guessed that to Carol, and to some extent myself as well, the figure standing there in black pants and gray shirt with black curly hair and gleaming eyes was a dark cloud on the horizon of our sunny day.

Introductions out of the way, Pope launched into his spiel, smiling and telling us with great enthusiasm and raised eyebrows that this was the chance of a lifetime, especially for the kids! Man, the Walrus Islands, the greatest walrus haul-out in the world! And who knew how long it would stay open and free as it was now? Some corporation was bound to turn it into a tourist trap. But we'd be able to sail right in and park and go beachcombing and maybe—probably—find some ivory! He had just bought the *Diane,* so the old *Otter* would be all ours, plenty of room for the whole family. And Brewer had been out there a couple of times, knew the bearings and everything we needed to know about catching the tides right and all that. Pope now put on his best serious-and-sincere face, addressing me but aiming at Carol.

"It'll be a piece of cake, Bob, a real treat and a great way to cap a great season. Educational too, for the kids. —And nothing to worry about, no way we could get into any sweat, what with three boats running together. Hell, it'll be a *picnic!*"

My interest perked up. I had heard about the Walrus Islands, a major concentration area of the Pacific walrus. They hauled out on those islands at this time of year in great numbers, thousands of them. It would be a spectacular sight. The great herds of Africa had mostly gone the way of the passenger pigeon and the buffalo. The walrus would probably follow suit before long or they and their islands would at least be turned into money. Yes, this probably was a once-in-a-lifetime opportunity to behold one of wild nature's spectacular events. —But on the other hand . . . those islands lay somewhere off the coast beyond Cape Constantine, out in the Bering Sea. The spirit of *Adventure!* at the moment had deserted my sails; they hung limp in the stagnant air of my doubts. A smallish voice inside me kept whispering, "Picnic my ass."

At this point came a surprise. I had been hesitant in my response, ambivalent about the whole thing, but not wanting to come off looking weak-kneed, failing Pope's challenge right off, when Carol turned to me with a bright smile and said, "Oh, let's go, Bob. Gene's right. It's a fantastic opportunity. The kids will love it—the boat ride, and seeing those wild animals in their own world. No zoo can compare with that."

I rolled my eyes in her direction, my head not turning, as was often my way, looking sideways. Did she mean that, or was it a very heavy sarcasm intended to expose the absurdity of taking small boats out into the Bering Sea, where great ships founder, to have a *picnic* at the Walrus Islands. Could be. She was capable of that. But then, we really did used to take Stevie to the zoo a lot. There was something about the animals, even in a zoo, we wanted him to see. Carol had taken a look at Jim Brewer and—failing to give sufficient weight to the fact that he had lived in wild Alaska for a long time—decided he was a sober and responsible man, someone to be depended upon. And she saw the bright eagerness leaping about in Jon's and Sally's eyes and Steve perched on the edge of his seat ready to board. So maybe that was it; she really did think it a good idea. But it could be, just possibly, that she very well knew what Pope was expecting of her—timid middle-class funk—and wanted to trump him, show him she was not to be placed in that box.

Whatever. The die was now cast. I was off the hook. No way could I be the one to veto the plan. We were going to the Walrus Islands.

The following day broke fair and balmy, with hardly a stir of air. The weather apparently was playing into Pope's hands, giving me no excuse to cop out on that account. The weatherman too appeared to be part of the conspiracy: The forecast was for clear skies, mild temperatures, and no mention of any pending storms or rising winds. We gathered down at the dock, looking like a party of vacationers or tourists—clean clothes, Carol and Teresa in colorful bandannas, children in hand, and no one in hip boots. Nushagak Bay, widening out to the horizon, seemed half asleep. Sea and sky wore an aspect of azure innocence, as though incapable of being roused to any expression more vigorous than a sigh. Of course, I knew better, but I allowed myself to be beguiled into thinking that all the rough stuff was behind me now, back there with the fishing.

The three boats were tied together off the dock, all shipshape for their new identity as pleasure craft—no nets in the stern, no blood or slime in evidence, not even a fish scale annealed to the hull. Brewer's new fiberglass boat, aptly named the *Gem,* was white with baby-blue trim. It had a flying bridge with a curved, tinted windshield and a dual set of controls up there. The impression it made was of a handsome naval officer in dress whites assigned to escort us to our picnic at the Walrus Islands. Very comforting. We were in good hands, back in the civilized world.

Even the tides were congenial. We moved out on the ebb about midmorning, an hour suiting the comfort preferences of vacationers. Back there in the fishing season it seemed that the powers that be had favored scheduling the starts of open periods at such hours that required us to catch the ebb some time in the middle of the night, usually in the face of pelting rain and angry seas. But that was long ago, in another country. We were in Beulah land now.

The bay was so passive and indolent we were able to tie up and run together. Brewer and his partner Gene were up on the flying bridge, steering for all three boats, and Steve was up there with them enjoying the view. The sun was already high and hot, and the breeze of our cruising felt just right. Carol sat on deck wearing a sporty outfit of slacks and blouse. The three smaller kids stood at the gunwale near her looking out. Beth was still so small she had to stand tiptoe. The breeze stirred gently through their hair. Teresa stepped across from the *Diane* and sat near Carol, the two women chatting about kids and Dillingham and whatever. Pope and I stood at the wheel of the *Otter* munching on salami and saltines and drinking beer. The scene might have been staged for a travel agency commercial. I was really pleased at the way things were going. Maybe we really were sailing into a new dispensation. I wanted Carol and the kids to like Alaska, not fear it.

About an hour or so later—it would be at least a ten-hour trip, something else I hadn't realized—as we were passing Protection Point (there was a clue in that name) on our way to rounding Cape Constantine, with the vast reaches of the Bering Sea opening before us, a wind started picking up out of the southwest. The boats began to jerk against the lines tying them together, impatient of the restraint now that the sea was to be dealt with. Periodically a geyser of salt water shot up between the hulls. The day all of a sudden was no longer balmy. And Carol no longer felt sporty. The youthful azure sky was fast aging into sullen gray, and Carol was looking a little peaked as she bundled the kids into jackets.

The smallish voice inside me was saying, "What did I tell you? Picnic my ass."

The boats were banging together too hard. We had to untie them. I assumed we would stay fairly close to one another, remembering Pope's assurance that with the three of us running together there was no way any of us could get into some trouble we couldn't get out of. The seas were building, great long ocean swells, but not cresting . . . yet.

The *Otter* was old and not well maintained. That wasn't Pope's way. He preferred to respond to emergencies rather than prevent them through proper maintenance. More exciting that way. Awareness of his modus operandi was one of the factors that had made me hesitant about the trip. I recalled that the bilge pump was temperamental, unreliable, and that the engine tended to overheat if called upon to perform beyond cruising range. I wasn't sure about the radio either.

"So," said the little voice inside, "now you're getting it. I tried to warn you. You heard, but you didn't listen."

As if to emphasize the sagacity of the little voice, the *Gem*, our coast guard escort and guide, was beginning to pull ahead, rapidly becoming only an occasional flash of white on all the gray foil of sea and sky. Heavy spray, but not yet any green ones, was coming over the bow and hitting the windshield as we dipped and came up out of the troughs. Each time the windshield cleared it seemed the *Diane* too was getting smaller, pulling ahead. It was evident that the only thing about the day still balmy was myself. I looked astern and wasn't at all sure which direction to head in should a retreat become prudent. The thin sliver of land I could see was lying low, shrouded in mist, appearing and disappearing, the entrance to Nushagak Bay not apparent. The thought of being alone out on the Bering Sea in a boat of questionable seaworthiness, without chart, bearings, or even a tide book, was not cheerful. But things weren't all that bad yet, I told myself. "Wait awhile," said the little voice.

Within the hour Carol took the three kids below, where they all got miserably sick. Steve wasn't feeling all that good either, but he stuck it out with me at the wheel. We were back in the old game of playing the waves, engaging in intimate relations with the sea. We worked the wheel and throttle as best we could to soften the encounter without losing visual contact with the *Diane,* which fortunately wasn't nearly as fast as the *Gem.*

All appearances to the contrary notwithstanding, Brewer and Pope weren't simply abandoning us. There was just this unspoken and unexamined assumption that we all knew what we were do-ing. It was simply the Alaskan style. But as a matter of fact, al-though my salad days were behind me, I was still lingering in my lamb-chop days. Lamb-chop days are when you believe "they" will look after you—friends and neighbors, the authorities, the state or federal government, the armed forces, the good Samaritan—while in reality the lamb is being led to the slaughter, to become chops at the banquet of the gods of this world, who are known to enjoy a feast of fools. For the fact was that as a lamb I didn't even think to consult the charts before starting out, to see whereabouts in the Bering Sea the Walrus Islands were located. After all, this was to have been an outing, a pleasure cruise, a picnic. It wasn't supposed to turn into another *Adventure!* Alaska is indeed a land of rugged individuals because all the others would have fled or been served up at the celestial dinner table.

But once again I was in the shoot and had no option but to stay the course. The only place I knew I was, was behind the *Diane* somewhere in the Bering Sea. "Walrus Islands" was only a name floating in the uncharted void of my mind. I had no mental image of how those islands related to Cape Constantine or Nushagak Bay. Though they had names, these airy nothings, they had no local habitation in my head.

The hours passed on the cutting edge. Either Pope was hanging back for us or we were keeping up with him, even though the *Otter* had begun to run a fever, the temperature gauge registering way too high. We had to slow down and fill the water tank periodically. We never quite lost sight of the *Otter,* but the *Gem* had ceased sparkling on the waves hours ago. Then Steve, who was steering, leaned forward intently, trying to make out a coherent image through the spray on the windshield.

"I think I can see the islands," he said.

I stood next to him, peering ahead. Yes. Small flat-topped mounds broke the horizon in the near distance. Surely the Walrus Islands. Good. Good. If the engine overheated too much and I had to drop back altogether to let it cool and if Pope didn't notice and kept going I'd at least have a target to shoot for.

The waves were slow and massively powerful out here in deep water, very different from the short chop of the bays. It made it easier to play them right, so that we didn't get knocked around so much. But it wasn't much easier on sensitive stomachs or inner ears, whichever is responsible for seasickness. Carol and the kids remained below, too sick to care.

We reached the tip of the first island about half an hour later, seeing no walruses. Up ahead, the *Diane* didn't stop. She seemed to be nose-diving through some unusually big waves. As we entered the passage between the first and second islands we started getting hit too—by what looked like some of the nastiest water north of Tierra del Fuego. The waves in that chute came on not simply as the impersonal sea, so much salty water propelled by such and such a velocity of air currents, indifferent to us, without malice aforethought. No. These waves came around the island like a mob of fanatics bent on obliterating a congregation of the wrong persuasion. There was that kind of single-minded fury in their onslaught. When the vanguard hit us I throttled way down. They had enough animus for both sides. I would not add the *Otter*'s momentum to the impact of our diversities. Resist not evil was clearly my best course. As long as they were so worked up I'd remain cool. I'd play dead in hopes of muting their wrath in accordance with the principle that there's no point in beating a dead horse. Or boat.

There was nothing I could do for Carol and the three little ones other than ask Steve to go below to see that they didn't get knocked around too badly and tell them that we were almost there. I caught a glimpse of the *Diane* moving along the lee of the island, a big one (Round Island, though I didn't know it at the time). Sheer rock cliffs rose abruptly out of the water. When we came abreast of them it was as though the cavalry had arrived and driven off the renegades. Whereas a minute ago the waves had been at our throats, the sea now gently rose and fell like the breast of a sleeping woman.

The sun found an opening in the clouds and threw a warm light over the scene. And what a scene it was. The cliffs were aglow with all the rich hues of the Impressionists' palette. Every niche and crevice was dotted with seabirds, and the air was alive with them whirling and slashing across the high rock face. Then as we moved in closer we saw the walruses, hundreds of them hauled out along the boulder-strewn ledge of a beach. They looked like boulders themselves—earth-colored mounds interlaced with the ivory of their tusks. At our slow approach bunches of them waddled to the edge of the ledge and dove or plopped into the water, which was deep and clear. Some of them bobbed about, looking at us. Others swam off under the surface. The water was a liquid transparency and we could see them several feet down streaking away like torpedoes. On land they looked hopelessly slow and awkward, but in the buoyancy of the salt water they darted, twisted, and turned as quick and agile as minnows.

I called down and told Carol what was happening above deck. She gathered herself together and they all came up to see the walruses. This was something a little seasickness wasn't going to obviate, something rare and wonderful that would strike deep and always be remembered. What an impression those wild walruses made on the kids' wide-open minds. Their queasy stomachs were forgotten as they stood like statues watching the walruses there in the water all around the boat and along the beach, waddling to the edge and dropping in with great splashes. This wasn't anything like seeing animals in confined spaces behind bars or windows in a zoo. These walruses were free and in their natural habitat pursuing the lifestyles that had been instinctive with them since ancient times.

How awesome and strange they must have seemed to the kids—and to me. I confess that the image of the walrus I'd carried in my head most of my life was of an amiable, goofy critter somewhat resembling Wimpy, the hamburger fiend in the old Popeye cartoons—bald, dopey-eyed, with a large brush mustache and about the size of a rotund man. So I too stood there wide-eyed with wonder. For these animals were enormous and not at all "goofy." Some of the bulls were about twelve feet long and would weigh in at three thousand pounds or more, with thirty-inch tusks, each one a good twelve pounds of solid ivory. More than that, seeing them in the wild brought home to me a sense of the primordial world teeming with such magnificent creatures as the walrus, the world in which our ancestors had evolved, in which human nature had formed. Such creatures as these, and such a scene as this, had become part of our makeup, and now our kind had been ripped out of it, torn away and bleeding at the roots of our being, rendered insane in the context of our artifacts, thrashing about with murderous confusion.

We needn't fear these walruses, so many of them surrounding the boat. I've heard stories of wounded or enraged walruses attacking kayaks, *oomiaks,* or other such small vessels, and I'm sure that if they did they could easily swamp such craft. The *Otter,* however, was out of their class of confrontation. She was old and some of her technologies were in bad repair, but she was still large and sturdy. A walrus is not a Moby-Dick. In the age-old debate between fight or flight waged in the animal mind, flight in this case emerged the obvious victor. Their shimmering hulks streaked away from us as we moved slowly along the beach.

We and the other two boats before us were, unfortunately, badly disturbing these mammals. Walruses when panicked sometimes trample one another getting to the water. Calves especially are liable to be crushed in the stampede. But at the time we were ignorant of that. Actually, disturbance at a haul-out site was one of the lesser impacts the walrus had to endure. They were still being killed illegally—poached—for their ivory and, rarely in modern times, for their meat and hides. Occasionally a wounded walrus would escape only to die later and eventually be washed ashore by a big tide. It was such a prize that Pope, Brewer, and Gene hoped to find beachcombing.

The ivory was worth going after, not necessarily because of its dollar value but as a palpable symbol of the great animal—so long as it was taken from one already dead from causes other than yourself. And it wasn't only the tusks these beachcombers hoped to recover. There was also the *usik,* the core of the bull walrus's penis, solid ivory and a couple of feet long. One of my soft-spoken native pals showed me one once back in Dillingham. He explained that that was why walrus cows seemed so contented and the bulls so self-assured and macho.

Just as there's more to harvesting a moose than the shooting, there's more to collecting walrus ivory than the finding. The treasure isn't just lying there on the beach all smooth and clean from sun and rain. It's firmly embedded in the voluminous folds of the now long-dead and rotting carcass. Animal cadavers of ample size give off pungent gases as they decompose, which, while attractive to scavengers, are intensely noxious to the civilized nose. And although the bodies of living animals are often pleasant to the touch—the flank of a horse, the fur of cats and dogs—the flesh of a dead walrus that has lain in the sun for months would normally be a thing to shun. To advance in the face of such deterrents requires that your desire for the trophy be stronger than your revulsion of its context. It would have to be a case of mind over matter, or mind over stomach. Having "a strong stomach" really means having a determined mind capable of discounting the urgent messages being sent by the stomach.

We pulled up alongside the *Diane,* moored in a quiet cove of the beach. When we cut the engine a cascade of seabird cries poured down upon us from the cliffs above. Those cries filling the air so abruptly reminded me of the sudden crash of cymbals and horns in a Stravinsky composition, startling and at first unnerving. We all stood craning our necks gazing up at the flashing wings. Pope's voice cut through the din.

"Come on, you guys, let's go find us some ivory."

He and Brewer and the other Gene were standing on the beach. That we had been able to follow, had made it to the islands without being shipwrecked, to them was apparently a matter of course, not worthy of comment. Self-reliance in the face of a certain element of risk was taken for granted. And after all, the Professor wasn't some kind of tourist. He was Pope's partner, had fished Bristol Bay and wintered in the bush. He wasn't *chechako* anymore.

For the while, Carol would stay on board with the kids, slowly recovering. But Steve and I were ready for some beachcombing. We were trudging along in the direction the intrepid trio had gone, slowly picking our way among the jagged rocks and boulders, stopping to inspect some bones lying about, when the pungent odor of ripe carrion snaked its way up our nostrils and registered on the alarm panels of our brains.

Red alert. Cancel all plans. Vacate area immediately.

"Wow," said Steve, stopping dead in his tracks.

"I think they found what they were looking for," I said, backing off.

The three scavengers had disappeared under a natural rock arch that followed the curve of the beach. Steve and I had been about to enter the arch when the rank odor wafting through the tunnel had assaulted our sensibilities. Now here came Pope in his baggy black pants and ragged black jacket returning with a smile of triumph. What luck! They had stumbled upon the carcass of a big bull wedged among the rocks. Good big tusks and no doubt an *usik* to match. It was too late that evening to set about cutting them out, and all three of the scavengers were hungry. (Now that's a dauntless appetite.) They would perform the operation tomorrow after breakfast.

Some tomorrows never come. The whiff I'd gotten assured me that as far as I was concerned, which was at a large distance, the tomorrow of the walrus autopsy would never arrive. I would be elsewhere and otherwise occupied, thoroughly indisposed at the time. I had no special yearning for the objects in question, so my stomach and I were in full accord: no going near the cadaver. For my stomach and me the end in no way justified the means. Were Pope and the other guys to regard my defection from the John Wayne mandate as a failure of nerve, that would be all right with me. I had resolved that in this instance I didn't care what the Duke might think or say. "Well, all right, pilgrim, but if you're figuring on settlin' in these here parts you better see about gettin' yourself a little grittier stomach."

Next morning after a leisurely breakfast, the day sunny and bright, Carol was thinking about going ashore with the kids and Steve and me for a little beachcombing, which she really enjoyed and knew the kids would too.

Then Pope and the others, who had hopped ashore earlier, appeared from around some big boulders. They each carried a trophy, two tusks and an *usik*: caked blood with shags of rotted, pungent meat hanging from the ivory. Carol almost suffered a relapse. The kids didn't know what to think or feel, but they inclined to their mother's reaction. The ivory hunters squatted near the water and set about cleaning their spoils (what's in a name?), the air around them ripening. I had no idea what was wrong with their noses. The Durrs decided now was the time to set foot upon the beach and go off in search of other kinds of treasure. In the direction opposite to where the dead walrus lay.

The air was filled with the birds' cries and we could hear the surf booming on the windward side of the island. The sun was warm and the breeze fragrant with the sea, and I was thinking that this part of the excursion might almost qualify as a picnic of sorts. I addressed my little voice inside with a bit of a smirk! "So what do you say now?" To which the voice replied, "It ain't over yet."

Carol and I walked ahead, with Beth riding on my shoulders spurring me on with little kicks to the ribs. She was still tiny. Her brothers and sister called her "The Bug," good-naturedly, as though that were a title of distinction, which was how she took it. Jon and Sal came along behind us, picking up seashells and marbled stones and colorful pebbles, which they showed Beth. Steve found what must have been a walrus vertebra, bleached white by time and weather and about the size of a teakettle. There was a rightness of sculpted form to it. I could imagine it atop a pedestal in an art gallery. Jon spotted a bit of broken-off tusk among the rocks. It was a prize he hung on to for years.

But the really exciting find lay around the bend in a small grassy pocket among the rocks. It was like uncovering treasure, as if a pirate chest had washed up and broken open. Japanese glass buoys lay scattered among the clumps of grass. Most were about the size of a baseball, a few softball size, and one as big as a basketball. The thick glass was tinted shades of bottle green, lime, and amber, each one enmeshed in a skillfully knotted web of twine. Collecting colored eggs on the White House lawn at Easter was as nothing compared with this. These were giant Easter egg jewels from the land of Hobbit.

The kids of course pounced on them, rummaging through the clumps of grass. Each one found was worth a shout. They gathered them into a pile. Steve made a sack out of his sweater, and everyone carried a few by their twine strands. We returned to the boats laden with real booty. Some of those floats still hang in a cluster here in my cabin and look rather magical against the muted gold of the logs. They often call my mind back to the Walrus Islands and what we found and learned there.

We accepted our bounty as ample compensation for the rigors of the trip out, and I addressed my skeptical voice: "So what do you have to say now?" To which the voice replied, "You going back the same way you came out?"

Hmm.

The holiday ended abruptly when I was awakened by the sound of clanking metal, the smell of gasoline, and the voices of men attending to business up on deck. It brought me for an instant back into the fishing season. Especially familiar and unwelcome was the ache of sleepiness denied by the overruling mandate to run with and never against the tide, especially not in Bristol Bay, whose tides are notoriously big and powerful. Calculations were that to ride the tide into Nushagak Bay and on up to Dillingham we had to depart the Walrus Islands at about three in the morning. Very familiar.

Carol opened her eyes and looked at me. "What is it?" she asked.

"I think they're gassing up out of the drums for the return trip."

"Already?"

Yes indeed, my lady. Time and tide wait for no man or woman, and certainly not for sleepy vacationers who think they're in Florida. Apparently Pope had neglected to mention the itinerary of our outing, had there been one, and I had neglected to ask. Or maybe Teresa had become bored and bitchy. She hadn't stepped foot off the *Diane* the whole time, "catching up on a little sleep." Or maybe Brewer and the other Gene had business to attend to back in Dillingham. Whatever. Our one good afternoon beach-combing seemed like a small morsel set between two layers of hardtack. But then, just to have seen these walruses and the islands! That was worth the price of admission.

I told Carol to stay put, just go back to sleep. Sally was sitting up in the bunk she shared with Jon, looking around wide-eyed but mostly still asleep. I kissed her and laid her back down by her brother, who remained oblivious to the world of adult concerns. Beth, sleeping with her mother, was too young and secure to be bothered. Steve was getting into his clothes.

Steve and I went up on deck into the glare of the picking lights from the *Diane* and *Gem* (the *Otter* had none) to help with the gassing up. Then the engines rumbled into life and the three boats pulled away, moving out slowly along the beach. It was early dawn, the air cool and damp, smelling of the sea. Walruses dropped into the water at our approach. We could see their shadowy forms gliding away under the surface. Brewer and his partner were up on the flying bridge watching them, their white caps muted in the dim light. On the *Diane,* Pope stood with a leg up on the gunwale and a hand on the wheel, leaning out to gaze at the great beasts, no doubt absorbing some of their strange life into himself. Steve and I were doing likewise. I was hoping these creatures would always be able to haul out undisturbed at these pristine islands. Even if their protection required that people no longer could come out here to be among them as we had it would be important to know they would be there in the course of their migratory rounds. Their loss would gravely diminish human life, as have all the wildlife losses around the globe, even for the commercial people who don't care.

The Bering Sea was much quieter on the return trip. Steve and I spelled each other at the wheel while the rest of the family slept below. The *Otter* was overheating again, but the *Diane* stayed in sight. I had mentioned the overheating problem to Gene, reminding him of what he already knew. The hours passed easily enough, even with the familiar weariness from inadequate sleep.

Finally a low headland emerged on the horizon off the port bow: Protection Point and the wide entrance to Nushagak Bay. All right! Their calculations of wind and tide had been correct—something I had worried about a little without mentioning it to anyone. It wouldn't have been pleasant to have floundered around lost in the Bering Sea until we ran out of gas and bumped up against some unknown coast or, worse yet, got caught in a storm, the other boats nowhere in sight. "That's the sort of thing I had in mind," said the voice.

I slowed down to avoid any further overheating. The *Diane* started to pull ahead and was soon out of sight. That was all right. I was familiar with Nushagak Bay, as Pope knew.

When we neared Clarks Point I spotted a few boats tied together off a flat scow: the *Diane*, the *Gem*, and the white hull with dark blue trim that signaled the *Wanda B*, Kenny Brandon's gill-netter. A fishing buddy, Kenny was a charter member of D Inn Crowd, famous among the bars, and a high-liner. Pope and Brewer would naturally have stopped to hang out with him for a while. I turned the *Otter* into the tide and pulled up alongside the *Diane*. Pope and Kenny's partner, Louie Hereshka, handled the bow- and stern lines and I cut the engine. Carol and the kids had been up for the past few hours, and here came Teresa stepping aboard with a big smile to chat with Carol. Steve and I hopped over onto the *Diane* to join the guys, who were lounging around in the sunshine and passing the customary jug (no, Steve didn't drink). Kenny looked at me with those lazy, smiling eyes of his and handed me the jug. Pope beamed. "Ain't this the life!" he said.

"I second that," said the little voice.

Shortly after the Walrus Islands excursion we flew back to New York and my professorship. Our only firm plan as regards our possible future in Alaska was that I would return to Bristol Bay for the season of 1966 to fish my boat *Port N Storm:* make my own decisions, learn from my own mistakes. I had to feel confident that I could play the fishing game on my own and not just in tandem with Gene Pope. Actually, Pope had taught me a lot more about cutting loose and partying than he had about fishing—and much of what I had learned from him about commercial salmon fishing fell on the riskier side of the vocation.

So we were determined to go slowly and deliberately toward the new life we had envisioned and now had had a taste of at Nerka. Carol and I would mull it over, privately and together. For the next couple of years a leitmotif wove through the background of our lives: To go or not to go. That was the question. By the summer of 1968 the leitmotif had become an occupying force in my mind. I had done okay on my own in '66 and with Pope again in '67, when the *Diane* made seventh high boat in the Nushagak fleet. The desire to go had become obsessive in me. We put "the farm" up for sale but had no takers through the summer, and by September, when it looked like we could close a deal, the question—To go or not to go—became focused on the fact that by any prudent calculation it had become too late in the year to be burning bridges and heading north to Alaska.

3

We're Bound for the Wild Country

The only surviving photo of the trip north.

(September 1968)

To go or not to go. That was the question.

Early September, the leaves and grasses just starting to turn, yet really like summer there in upper New York State: shirtsleeve weather, Indian summer. But in the north country—the vast Yukon Territory we'd have to cross on our way to Alaska, and in most of the Great Land itself—September meant probable snow and subfreezing temperatures. But we were experienced automobile campers and liked traveling and camping in the fall, when the campgrounds weren't crowded. By camping out most of the way and fixing our own meals we'd save considerably on expenses, and we'd be moving through a lot of wonderful country—and moving fast. I was ready to put in long hours behind the wheel.

For the poet T. S. Eliot April was the cruelest month because he saw the promise of spring's new life doomed in the spiritual wasteland of America. But for me, on the brink of bolting the reservation for the promise of new life in wilderness, September was the cruelest month because its ambivalence in the seasonal round was so tantalizing. Any month before September would be good to go, and any month after September unthinkable. September itself though, early September, was neither the one nor the other. Like Janus, guardian god of portals, patron of beginnings and endings, it faced both ways, offering no oracular assurance as to the best thing to do. It might work out okay to chance it and just go, if the prospective buyer of our place came through, as seemed likely, finally, after we had tried to sell all summer. We might sneak past the real bad inland weather, the Yukon's snows and falling temperatures, maybe, with a little luck. But then again, we might run into early and confirmed winter weather.

Prudence, that rich ugly old maid I had such difficulty warming up to, sternly admonished me not to do anything foolish, to stay put. It was simply too late in the year to be thinking about starting out on a journey of that size, from New York State to the Lake Iliamna wilderness of Alaska: in a seasoned Plymouth Valiant ("valiant" all right, but wasn't discretion supposed to be the better part of valor?) all the way across Canada to the West Coast and up through British Columbia to the start of the Alcan Highway heading north, and if we made it into Alaska, the short airplane hop out of Anchorage to Lake Iliamna and *then* to start building a home, with winter around the corner.

"Maybe we should wait till next year," Carol suggested reasonably and mildly. She knew I was straining at the leash. "We could leave in the spring and have warm weather all the way—and time to build a cabin."

Yes, of course. That would be common sense. . . . But Zen says life is dancing in the houseless void. Could we dance to that tune? Should we even chance having to try? Common sense doesn't dance, it sneaks along. Yet if we didn't go for it this year we might not get to go at all. A lot can happen through a year's delay.

There's a photo of me taken that September of 1968, by Steve, I think. I'm sitting on a bench between two silver maples by our white farmhouse, unconscious of the camera, leaning forward, head bent, elbows on knees, hands loosely clasped, gazing sightless at the ground before me: To go or not to go. A question weighing on my mind as heavily, it seemed to me, as that which had bedeviled the Danish prince. Well, if we didn't get a buyer pronto it would all be idle speculation.

And then suddenly the poet W. D. Snodgrass, a colleague, showed up ready to buy the farm if I would take the mortgage, to which I agreed. Was this the signal I needed to risk it all and go for the gold? I was eager to believe so. I see myself then as a man under sway of some force capable of overwhelming his normal provision of reasonable caution. After all, I'd never been prone to foolishness, though often enough capable of it. My whole past history suggested I was reasonably intelligent, able to make appropriate common-sense decisions, not blindly driven by emotions or psychoses. So why was I wanting to do this foolhardy thing? For I definitely felt a compulsion to go ahead and do it, devil take the hindmost, contrary to all prudent deliberations.

But that was the point. Something in contradiction of prudent common sense was at work in me, something from outside the stockade of the conventional wisdom. That something was what was drawing me northward away from civilization, something from the hinterlands of consciousness, a blind, impulsive thing right out of primal chaos pulling me in the direction I had to go, drawing me to itself. I was caught up in a teleology.

For why in the world otherwise would anyone in reason want to do such a thing? That's the question I often sensed hanging in the air, especially in the beginning when people would ask me about the whole idea. And it's the question I asked myself then, and recurrently. I was always trying to winnow out the pat answers and put the fashionably idealistic ones to the test in the privacy of my own ruminations, always trying to get down to bedrock. I wanted the truth and was determined to resist the ego's propensity to accord it to self-congratulatory theories. What was pushing me—or drawing me—so hard, hard enough to make me want to undertake that kind of radical venture?

Many men, and some women, in the seething cities and tight

work-a-day suburbs daydream at times about just leaving it all and taking to the woods, returning to a simpler, slower life. But with rare exceptions they don't do it; they stay put, embracing the devils they know rather than risking the demons they imagine. With the majority, of course, the thought never crosses their minds. Their desires are fixed on goals lying in quite the opposite direction: on having more and better of all that city and suburb offer. The idea of starting from scratch in the houseless woods at midlife and in midstride of a successful career, family in tow, would strike them as preposterous—more than that: as a particularly incomprehensible and somehow reprehensible species of dementia. I saw some of my colleagues become upset, as though threatened, when in conversation I introduced the notion as a serious proposition for their consideration.

I had just turned forty-three that summer of 1968, a man in his prime, firmly ensconced in the catbird's seat: tenured full professor of English at Syracuse University, on good terms with my colleagues, liked by my students, with a schedule that took me off my thirty-five acres of fields and woods and away from my white farmhouse and into the city to teach and keep office hours only three days a week, Tuesdays, Wednesdays, and Thursdays, leaving me a four-day weekend—with papers to grade and classes to prepare for, yes, but on my own time and doing it up in the quiet shack I'd built at the edge of my woods, at the table looking out onto the hay field sloping down to the house and, on the other side of the gravel road, sinking to a line of brush down where the creek twisted, and then up the far fields rising to the thin rank of trees at the crest. In the winter, sometimes with the wind gusting snow against the window, I fed chunks of beech and maple into the potbellied stove that easily heated the small building.

And with lots of time off besides, long summers, long Christmas and Easter vacations, midsemester breaks, and miscellaneous holidays at regular intervals. Not rich, but not poor either.

Comfortable. Secure. A respectable middle-class life, with even a little professorial prestige to stroke the old ego. And a family to fit the picture, a fifties family, apparently, Ozzie and Harriet and the kids, with a touch of *Father Knows Best*. A normal American family (though by 1968 that hut of rough boards at the edge of the woods had become known to my friends as the Psychedelic Shack, a title bearing implications incommensurate with "normal" in mainstream America, being the site of ventures into the wilds of consciousness lying beyond the bounds of social conditioning). My wife Carol, a real-life devoted mother and mate, albeit with her own kind of spirit and strength of will when we argued, as indeed we did, but basically quiet-natured, gentle-natured, with a soft kind of brown loveliness, a woman satisfied with her life, more or less, even a little proud about her professor husband, whom she thought handsome to boot, and proud too of her four children, who she knew were beautiful and happy.

As much can be said, really, of our marriage: basically quiet-natured, good-natured, with a tight unconscious connection between us, an identification that persisted on its own, calm and steady beneath the occasional squalls vexing the surface (most of them, I now concede, probably generated by my subliminal restlessness, behind all the usual everyday stuff a part of me always looking and listening for that something missing, something forevermore about to be, without clearly knowing what, the thought passing like a shadow over both of us at times that it could be for someone instead of something else).

So there was the shack at the edge of the woods and the pot-bellied stove and the fact that I chose to live on a onetime farm thirty miles from the city, in an old house without central heat or hot water for the first years, freestanding cast-iron fireplace stoves heating downstairs and a little heat rising through grates to the bedrooms upstairs. My colleagues lived near the university in solid houses with all the creature comforts, all the twentieth-century shit, as I was wont to put it even then, feeling some amorphous contempt for the general insistence on all that. Was that what life was for, to be safe and a little fat and own nice things? What about the Great Mystery, and what about the wolves?

I hunted and fished in season avidly, almost obsessively, not only on weekends and during vacations but often squeezing in a half hour at a hedgerow or trout stream on the way home, as though the literal game or fish was that something I sought. On a Monday or Friday through the winter, when big Oneida Lake was likely to be void of other fishermen, I'd walk out on the ice to the middle, chop my holes, and sit there jigging for jack perch and walleyes, listening to the wind whispering into my ears. Those days when I came back with a brace of cottontails or a string of fish and laid them on the kitchen table did I not feel an odd sense of triumph, a curious pride, that was absent when I laid my paycheck down?

Also, at least once a year I went off to camp in the Adirondack Mountains for a few days, usually by myself but sometimes with my oldest son Steve—in the autumn after Labor Day, when the campgrounds would be deserted. We'd set up a simple lean-to camp by an open fire, the wind off the lake cold and the waves hushing along the pebbly beach. During the night the cold would wake me and I'd feed night wood onto the coals, the stars big and bright. As the flames grew, the heat would slowly put me back to sleep. I loved all that. I felt right. The tiresome movie with sound track in my head starring me as hero/villain would fade away and become silent, and there was just the night, the wind, the waves lapping, and the small fire close in crackling, sounds quieter, more quieting than the silence itself, like a wordless Zen parable emptying my mind, so that there was no other me than the naked night.

I don't believe I thought about it in quite those clear terms back then, connecting dots. It took me a quarter of a century to begin to realize what had been going on in me. As a matter of fact, it can take a lifetime for a man to come to know himself *(nosce te ipsum)* in terms of those delicate inner dimensions, the accumulation of those small experiences his gross conception of himself, the ego/superego syndrome of conditioning, had blocked him from recognizing as crucial to the growth of his real self. Keats said somewhere in one of his letters that life is a "vale of soul making," meaning by "soul" one's unique identity, which I believe he understood to come from and be molded by the universal creative energy, what the Indians called the Great Spirit, the divinity that shapes our ends, rough-hew them how we may (as Shakespeare put it in *Hamlet*).

At the time, I was governed by emotion and impulse. Cautious reason and common sense couldn't withstand the thrust of the desire that had grown in me over the years. Looking back, I've come to see that I had always wanted to live in the great north woods, even as a boy glued to the radio, thrilled by the howling wolves at the start of each episode of *Renfrue of the Mounted*. Was it Freud who concluded that only a life built upon childhood dreams could know fulfillment, that the money-and-power thing couldn't do it because it had never been a childhood dream?

What were reason and common sense anyway but the echo of our culture's mind-set? And wasn't it exactly that adolescent, repressive mind-set and the "reality" it projected that I wanted to get free of by turning back to raw nature? So why then be intimidated by its tinny voice, why bow before the preaching of its paranoid mentality perpetually calculating the odds? Nature hates calculators (Emerson said that). And Thoreau warned, "Who but the Evil One has cried 'Whoa!' to mankind?" And didn't Blake condemn society's denial of the gallant heart everywhere in his writings? And Wordsworth and Whitman, D. H. Lawrence and Henry Miller, and so many of our greatest visionary writers the same? These were the men to be listened to, not the captive legions standing up to their lower lips in shit murmuring, "Don't make waves. Don't make waves."

Always and everywhere what you hear is "Take care now. Be

care-full." Well, no thanks. Already got my fill of care. Don't need no more. Take care. What kind of advice is that? Is that wishing someone well? Damn the torpedoes of care. Full speed ahead! "Foolhardy" be damned. Better foolhardy than dead man walking. I go with *corage*—courage, heart, spirit. We're bound for the wild country.

Everything happened fast now. We'd travel light, just our camping gear, cold-weather clothing, and a few miscellaneous items. We stuffed everything into the trunk and onto the rack on top. Other things we'd need in Alaska or couldn't part with we packed in boxes and shipped to the village of Iliamna, which lay directly across the great lake from Pope-Vannoy Landing, Gene Pope's home site, our ultimate destination. The rest of our possessions, all the furniture, tableware, and so forth, went with the house as part of the deal I made with Snodgrass.

The bulk of my library I sold at hasty-departure prices, and what I didn't sell I left with the house. Snodgrass was a good poet and ipso facto in my estimation a good man, so I was content to leave those books in his good hands. Certain volumes, leather- or calf-bound eighteenth-century sets of Fielding's and Sterne's novels, for instance, a seventeenth-century edition of Quarles's *Emblemes,* a sixteenth-century copy of Plutarch's *Lives* in Latin, and other such fairly rare and valuable books I donated to the Syracuse University library, perhaps in part as a conciliatory gesture apologizing for my abrupt resignation, which was really almost a reprobate action according to the tenets of academia. Our last-minute telephone good-byes to friends and colleagues, softened a bit by vague talk about coming back, also probably belonged under the heading of reprobate or at least bad form. We used the same subterfuge when letting our folks know what was happening. The actuality of our going, after all the speculation and talk, was too sudden to be painful. Everyone was just . . . stunned.

I was like a man possessed. Everything there in upper New

York State that had seemed so close and solid now looked far away and granular as an old photograph. The Plymouth was loaded and we were about to climb in and drive off—just drive off to Alaska—when a car turned into the driveway and stopped. It was Sally Dike, an old friend and colleague, and now it was only a hologram of me that chatted with her and laughingly said yes, we're going to Alaska (I must somehow have forgotten to call the Dikes), yes today, right now as a matter of fact. She laughed nervously and looked a little confounded, as though she had just discovered a tear in the fabric of her daily life. She had dropped by to talk about some things of note concerning that life. I, however, was seeing her through the wrong end of a telescope and hearing a voice-over paraphrasing Shakespeare, saying, "But that was long ago, in another country, and anyway the wench is dead." Even the fact that it happened to be Friday the thirteenth was like water off a duck's ass to me.

Carol, a little bewildered, and the kids were swept up into the rush of our leaving. Jon remembers it this way:

The day Snodgrass bought the farm I was down at the reservoir fishing for sunfish with my friend Joey Adams, enjoying the last of New York's summer weather. I'd be going back to school soon. I rode home on my bike, and when I walked into the house I knew right away that something had happened. Everyone was excited. Sally rushed up and told me the news: The house was sold and we were going! My head got dizzy thinking about huge rainbows, great northern pike, and giant salmon. I was ready to leave the land of sunfish.

The excitement of our going continued like an undercurrent to the tedium of the long days of driving. There was a song we burst out with almost every day that became the theme of our journey. It was a song from America's pioneer days, the westward ho! days when according to the idealistic spin we put on it the pioneers felt they were leaving society and its strictures behind and striking out for the freedom of the frontier:

> *Far across the wild country*
> *Away! Come along!*
> *Hiyup-a Susanna! We're leaving today.*
> *We'll cross the wide prairies, o'er mountains we'll go.*
> *And we're bound for the land of the Sacramento!*

The words go to a spirited tune, full of energy and the fresh air of open spaces. We changed the last line to "And we're bound for the land of the ice and the snow." Also, the next stanza is filled with images of gold—the precious metal—which was what the majority of the early pioneers were really after, that or ownership of property, not the wild land itself, which was what we were after. To most of the first settlers, just as the Indian was nothing but a murdering savage, the "dirty Redskin," wilderness was nothing but wasteland, land wasted until fenced in, plowed, mined, and stripped of its forests.

We were content to leave that stanza out of our picture, exercising a deliberate suspension of disbelief on behalf of the pioneer. We wanted to believe in the American mythos about the pioneer as presented by Hollywood and the popular media, even though we had learned that it didn't square with the historical facts. The gap between fiction and fact, rhetoric and reality—often enough, between outright lies and truth—was a feature of mainstream America, its politics especially, I wished to leave behind.

I drove ten–twelve hours a day trying to beat the calendar. Every day into September advanced the possibility of getting bushwhacked by the weather in the Yukon. I had calculated that we probably wouldn't have time to put up so much as a one-room log cabin before the snow and cold hit, even in the Iliamna country, which, being surrounded by big bodies of water, would be much milder much longer than the inland territories. Every day counted.

In anticipation of all this I'd ordered one of "Bucky" Fuller's geodesic domes. With Pope's help we could erect it in a few days. It was supposed to arrive at Iliamna about the same time we did, or soon after. We'd haul it and our other gear across the lake from Iliamna in the *Diane*. That was the plan. But as they say in Tierra del Fuego, there's many a slip between the cup and the lip. The future has a way of unfolding itself in unanticipated events.

In the meantime we pushed on across Canada. We could pull into one of the provincial campgrounds, set up the tents, roll out our bedding, and be sitting down to supper inside an hour. Some of the campgrounds were crowded even back then and even that far into September because of Indian summer across the plains, but we usually managed to find a campsite off by ourselves a ways. When we hit the Alcan, farther north and further yet into September, crowds would be the last thing we'd have to worry about. Cold and snow would be the first.

We marveled at the great stretches of flat land through the Canadian prairies, mile after mile of cropland, with isolated clusters of buildings enclosed in islands of trees and shrubs for protection against the winds. The vast checkerboard acreage was crisscrossed by gravel roads straight as a ruler that met at right angles. And nary a billboard to clutter the open expanse of the land. Canadians are close neighbors to Americans but seem to have contracted a less virulent strain of commercialism, retaining a healthy respect for the land's dignity.

The last time I traveled by car to Alaska was in 1966, the summer I fished *Port N Storm* with my old New York friend Bob Henrie as partner. We had plenty of time to get to Dillingham before the season got under way, so we took the scenic route through British Columbia. It wound through the spectacular Rocky Mountains, a landscape as grand as any on earth, worth the couple of extra days' travel it cost us. But this time we were racing the clock, or more exactly the turning of the seasons, so we headed straight up out of Dawson Creek, passing through

Fort Nelson and Fort St. John—cowboy country—and across into the Yukon by Watson Lake.

The farther north the road took us the more the feel of the land and the look of the people changed, in subtle ways taking on the flavor of the frontier, as though we were traveling back through time. I had witnessed the transformation before, but it was still exciting because I was seeing it through the eyes of the family—and because this time I wasn't just passing through. I was out to enter the life the changing landscape and people hinted at. I should admit that some of the excitement for me, the Great White Leader responsible for whatever might befall us, was of a more uneasy kind as I watched green turning to russet and brown and falling leaves forecasting the falling white flakes soon to follow—an excitement making my foot go heavy on the accelerator.

Jon captures all this as it struck his carefree mind then:

After we crossed the Great Plains and started heading north I really had the sense that civilization was being left behind. The gas stations started becoming little more than a pump in front of a log cabin with huge moose antlers over the door, and one time there was a big bear hide on a wall. The men began looking different too, not so smooth and clean, more rough and weathered, which I guessed was the look of northern backwoodsmen—which they were! As we drove farther north days passed like weeks and we moved fast into autumn and the coming winter. The leaves were all turned and almost all gone and then there were snowflakes in the air, whereas a week earlier it had still been solid green and warm in New York.

By about the last week of September there was heavy frost on the ground in the morning, puddles were glazed over by a sheet of ice, and we were changing into our cold-weather gear. One day when we broke camp the sky had the leaden look of snow, and by midmorning the first flakes were swooping up off the windshield as we drove into them. The frozen road whitened quickly and after a while even smoothed out a bit.

We had been seeing fewer cars on the Alcan, and now we rarely saw any at all. The tourist season was over, the campgrounds deserted. Everyone except an occasional Alaskan going south and the mad professor and his family heading north had abandoned the wilderness expressway. Many of the filling stations had closed and most of the roadhouses. We never passed one without topping off the tank. We didn't exactly pray or hold our collective breath, but we were rooting for our valiant Plymouth to keep on keeping on. I knew next to nothing about automobiles but at least had put on four new tires and had our local mechanic check the car out well before we started.

Steve sat up front with me, Carol with Beth and Jon and Sal fit nicely in the back. The driving hours were long, but no one complained or waxed restless. Jon and Sal periodically engaged in the usual kind of fooling around. We talked a lot about the journey and speculated about the weather. But it was exciting—camping out, looking forward to the lunch breaks when we could stretch our legs or run around—and more than that, being on a journey, an adventure.

The deep forest stretching away on either side of the narrow strip of road now made its presence felt. Hour after hour it was there in our peripheral vision, the forest primeval, unbroken and clearly unconcerned about this one sliver of civilization passing through it. What we sensed in its presence we couldn't exactly say. It made no statements, gave no promises, muttered no threats. It stood silent and inscrutable, watching us go by—or so it felt, at least to me, and that only dimly; and dimly too it stirred memory of the metaphysical horrors. Was I ready to walk off into those woods? I knew in a way that this, what we half sensed in the vast forest, was where we were going, this was what awaited us over and beyond the down-to-earth practicalities of settling in. It would be a presence unlike any we had known in city, suburb, or countryside, a presence that could be daunting.

I kept this to myself. Why add to the potential of paranoia about the woods with something so amorphous? But I suspected that Carol was tuned into this a little now that the die had been cast and we were moving into it for good, not just as sojourners. If so, she never brought it up. Her talk focused on the pragmatics of our situation: time enough for the metaphysics later on. Jon, Sal, and Beth were without anxiety of any sort. For them it was pure adventure. They rested secure in the family bosom. I felt that Steve sensed something of what I did, but his sturdy spirit took it in without misgivings or complications.

The pragmatics of our situation weren't all that bad really. The temperatures were subfreezing but not subzero, as they easily might have been in late September in the Yukon. And the snow wasn't that deep yet that we couldn't get into the campgrounds. Most of them had some sort of central shelter with a stove or fireplace and picnic tables, and there was no longer any competition from other travelers for using them. At the end of the day's driving we moved right into one of those shelters.

Steve, Jon, and Sal, with Beth tagging along, could always find enough dead lower branches of spruce and charred chunks of wood from the other fireplaces for us to get a good blaze going in our shelter. Even if the shelter wasn't closed in we managed to stay warm enough. Carol got a hot meal going, usually something simple like franks, beans, and corn, while I inflated the air mattresses and laid out the sleeping bags. Paper plates and towels and melted snow made quick work of dishwashing. Then we sat around, close up to the fire, sipping on tea or cocoa and talking over the day and the prospects of the morrow. It wasn't long, with the cold air on their backs and the fire's warmth on their faces, before the kids crawled into their bags and drifted off. Carol and I sat up enjoying a last cigarette together.

"If our luck holds," I said, "we could make it into Anchorage in a few days."

"Oh, that sounds good." She looked up at me with those big, trusting brown eyes. I was home to her and, more than I realized, she to me. "So maybe only a couple more days of this inland weather. . . . I know it could get real cold. Or snow hard."

"Oh, yeah, it could. We've been lucky so far. Our guardian angel has been looking after us. He . . . *she* . . . believes in what we're doing." I smiled and put my arm around her shoulders. "Once we cross the border into Alaska, heading down toward Anchorage, we'll be moving out of the cold belt, farther south and with big bodies of water holding on to summer. Even in October, Gene tells me, the Iliamna country can be pretty mellow. That's our ace in the hole."

I could feel her relaxed against me. The fire crackled softly. I kissed her hair. "Yup, we're gonna make it, Lizzie Tish." All impressions to the contrary notwithstanding, "Lizzie Tish" was a term of endearment. Our marital problems seemed far away. We were very close. That was a big part of what I hoped for in going to this new life in the woods. I recalled that Nerka had been good for our relationship, and I had been aware of that.

Later, when the fire had died down, I was awakened by the cold on my face. Tending the fire was my job, so it didn't take much to wake me. Everyone else was sound asleep, only their noses sticking out of their bags. The stars were very bright, the surrounding trees a darkness upon the dark. It wasn't threatening snow, and I was sure we could handle the cold. We slept in our long johns, woolen socks on our feet. I fed the fire and crawled back into the bag next to Carol's warm body. The fire built up, crackling and shooting sparks. I leaned on an elbow, watching the flames.

Yes, it looked like we were going to make it. Still . . . three days, even one day, would be enough to stop us dead in our tracks if the sky opened and dumped on us good. And what would we do

then? Wait for the Mounties to rescue us? And then what? Go
back? Stupid thought. If we couldn't go ahead, we surely couldn't
go back. And to what, really? Six people and a dog to be taken in
by family or friends "until something turns up"? Not to mention,
as surely no one would, that the size of our folly would have become apparent to all, in their minds confirming the conventional
wisdom they lived by.

I don't remember that we debated the idea of going back at all.
It was as though we had glanced in that direction and seen nothing
worth considering. To my mind, common sense or "free will" really hadn't had much of a say in the matter. Something else had
written and was now directing the drama. We were simply playing
out our parts, knowingly or not. Mostly not. The deeper into the
bush life I got, the more strongly these thoughts were confirmed in
my mind. We were nature's children, her minions. The idea of
conquering or even controlling her was a joke. She wasn't ours, we
were hers. Her will be done.

Our good luck held, and we crossed over onto Alaska's pave-
ment at Tok within the next two days. The road on down from
Tok through the flat landscape around Glenallen was white with
snow, but the snowplows had been busy and we moved along in
good shape and high spirits. Then the terrain changed abruptly to
mountainous, black craggy cliffs and white peaks all around. The
road twisted and turned, rose and fell sharply. Of course, there was
road work to contend with. The girls in hard hats and orange vests
holding traffic signs seemed oblivious to what struck me as some
perilous detours, and I was thinking, ain't that just like Alaskans?
"Been around danger so long, seems like safe to me."

Anchorage then was more of a big town than a small city. It
was open and spread out, the main streets broad and not crowded,
parking spots everywhere. Many of the side streets were unpaved.
A disproportionate number of pedestrians wore plaid shirts and
leather boots and carried backpacks with fishing rods sticking up.
But all this was like the innocence of children in a dysfunctional

household who would soon enough become just like their parents. The signs were clearly in place that Anchorage would mature into a clone of all the stateside cities of comparable size, which I can assure you it has. If you're in Anchorage today you might as well be in Hoboken (except that in Hoboken you're not apt to bump into a moose on Main Street or a black bear on your back porch).

But out there, in the hinterlands beyond this city, still wild and undaunted, severe as a Zen master, was the enormous Alaska bush. We got a motel, did some buying of what we'd need, sold our valiant Valiant, with a pat of thanks on its indifferent hood, got on an airplane, and headed out there.

4

Lake Iliamna

Aerial shot of the dome and One Mile Bay.

(September 1968–August
1969)

So now the long and winding road from Morrisville, New York, to
Alaska had been traversed and we were aloft and flying into the
primordial world awaiting us, as if flying back through time. The
airplane rose fast, at an angle, and I leaned past Jon, who had
the window seat but wasn't looking out much; he was keeping himself together and frowning his way into all this new stuff. I looked
back at Anchorage, the last emblem of civilization we would con-
template for a long time. It was already just a small flat patch on
the land, all squares, rectangles, and straight lines crisscrossing: a
geometry of the linear mind, the meddling intellect that misshapes
the beauteous forms of things (as Wordsworth put it). Up ahead
there were no squares, rectangles, or straight lines but only the
rolling greens of unbroken forest and tundra reaching up into the
snows of the jagged mountains. And that was all there was to see—
no clearings, no power lines, no highways, no houses or barns or
pastures—until the long oval shape of Lake Iliamna hove into
sight, pale blue jewel amid the foil of the green land and snow-
capped mountains. We were looking out a window opening on
hundreds of thousands of years when wild nature was all there was.

Gazing down at the great lake from the air we saw no sign of a town, no roads, not even the wake of a boat. And in my inner vision Hemingway's Compton leaned back from the controls and turned and smiled at us, nodding ahead. That was where we were going, into that wilderness rolling and stretching away to the far horizons, mysterious and vast. We were embarked on a great adventure, a great life enterprise, to play our part in the archaic revival, to rediscover our true selves and our proper home.

"Ooo," I heard Carol's voice in my ear, "it looks so big . . ."

"The lake?" I asked. "Biggest in the big state of Alaska, over a hundred miles long and a good thirty-five across at its widest."

"No, not just the lake. Everything. The whole country. It seems like it could swallow cities, towns, highways, everything and everyone." She paused, then tapped me on the head. "—Too much, Bobby." (That was Carol's boilerplate for when she thought I'd once again gone too far out.)

"Yeah." I grinned. "I think we're a long ways from New York. Like on another planet—or in another time."

Little Beth was asleep with her head in her mother's lap, and Sally was still such a little girl herself. Carol too, in a sense, a little girl—I often referred to her as "little one"—though she was to reveal strengths I never guessed were in her. "The woods will bring out what's in you," old-timers said. If we made a go of it, the kids would be growing up in a very different world from the one their mother and father had been born into. I wondered, would they grow up a little on the wild side? So far, I'd never met anyone born and raised in Alaska who didn't have an air of the wild about them, females too, not just the males. Surely it was the influence of the Great Land itself, something like Rupert Sheldrake's morphogenetic fields molding them, with not enough people and rules and regulations on hand to damp them down.

That's what I wanted for my kids, a strong spirit, the kind of zest for life so obvious in all the vivid wild creatures. "How near to good is what is wild," Thoreau had written. I didn't want my boys and girls reduced by social conditioning to hamstrung well-adjusted citizens doing the Man's work for him. I repeated to myself one of my personal mantras: To be well adjusted to an insane culture is to be insane. Wilderness living could be dangerous, no doubt about it, but so could civilized living, not only in terms of systemic overt violence, but also in subtle, sneaky ways eating away at your life force.

The plane banked and as the wing dipped I caught a glimpse of the airfield and a few buildings. My mind filled with practical matters. Would Pope be there to meet us? He lived directly across the lake, at its widest part, and as we descended I saw that it was blowing and the water was white-capping. This wasn't a place where trains, buses, and aircraft kept fairly regular schedules. The kind of assured regularity people expect in society was alien to this place. This was the land of *Adventure!* and adventure by definition is unpredictable, out of uniform—especially, I knew very well, when Gene Pope was involved.

Pope wasn't there to greet us, but Bob Walker, owner of the Iliamna Lodge, had been alerted and came forward with a handshake and a weathered smile. He had the kind of look I'd come to recognize as typical of the seasoned bush Alaskan, a certain lean alertness and an easy style. He told us who he was and that he had been on the radio with Pope that morning and yes, my partner was probably about halfway across by now . . . if he had managed to get enough charge into the battery he'd used to call the lodge. Pope was a walking illustration of quantum physics's uncertainty principle, or maybe better, he was a Zen lunatic: Never mind your plans. Surrender to the impulse. You'll have a better time.

The lodge was a classic of its type, handsome in large golden logs and glass. It was spacious inside; one wall of the main room was all plate glass overlooking the lake. Walker catered to trophy hunters and fishermen from around the world. This was the big time for those sportsmen who could afford it. On the drive from the airstrip to the lodge Steve and I and Jon rode in the back of the pickup, Carol and the girls up front with Walker. There was dried blood and some matted hair on the pickup bed. Another pickup passed us, its back bristling with moose and caribou antlers and a pile of brown fur that said grizzly bear. We stared. Every one of those antlers looked trophy size. Big time all right. Big game, big country. It could fit the Adirondack Mountains, which had been the deep woods to me as a kid, in its vest pocket. The base of some of those giant antlers still showed fresh blood matting the hair. Just this morning or maybe the day before these great beasts had been roaming the woods and tundra where we were going to live. We were in the thick of it now.

Walker told us to make ourselves comfortable in the main room. We could enjoy the view and at the same time watch for the *Diane*. Just off from the gravel beach maybe fifty yards a cluster of dark rocks, one as big as a house, were fronting the incoming waves, which broke against them in classic tumult. The open lake beyond revealed no far shoreline. The clouds were dark and scudding over the water. Just the right kind of day for Pope to make the trip across. Call it a voyage. I could imagine him at the wheel, probably in the same immortal black jacket he had worn that first day back in 1964 when he strode into my life, and at the Walrus Islands too. He wasn't liable to the mania of owning new things. Backwoodsmen tended to take pride in their ability to keep old things going, partly no doubt because they weren't exposed to the barrage of manufactured wants deployed through the mainstream media. My family would be free of that in the woods. They would learn how little in the way of *stuff* it took to enjoy life.

The kids were quiet, but their eyes were wide open and taking it all in, picking up on the different look and feel of this place. We all stood by the big window gazing out, hoping to catch sight of the *Diane*. Ours had been a morning flight to Iliamna, so there was a lot of daylight left, even this far into autumn. Still . . . you could never be sure about Pope.

Carol was reading my thoughts. "You know, I hope he makes it pretty soon. It looks bad out there. Maybe he had to turn back or something . . . But I hope he shows soon, if he's coming for us today. I won't want to be out on that lake after dark." She gazed out past the rock islands with a little shudder. "I'm not sure I want to be out on that lake at all in weather like this." She was remembering our excursion to the Walrus Islands in '65 when the weather had turned sour and she and the kids had gotten so seasick she hadn't felt scared, only sick. Yes, but it wasn't another bout of seasickness she feared now. It was the great lake itself, immense as an inland sea, harboring all the awesome power of the sea, and all its indifference to the perpetuation of hominid life-forms.

Jon and Sal had been getting restless with the waiting. They wanted to go down and explore the beach. We would be able to watch them through the big window, so we let them go, cautioning them not to wander off. There they were below, two small figures from pastoral New York, with a different wind blowing their hair. Here's what Jon saw—and smelled:

There were strings of salmon swimming awkwardly, flopping about in the shallows, in their death throes, the males bright red with white rot spots and massive hooked jaws. Out on the water diving ducks dashed this way and that, restless with the gloomy weather. A cormorant flew low, skimming the water, then settled into the chop. A loon let loose its eerie call, and overhead a flock of Canadians were making their way south. It was probably all just like this a hundred thousand years ago.

Then there were the smells. I breathed in deeply, inhaling the scent of these strange new surroundings—the clean air, rain, and big water smells mixed with the whiff of rotting salmon, cranberries, the scent of tundra, Labrador tea, and much more I couldn't name. Years later when I had been away from the Alaskan wilderness for a long time at grad school, the first thing I did upon returning home was breathe in the smells. As I stood taking it all in I saw a small gray boat bobbing in the chop. I knew that it was probably Gene

*Pope, our taxi across the lake. I had hoped for something like an air-
craft carrier for the crossing, but the little gray boat would have to
do. Sally and I ran back up to the lodge, excited.*

Just before Jonny saw the *Diane,* Steve spotted it from the window. "I think I see him," he said, pointing past the big rock.

Yes, a little dot of a boat out there bobbing and wobbling and
disappearing in the bigger troughs. The *Diane.* And making a
proper entrance, like the classic opening of a horror flick showing
an old gabled house in a thunder and lightning storm. The Big Eskimo in the Sky didn't believe in easing into things, especially
when newcomers were at issue. He wanted them to know right off
what they were getting into. Sure, the lake could be sunny and
calm, but more often it was like this, or worse. A very large fresh-
water lake can be rougher and more dangerous than the salt waters
of Bristol Bay or the Bering Sea because without the salt to damp
them down to some semblance of order the waves are apt to go
berserk and run amuck.

Steve and I went out into the wind and down to the beach to
meet him. And here he came in that wading-right-into-it-whatever-
it-is rocking, cocked-shoulder walk of his, black jacket torn and
flapping in the wind, just as expected, and a smile so unconstrained it would have fractured the face of any normal person.
Well, we shook hands all around and even allowed ourselves the
liberty of a clap or two on the back. His curly black hair was
jumping for joy in the wind.

"How was the crossing?" I asked, and got the reply I expected.

"Just two degrees shy of flat calm for Iliamna Lake!" He gave
me his tight-lipped serious grin, belied by his twinkling eyes. He
liked to get a rise out of me, watch my reactions. "We'd probably
have to wait a month for a better day." It seemed to me I'd heard
that song before.

. . .

It was choppy out past the big rocks all right, but it did feel good to be on the bounding main again, riding the waves, the splash and dash of it. The clouds started breaking up and some sun came through, turning the spray off the bow into fans of diamonds. The wind seemed to be easing off. The Big Eskimo in the Sky was cutting us a little slack. Carol and the three small kids were down below, life vests nearby.

Carol and Gene had greeted each other in friendly fashion. Pope was ready to be on good terms with her, given the chance. He was good-humored and inclined to like people. Despite her inner certainty that safety and security could never penetrate the force field of mayhem around Pope and his doings, she was inclined to give him another chance or two and search out his good side, to see him more the way her husband did, if possible.

I noticed that Pope was spinning the wheel to port and starboard way more than usual and I was about to ask him how come when he looked over at Steve. "Hey, Steve, you're no landlubber. Come on and take the wheel." Then he assumed his sincere and serious look. "Oh," he said, "I forgot to tell you: The rudder is loose from its bottom hold on the skeg. Broke loose. So steering is a little tricky. You'll have to watch the water close and kind of anticipate the bigger waves that want to shove us broadside, and compensate for the floppy rudder. So you'll have to work the wheel a lot more."

Aha, thought I, we're off and running in *modus Genus Popeius*. Hang on, Hannah!

Gene broke into a smile and stepped away from the wheel. Steve took over and, no surprise to me, got the hang of it right away.

"All right!" Pope beamed at Steve. "You're captain of the good ship *Diane* now. Steady as she goes."

By halfway over, the water had calmed a lot, no more white caps, and the sun had broken through. I called down to Carol to come up on deck and enjoy the ride and the day. Jon and Sally popped up right away (in life vests on top of sweaters and jackets) and stood by me, with a hold on me and the boat. Carol came up with Beth, also bundled and in a vest, looked around, and, seeing nothing but water, no land, managed a wan smile nevertheless. I didn't bother her with news about a free-swinging rudder.

Within the hour we saw the massive rock, reminding me always of the forehead of a giant sperm whale, that was the landmark of Tommy Point, entrance to Intricate Bay, and we soon passed behind it and into the maze of islands and channels. The water here was quite calm. The islands were gorgeous with the dark spruce among the spattering clusters of golden leaves still clinging to the birch trees. As mentioned previously, because of all the sizable bodies of water in this region autumn and winter came on much more slowly than in the interior, which would be getting subzero temperatures and snow by now. That was something I congratulated myself for having counted on.

Pope-Vannoy Landing was a small clearing along the banks of a spawning stream at the far end of the bay. Two weathered, low-slung log cabins sat along the bank; the bigger one, with what looked like a couple of sections added on to the original cabin, housed Gene and his family. The smaller one, a one-roomer, was where Grant Vannoy, Gene's uncle, lived amid his books and practiced his esoteric philosophy, often discussing and arguing with his interested and indefatigable nephew far into the dark winter nights. The third cabin was the newest, the logs not grayed like the others. Gene and Grant had built it for Art and Patty, Gene's parents, who had abandoned their middle-class life to be near their only child, whom they couldn't talk into returning to Ohio.

During the fishing season of 1964 Pope had fallen madly in love with Teresa Prince, Albert's sister, and consequently broke off with Matrona, his native wife, an act that did nothing to recommend him to Carol and alerted me to the fact that wild did not necessarily mean nice or moral; wilderness and the morality of Western culture did not always jive. But I had come there to learn, not to judge; and I hadn't come with any steadfast allegiance to the moral teachings of Western civilization, which I had seen to be, more often than not, hypocritical and at odds with human nature. Wilderness—"Nature bloody in tooth and claw"—couldn't compare by way of savagery with the constant carnage and slaughter moral civilized peoples have been visiting upon one another—and of course upon the "benighted savages" whose lands or resources they coveted—down through history. It was one of my core observations that civilization warred upon human nature, and that was one of the core reasons why I left.

As regards Gene and Matrona, people break up and suffer the trauma of divorce in Middle America too. Matrona's case, however, was especially tragic. She had relatives and friends to turn to all over Bristol Bay, but after she decided not to shoot her husband she went on a bender in Anchorage and, as so often happens with these innocents from the back country, fell among the drunks, perverts, and drifters who hung out in the sleazy bars along Fourth Avenue and, as I heard the story, was found one day in a back alley, sexually violated and beaten to death. Indigenous peoples have suffered physically and spiritually at the hands of the white man everywhere and at all times, including today. The Upik Eskimos, Inuit, Aleuts, and Athabaskan Indians of Alaska are still treated like second-class citizens regardless of all the egalitarian political rhetoric and the natives' intelligent efforts to lay claim to their ancient rights. I don't know that this tragedy can be laid exclusively at Gene Pope's feet.

His band of ragamuffins came running as we tied up. There was no mistaking them for anything but bush kids, dressed in whatever miscellaneous rags they could find to put on. The youngest boy, Junior, about six or seven, came clomping along in a pair of his father's mukluks, looking something like Mickey Mouse around the feet. There were two other boys, Billy the older and Tommy the younger, about twelve and ten. The two girls, Sharon and Dolores, were bright-eyed, tanned, and quite beautiful, the

mix of white and native having worked its typical magic in that regard. Dolores, the oldest of the bunch at fourteen, was radiant
with happiness, ebullient with energy. She wore an old print dress
and was barefoot even though the air was cold with autumn and
all the Durrs had put on sweaters and jackets during the trip over.
Her vitality and joy at meeting us apparently was all the warmth
she needed. We must have looked like celebrities to her. As time
would attest for us, she was sweet-natured, without a derisive
bone in her body. The third girl, Marlene, seemed unusually shy.
We learned later that the year before she had wandered into the
dog yard and been attacked. Her scalp had been torn off, and she
had to wear a wig after she recovered. Most sled dogs are as
friendly as any other kind of dog, and yet this sort of thing seems
to happen a lot in outback Alaska.

Teresa followed, her baked-apple cheeks all bunched into a big
smile. She greeted me: "Professor! I can't believe you actually
came! And Carol . . . and the kids—getting so big!" She went up
to Carol as to a long-lost sister and gave her a bear hug. "Oh, it's
so great to have you here." Carol returned the embrace, smiling
and saying friendly things. I knew my little lady had her doubts
about Teresa: Was this a genuine expression of the old-time Eskimo warmth I'd told her I had found so often among the native
people, or was this the spider welcoming the fly into its web?

The thing about Teresa and so many of her people struggling to
know themselves in the modern world that had been thrust upon
them was the ambiguity or ambivalence of their feelings and attitudes. I'd seen native men in Bristol Bay turn, under the influence
of alcohol, from jovial to nasty in the course of a few hours, the
threat of violence coming into their eyes and demeanor. By 2:00 or
3:00 A.M. in any of the bars you could be assured of a fight breaking out, hopefully not involving yourself, another goddamned
white Outside fisherman ripping off their fish. A real-life Dr. Jekyll
and Mr. Hyde scenario. Carol sensed this about Teresa and was
friendly but wary. Under sway of my excitement at being there,

I assumed it would all work out amicably. After all, this was a different life, devoid of the stresses and petty grievances germane, it would seem, to city and suburban relationships. The natural world would surely have its salubrious effect.

The Durr kids were oblivious of any undercurrent of tension and went on their merry way exploring the Pope kids' world—the set-net with the thrashing of the caught salmon, turned rich red or mottled pink after so long in fresh water, beheading, gutting, and splitting the fish to the tail, tossing them into the brine and then hanging them in the dark smokehouse that smelled of wood smoke and the dried salmon already hanging there; fishing for rainbows off the mouth of the creek or picking the last of the berries; these and so many like wonders of this new life any child would inevitably be caught up in.

Art and Patty, with Grant trailing a bit behind, came down the dirt path smiling and looking Middle American, except for Grant. He was slim but sturdy and a little stooped, with long gray hair and long gray beard, nondescript clothes—the classic sourdough old-timer. Beyond a handshake and hello, he said little, looking out at us from among all his hair. For reasons resident in the singular imagination of a young boy, Grant impressed little Jonny mightily. I'll let him take you inside his mind as regards Grant Vannoy:

As I was a ten-year-old new to the wilderness and its denizens, Grant somehow both awed and terrified me. I remember him now decades later as a mixture of Walt Whitman and Gandolf. I can still picture him, gray hair and beard, gray eyes, pipe clenched in his teeth and often an older model Ruger Blackhawk .44 Magnum on his hip. To me he was the consummate frontiersman.

Nobody really knew much about Grant's life before he moved to the bush to live near his adventurous nephew. There was talk that he had once been successful in the Outside world, a ladies' man, and drank too much. Like so many people who end up in the bush and fall in love with it, Grant didn't talk much about the life he had walked

*away from. I imagine there were secrets and regrets about his life be-
fore Alaska which he took to his grave. He sometimes had that sad,
faraway look of a man who traffics with ghosts.*

*In 1968/69 Grant was in his midfifties and fully content with the
simple bush life he had found. He hunted, put up fish, picked
berries, gathered eggs in the spring, and grew a huge garden. On
summer evenings we would often see him sitting in his potato field
smoking his pipe. Us kids would joke that he was watching his potatoes grow. Looking back now, however, I realize that he was very
much a Zen man.*

*Grant was the community watchman, at least for all us kids. He
would tell us in a soft voice not to play somewhere because the ice was
bad or not to fish a certain stream because a grizzly was currently
working it. In the summer our dad and Gene were away fishing in
Bristol Bay, and Grant became the necessary jack-of-all-trades—
carpenter, gardener, and medic. On Saturdays we would often load
everyone into skiffs and find some special place among the islands to
have a picnic. I can still see Grant sitting on a log smoking his pipe. I
got the feeling he enjoyed watching us run around. If he didn't like the
way the weather was shaping up he would tell us it was time to go or
maybe not even say anything but just point at the darkening sky.
Everyone would then start packing things up and get into the skiffs.
No one argued with Grant.*

*His greatest passion was reading. He welcomed the coming of
winter after the busy summer months. The long dark gave him the
time to read. In this way he was one of the most fortunate men I've
ever known as all he needed to experience real contentment was a
warm cabin and a good book. In his later years he lost much of his
sight from reading by the dim light of kerosene lamps.*

*Nothing smelled like Grant's cabin. It was a mixture of wood
smoke, wet wool socks, gun oil, smoked fish, strong black tea, and
pipe tobacco. To this day, I can imagine opening the door. I feel the
rush of warm air and the smell, which was never displeasing, it was
just . . . well, Grant's cabin.*

Having grown up in the wilderness, I can tell you firsthand that kids don't need big thrills, fancy parties, and piles of toys to be happy. The outdoors and a kid's imagination can provide all the thrills and entertainment needed.

That's how it was on Halloween 1968. The Pope and Durr kids were having a time terrorizing the three-cabin community of Pope-Vannoy Landing. It was a miserable cold, rainy, windy night typical of the Alaska peninsula in late autumn. I was in the middle of a flanking maneuver around the girl part of our gang when I passed by Grant's window. There he sat, imprinting my mind with an image I'll remember till the end of my days. He was sitting at his table by a kerosene lamp, reading. His pipe was clenched in his teeth, and the ever-present mug of black tea rested on the table. I watched him for a full minute, with the rain hitting the window, distorting the image. Then I turned and looked into the darkness that stretched away uninterrupted by the friendly lights of houses. For a minute I felt the true depth of the wilderness I was now a part of and I felt awfully small. I glanced once more at Grant in the lamplight, then turned to continue stalking my adversaries. I was sure glad Grant was nearby in case the dark tried to swallow me up.

Grant's brother-in-law Art was also slim but looked like someone in Ohio on a weekend about to mow the lawn. Patty too was neat and clean, almost starched. Unlike her husband, she was a robust figure, and I could see where Gene had gotten his physique and energy. She was solicitous of our comfort and eager to extend some hospitality to her son's friends, the Professor and his family. Patty didn't like or approve of some of her son's other friends, but she welcomed the Durrs with bright eyes and open arms. We looked like the people she and Arty had left behind in Ohio, and I a bona fide professor no less—surely good influences on her son and grandkids. Pope apparently had not told his parents about those wild heavy-drinking parties he and the Professor, as charter members of D Inn Crowd, had vigorously participated in down on the fishing grounds. Nor had he mentioned the stash of homegrown pot the Professor had brought along, which accounted in part for Gene's present state of glee.

Pot was a new mind-bender in Bristol Bay, introduced, I must confess, by me in the season of '67 along with the information that certain species of morning glory seeds were powerful psychedelics capable of taking one into dimensions of reality of which booze, hitherto their only psychotropic substance, was ignorant. But I didn't feel guilty about that. I was doing them an important favor. The native population was being whacked hard by John Barleycorn, fueling violence, wrecking lives, but pot wasn't addictive like booze, had no serious adverse effects on body and mind (providing you didn't work around buzz saws and the like when stoned), could in fact be beneficial: the uses of marijuana in medicine, its calming, relaxing effect, and the fact that, unlike alcohol, it did not conduce to violence but to laughter. It worked that way for those of D Inn Crowd who tried it during the season of '67. Of course, pot would have arrived in Bristol Bay sooner or later in any event. I just played Marco Polo. Pope was one of those people, of whom I was not, who could smoke pot all day long, from waking to sleeping. So the hills were alive with the sound of his barbaric yawps, no doubt gladdening the hearts of all the wildlife who heard.

All the Pope family urged us to build on a piece of their land, but Carol and I declined, wanting to be more alone and fearing close proximity might breed tensions between the two families. Gene, Steve, and I went looking for a good spot to build on, cruising the shoreline in the *Diane*. It didn't take long. Gene recommended a sheltered cove off the main channel that ran past Pope-Vannoy Landing and to the mouth of the Copper River (home of trophy rainbow trout). The channel was long and wide enough to get choppy in a good wind, but the cove was a quiet harbor in all weather. A knoll rose from its banks about twenty-five feet high. It was covered with spongy, multicolored tundra without any trees at its crown. The view from the top was grand, overlooking a wide expanse of the islands, channels, and passage-ways of beautiful Intricate Bay.

That settled it; that dome of tundra would be the site of our wilderness home. In reason, we should have regarded the fairly steep climb to the top as a negating handicap. Gene kind of men-tioned that, plus the exposure to the wind. But that view! No cas-tle overlooking the Rhine could boast its equal, because the world spread out around the castle would all be tamed and carved up by hordes of people, whereas our view surveyed nothing but aborigi-nal, pristine nature. No other humans lived in Intricate Bay. The nearest human population was in the native village of Kakhonak, about twelve miles from Pope-Vannoy Landing, half of them down the open lake.

Not only were there no other people living in all the square miles of Intricate Bay, there wasn't a settlement or even a cabin along our side of the great lake until its northeast end, where Carl Williams and his wife kept a household and outbuildings during the summers on the site of what was once the native village of Pile Bay. Carl transported fish boats on his big flatbed across the mountains from Iliamna Bay on the Cook Inlet side to Lake Il-iamna and back again.

The first few days we bunked with the Popes. Gene somehow produced a large metal bed for Carol and me; his kids made up pads and bedding in the back rooms for Beth and Sally; Steve and Jon slept on the *Diane,* using the oil cook stove for a little heat. We all ate together, in shifts, mostly salmon with Grant's potatoes or sometimes rice or our beans. Healthy and tasty too. Breakfasts were either pancakes or oatmeal. Lunches were apt to be peanut butter and jelly or leftovers. Even with Gene there with his generous nature to monitor things, Carol noted that Teresa usually managed to dole out more and better of the grub to herself and her girls, Gena and Roberta. (Pope didn't believe in planned parenthood. Let the chips fall where they may.) Food was not that abundant at Pope-Vannoy

Landing, not because the country couldn't provide but because Pope wasn't an ambitious provider. He liked to talk and laugh, all the more so under the influence of pot. "Fetch me another cup of coffee, woman!" he would call out at intervals, which Teresa did, with something of a sour demeanor. Carol maintained a straight face, but there was no mystery as to what she thought of that.

After a few days at the Popes'—waiting, somewhat anxiously, for word that our geodesic dome had arrived at Iliamna—we set up our tent, big enough for all of us, at the base of the knoll in what we named One Mile Bay because it was about a mile from the Popes'.

Autumn was passing, the birches were all but bare, and the lake was beginning to freeze. Thank God for all the surrounding big waters holding winter at bay, slowing the Coldman's approach. We had to cross over the big lake, back to Iliamna, to get the dome, our food staples, some mailed packages, and the Franklin stove my imagination wouldn't let go of, though I was to learn that such a stove wasn't best for real cold country. But an open fire dancing before us while the wind howled outside! Gotta have that stove. I wasn't in Alaska on practical matters but for the poetry. Nevertheless, my mind was preoccupied with one matter of crucial practicality: getting a house of our own to winter in. We could probably get the dome up—the panels bolted together, the seams taped (we'd need a mild, sunny day for that) in just a few days, but no word had come from Walker that our domicile had arrived. We had no time to lose. I had the plans, so we knew the dimensions. The dome would have to sit on a platform. We got to work on that.

The knoll was fairly flat on top, but we leveled the needed dimensions further. Now for the platform. You can't set a building on the ground and expect it to last or even remain level. We needed logs, and they would have to be carried up that hill on our shoulders. What we wanted were standing dead spruce, which would weigh roughly half of what they did when alive. When we found one of about the right diameter, we'd fell and limb it, cut it to size, lasso it with a stout line tied to the *Diane*'s stern cleat, drag it into the water with the boat, tow it to the foot of the path up the knoll, gird up our loins like men, and bull it up to the top on our shoulders, one sixteen-foot log at a time for a total of twelve.

Arms like knotted manila rope, chests like bison, legs like mountain goats, and lungs that could huff and puff with the best of mountaineers. Three men in very good shape, even the oldest— not so far gone at forty-three: as regards strength and endurance, probably still in my prime. We dug holes for the footings, flattened the section of log that would sit atop a post, and spiked them down. Flattening the topsides of the logs with axes and leveling them to take the two-by-fours and plywood for the floor ate up a lot of time. But we were ready when Walker radioed that the dome and the rest of our stuff had at last arrived.

The skies cleared, metallic blue without blemish, and with the clear skies the cold descended upon land and water. The tundra was crisp with frost in the morning, and ice was forming in the shallows. Freeze-up was starting in earnest. We'd have to hustle to make it across to Iliamna and back with the dome and everything before the ice in the shallower channels got too thick to smash through.

Gene, Steve, and I set out the morning after we had all enjoyed a moose-steak dinner. Carol, Teresa, Art and Patty, and Grant and all the kids stood on the shore to wish us luck. What was Carol feeling? I had the sense that it was pride more than anxiety when she came over to kiss Steve and me bon voyage.

It was a clear, brisk day, and I was relieved that it wasn't blowing. Pope had managed to reattach the rudder to the skeg, and that was comforting. But even on our way among the channels of Intricate Bay we had to break through some thin ice. Oddly perhaps, we didn't worry about that. We were young, hale, and hearty, and it was just *Adventure!* Would I rather be sitting safe and warm in my office at Syracuse University preparing for class?

I was always proud to have my number one son Steve at my side, and number two son Jonathan already showed signs of becoming a good woodsman (which he has). Should I want them to become doctors or lawyers or businessmen sitting in stuffy offices in crowded cities breathing bad air while exercising mainly the left lobe of their brains instead of living this kind of life out in the open? They'd make more money, but would they have more life? There's more to life than accounting. Our greatest American poet, Walt Whitman, expressed the fact of the matter succinctly:

> *Now I see the secret of the making of the best persons,*
> *It is to grow in the open air and to eat and sleep with the earth. . . .*

> *Here is realization,*
> *Here is a man tallied—he realizes here what he has in him. . . .*

The trip across was easy, but when we got to the other side, at Iliamna (formerly Severenson's Landing), we couldn't reach the beach. Ice had formed along the shore of the cove too thick for the *Diane* to break through. We were stopped about twenty yards offshore. Pope backed the boat up and drove at the ice. Commercial hulls of *Diane*'s vintage were strongly built, the bowsprit thick and made of ironwood. But no use. We broke through the thinner fringe ice and then were stopped. All right then, that meant the ice was thick enough to walk on. Pope pulled up broadside, and we tossed the bow anchor and a stern hook onto the ice, then jumped over the side to drive them in enough to hold the *Diane* in place.

"Okay," Gene said, "let's get your shit, slide it to the boat, and haul ass. It's now or never."

As mentioned, we had broken through the outer fringe of thinner ice. Where we were stopped the ice appeared to be at least three or four inches thick, enough to hold quite a bit of weight. Steve stayed aboard to watch the mooring lines should a wind come up, while Gene and I walked to shore. Bob Walker and several of his hired hands had gathered there, ready to help if they could. We used Walker's truck to get my stuff to the beach. The dome came in triangular sections, nicely packaged to take some rough handling. Once we got a section onto the ice, one man could slide it out to the boat. A couple of Walker's guys helped. We'd lift the sections up onto the *Diane*'s gunwale, using it as a fulcrum, and Steve would tip it into the stern hold. The same held true for the plywood, tied together, set on edge, and slid along by two men.

Then came the pièce de résistance, as they say in Tierra del Fuego: the crate with the largest size of Franklin stove packed inside. It was very heavy, maybe too heavy for the ice, especially since it took both Gene and me to push it along, adding up to a lot of concentrated pounds. I was breathing hard. The ice could crack and give way at any instant, which could turn out to be more than just a dunking in ice water, what with that big dead weight going down with us. Okay, come what may, that's the deal. We kept on shoving.

Unreasonably, I wanted that stove in the dome despite whatever risk it represented at the moment. As we neared the boat I noticed there was a film of water on top of the ice that hadn't been there before. It helped us move faster, but it meant the apron of ice was sinking a little, and it got deeper as we neared the edge by the boat. Nevertheless, it wasn't cracking, breaking up, just the whole thing slowly sinking under the weight. We got to the *Diane* and the water was ankle deep. Walker's guys stayed on shore, not wanting to add their weight. Our adrenaline must have been right up at the top of the gauge because Gene and I in synchronized movements pulled the two hooks, threw them on board, and without pause lifted that crate—it probably weighed nearly three hundred pounds—right onto the gunwale with one heave—with the ice sinking and the water coming up our boots to our knees. Steve held the crate balanced on the gunwale, and Pope and I kind of beamed up into the boat. The three of us then set the box down. The guys on the beach were whistling and cheering and holding up the victory fingers. I could almost hear it on the air: "Now if that situation ain't just like Pope. Well, good luck to *you,* Professor!"

We waved, Pope doing the boxer's victory gesture, hands clasped over his head. Then he started her up and we pulled away and headed back across. But as it turned out we weren't done with the ice yet (or vice versa). For one thing it was building up on the hull. I doubted we would have made it if we had had to run the length of the lake instead of just across. The ice buildup made me nervous— something about it gave me the shivers, and it wasn't just its temperature. But I could see Tommy Point ahead, we still had enough freeboard, and there would be minimal splashing in the sheltered channels of Intricate Bay.

So we had my stuff aboard and had made the crossing okay, the weather holding fair . . . and cold. We were in the open bay behind Tommy Point when the engine quit. The *Diane* glided to an eerie silent stop, my heart in accompaniment.

"Shit!" said Pope.

"What?" I asked him.

"What with all the shit and shinola back there I forgot we might need more gas to make it all the way. Well, fuck a duck."

"Yeah, we're the duck," I said, "Daffy Duck." I was a little more than a little dismayed. Out of gas. My home and food and whatnot on board and we're dead in the water many miles still from Pope-Vannoy or One Mile Bay, the ice thickening in the channels with every passing minute.

Pope looked over at my downcast features. "I bet you think we're *fucked!*"

"We're not?" I responded in a flat tone. "What do we do? Hop overboard and push the boat to shore? Or float around until the Coast Guard or Sea Scouts rescue us?"

Steve stood back, waiting to see eventualities. He wasn't prone to anxieties.

Pope said nothing, just gave me his tight-lipped grin. He went below and came up with a can of nuts and bolts and some oily rags. "Here, you guys clean these up as good as possible. —We ain't done yet, mates." We did as directed while he was crouched over the engine with a wrench. "Okay," he said. "Hand me them nuts and bolts."

What he did was to place those nuts and bolts in the carburetor's settling bowl (I think he called it that), thereby raising the level of the remnant gasoline enough to start her up. He had drained the fuel from the cook stove and poured it into the gas tank; the boat could run on that fuel for a while, but it had needed real gasoline for starting.

Okay. I'd been in tight spots before with Pope, and he had always found a way out. I think tight spots squeezed him into coming up with something unimaginable. This was no exception. "Alaskan ingenuity" triumphed again, a little. Pope was grinning. I was learning not only what to do but how to take things in stride, with a head cool enough to be capable of ingenuity.

The engine started, with just enough of the fuel oil behind the gas to push us up against the shore before the engine went dead. And now what? It was almost dark and the cold settling down hard. I wasn't even sure in which direction Pope-Vannoy lay or what kinds of water and land lurked in between.

"Okay, mates," Pope said, "the situation is simple. We need some gas, and after that I know two channels that should still be open. It's about a five-mile walk-and-wade from here to home, so it'll take some time getting the gas. Either of you want to keep me company? —You know, get in on the *Adventure!*" As he belched the magic word *"Adventure!"* he thrust his head forward, eyes bulging, mouth in a tight grin, clenched his fists, and swung his arms across his chest in that same weird gesture I first saw him perform back in '64 on the old *Port N Storm* the day I met him. The gesture still startled.

"Can you find your way in the dark?" I asked. (It was a rhetorical question; I knew he'd say he could—and probably he could.)

"Sure!" And then he let out a laugh that rocked the boat. "I think so . . ."

"I'll go," said Steve. "Oh, no you won't," I thought but didn't say. We weren't in Alaska to secure our security. They were both smart and strong. They'd make it, one way or another, sooner or later, though it would be a tough round-trip. As for me, I wasn't needed and I was tired. Five miles in the dark through the bush without so much as a trail, with muskeg, streams, and whatnot to negotiate, didn't present a prospect I felt I could embrace at that time—though I now know that if my going had been unavoidable I would have and could have done it. You learn that you have reserves that can be called upon in dire straits. These straits were inconvenient and uncomfortable but not dire. Yet.

"I'll mind the *Diane*," I said, "keep the bears at bay." At the last minute I'd brought along my Ruger .44 Magnum. My Boy Scout training once more. However, my training in this instance at first appeared to be wanting in one particular. I should have known there'd be no food on board and that we wouldn't just go, come back, and sit down to dinner. The cupboard was indeed bare. Not even a box of Sailor Boy crackers. And it was getting colder and darker by the minute. No food, no heat. Too bad, Professor. But at least this wasn't the *Titanic*—lots of food and luxurious appointments but too much salt water. Whoa! Wake up, Professor! What's in some of those boxes on board but *food!* I turned on the DC light long enough to find a carton of canned beans. Out came my hunting knife and—the *Diane* did have some forks and spoons on board—those cold beans tasted just fine. I grabbed both sleeping bags and crawled into the top bunk, the lower bunk being packed with boxes, and prepared to play the waiting game.

The silence closed in, a palpable presence, the darkness concealing its features, the cold probing but so far not penetrating. I was a light sleeper. I'd hear a bear before he could reach the boat. But mainly what I sensed was that there was nothing enveloping me but raw, unmitigated elemental nature and that the operative word was not "cuddly." Don't look back, Dylan cautioned. And I didn't. The thought or image of my cozy upstairs bedroom in my erstwhile farmhouse back in New York never crossed my mind. The here and now of where I was and what was in the offing absorbed all my attention. My thoughts were with Steve and Gene picking their way through the dark woods. I was into it, and probably revved up to the point where the metaphysical horrors could find no weak spot of entry. This wasn't just another camping trip, a kind of vacation from which I would soon return. This was what my life was now all about. This was the real thing. No security blankets available. A sock in the kisser for the metaphysical horrors.

And make it they did. From where they had come out across the big channel from Pope-Vannoy, their combined lung power had been enough to rouse Art and Patty, who had been worried and wakeful. Art picked them up in the skiff. Next morning, Gene filled a five-gallon G.I. gas can and strapped it onto a pack-board. For the return trip, Art, with the shallow-draft skiff, was able to get them to within a couple of miles of the *Diane*. I heard them coming—more exactly I heard Pope's voice—from way off. Yeah! I thought, we'll make it back after all! But that thought, alas, was premature and unfounded. This last cold night was all the Coldman had needed to finish his dirty work. He wasn't yet up to full strength, but he was strong enough.

Pope was at the wheel, Steve and I standing next to him, peering ahead. And then we saw something. It looked like a thin line of mist or fog lying straight across the channel. It was ice.

"Shit! Piss! And corruption!" Pope roared.

We were in the main channel home, the widest and deepest. What were the odds that any of the smaller, shallower channels would be open?

Pope gunned it. Maybe if we could ride up onto it, the ice would open under our weight. We held on, and as we got close the ice got tough-looking. It had formed across the narrows and was spreading out from there. We broke through the fringe of forming ice, rode the bow up a little, and slid back into the water, the ice remaining solid, impassive, offering no apologies, expressing no sympathy. In the real world, forget Hollywood. The only happy ending you're guaranteed is death. Stay focused on the fundamentals of the moment. I wasn't thinking this. I had been absorbing it from that cryptic Zen *roshi* we call nature. A wordless transmission.

Pope tried the other two channels. No go. Our last hope of getting through was "the shoots," a shallow connection to the main channel that for reasons of physics I didn't understand stayed open with running water for days after everything else was iced up. It flowed into the main channel at its broadest and deepest, which would probably still be open enough to sneak across. Gene found the shoots, and we inched ahead cautiously. In the spring, when all the waters were high with runoff a fish boat could make it through, just barely. But not this late into the autumn. About halfway down we started hitting bottom and were stopped dead. We were now only a few miles from Pope-Vannoy as the crow flies. But we weren't crows, and to get around to within shouting or even shooting distance of Pope-Vannoy would mean another several-mile walk overland. Not even Pope could muster the enthusiasm. We had run out of horsepower, everyone tired.

We decided to build a fire on shore and rest up, maybe doze a little. We used the mattress from the boat and bunches of dried grass to curl up on with the two sleeping bags stretched out over us. The cold pressed down, but our driftwood fire held it at bay. The water running over the rocks murmured to some part of me about peace at the heart of existence, but my surface mind was troubled by the fact of our house and supplies being stuck here. For one thing, some of the foodstuffs would freeze before we could get them. "Just keep them frozen till you're actually going to eat them," Pope advised. "They'll be okay, most of them. And hell! We already got moose meat, smoked salmon, Grant's potatoes, and rice. We're in good shape!"

We talked some and dozed off a little, resting up, then made our way to a point of land within sight of Pope-Vannoy. Shots from the .44 Magnum brought Art in the skiff, the main channel being still open from the wind pushing the water, except around the edges. As for the *Diane,* she would have to stay right where she was till spring. After everything froze solid and we got the dome and other gear to our bay Gene and I would come back to do some winterizing and covering against the snows.

Well, everyone was relieved we were okay. Any number of things could have happened. This country had claimed the lives of many over the years. Art, Patty, and Grant were well aware of the dangers intrinsic to this beautiful land, and Carol intuited it, but they didn't dwell on it, especially not with the kids around. Kids nevertheless are good at picking up vibes from grown-ups, and after the hugs and kisses when we got back I thought I noted a new look in the eyes of Sally and Jon: It had never before occurred to them that their father and big brother might possibly not come back to them. Of course, they knew little or nothing about the risks involved in the dangerous job of commercial fishing, so that never troubled their imaginations. But with this they were right on the spot. They had seen the concern in the grown-ups' faces, including their mother's, and heard the vague talk of possibilities. So when we showed up, none the worse for wear, the two girls jumped into my lap with kisses, and Jon stood looking from me to Steve.

The validity of the grown-ups' fears for us was confirmed not only by the lives lost to this wilderness country in the past but by tragic fatal events to come. In the years after we moved from Lake Iliamna, Billy Pope was taken by a sudden squall of a snowstorm when on foot trying to reach home from Kachonak. The consensus is that the dense, heavy wet snow blotted out whatever trail there had been as well as his vision and he got lost. His body was never found. A year or two later, Tommy and Junior didn't make it back from Iliamna, where they had been partying. Their skiff could manage the lake when it was relatively calm, but it's a feature of this country that a blow can come up very suddenly. The boys had probably been drinking, and the prevailing theory is that their beat-up old kicker quit on them and they broached and swamped. These were all fine lads, good-natured, good-humored, and of course savvy about bush life, but I suppose that, like their father, they tended to be reckless and daring. My kids had become close friends with them and were hit very hard by the news of their deaths.

Perhaps most tragic of all was what befell beautiful Dolores, she of the sunny, ebullient disposition. It happened several years after we moved and were settled on Back Lake, north of Talkeetna, our present location. She was married, with two small girls. I don't have all the details, but what got her could have gotten Gene and Steve on their walk in the dark (no flashlight) after leaving me with the *Diane*. The circumstances were eerily similar.

She was at Pope-Vannoy with her girls during freeze-up. I never got it clear, but for some reason she wanted to make the run across to Iliamna in the old fish boat she and her husband owned. She had been familiar with such rigs since girlhood, so that wasn't the problem. She was actually less than a mile from home, in between Pope-Vannoy and One Mile Bay, when the ice stopped her in some way preventing her from turning around and going back, or perhaps the engine had conked out. She must have decided she could make it to shore over the ice from where the boat, with the girls, was stopped. She'd just walk to within shouting distance and her dad would come for her. It must have been a cold day, colder than the one when the ice had stopped us, with a stiff wind adding the deadly chill factor. She broke through and, soaked to the skin, got to shore. But even with less than a mile to go, the wind drove winter's breath right through her. Hypothermia set in fast. When she was found the next day lying dead on the beach, her body was without most of its clothing, a phenomenon typical of hypothermia victims—as though the body in a last desperate resistance to the conquering cold opened all the valves, loosing the last of its heat. Her girls survived but were no doubt traumatized.

We all, my boys and girls especially (now men and women of course), still grieve for them in that distanced place where time takes you, where the grieving is quiet with acceptance. And I will tell you that from the start of our venture, fear of losing one of my family skulked in a dark corner of my heart, never mind my understanding that living is ineluctably risky business and that death is really reentry into the world of light. It's not the dead who suffer, they're in the land of bliss; it's the living who loved them.

For the next few days the skies stayed clear and the Coldman, no slacker, stayed busy, putting on muscle. The ice would soon support our weight and that of our gear. We wanted three or four inches under us. In the meantime, one or another or all of the Pope kids were always around, and in the evenings Gene, sometimes with Teresa, was dependably on hand. He had brought over a small tent stove, which did the job for us, although I had to get up and stoke it a couple of times through the night. In the evenings of their visits, we sat around the tent close up like animals, bodies touching, warm with the cold outside letting us know we were warm, and talked and under Mary Jane's influence laughed a lot. We didn't need entertainment or any of those Conveniences sacrosanct to Americans. Bodily contact in the warmth of friendship, talking, munching, and laughing, with subliminal consciousness of the overarching night beyond the kerosene light, was quite enough. Very easy on the nervous system.

As regards gauging new ice for its readiness to support our weight walking, it's not a simple, categorical exercise. Due mainly to springs and other tentative factors there can be weak spots in an otherwise okay stretch of ice. Steve was involved in an interesting and, really, rather humorous incident on the ice with Gene Pope. This is the story as Steve tells it:

One morning while we were waiting for the ice to thicken enough for the gang of us to go retrieve our stuff from the Diane *Gene and I set out on foot for One Mile Bay. An additional night of freezing had, of course, strengthened the ice, but it was still "iffy," no more than two inches at best. Common sense dictated that we spread out, Gene about twenty yards offshore, and myself another twenty beyond that. There were springs along the shore that created more weak spots than there were farther out.*

It was like walking on a plate-glass window. Every rock and sunken log along the bottom was on display. Dead and dying salmon eyeballed us as we passed by overhead. You develop a comical walking style in this situation. I was aware that my arms were floating out at my sides, as if that would make me lighter.

Gene decided that this was an opportunity to deliver some old-timer wisdom.

"Do you know how to get out if you fall through?"

I just shrugged. It seemed fairly obvious that you simply climbed back out as rapidly as possible. But, as we were to learn, very few things are that simple in the wilderness. What might seem obviously right at the moment could be dramatically wrong and the penalty imposed for the mistake nothing short of death.

"It's important to remember you can't pull yourself out. You have to swim out on your belly. If you try to pull yourself out you just keep breaking the ice until you get hypothermia." He had his sincere look on.

To my immense delight, at the very instant he finished the lecture, the ice around him cracked in all directions. For a moment he was standing in the center of a giant spiderweb. This caught his attention. He looked around excitedly for options, but of course there were none. As the ice broke beneath him and he went down into the water he laughed over at me and, I swear to God, he said, "Here, I'll show you."

He kicked and clawed and swam out on his belly, a perfect breaststroke, until he got back on ice that would hold him.

Pope's advice was undoubtedly correct, but when, on a hunt, I broke through, as I recall it I simply popped back out onto solid ice. No breaststroking, no swimming at all. Just popped back out like a spring-loaded cork. Don't ask me how come. Maybe it was a different kind of breakthrough.

The third day after we had gotten back, the fault lines in the ice read about three inches thick, enough to walk on. We decided to give it another day to add another inch, and then we'd tackle the task of getting our dome and gear from the *Diane* to the knoll.

It hadn't snowed yet, so the ice was crystal clear and perfectly smooth. Along the shallows, as Steve noted above, you could look down and see the weeds and sand and stones on the bottom. It was something like walking on water, a little spooky. We made sure the kids, ours and Pope's, walked well behind me, Steve, Pope, Art, Grant, and Carol, and everyone spread out; if the ice held the grown-ups it would certainly hold the kids.

It was a beautiful day, sunny and brisk. Of course the youngsters had to do some running and sliding on the way over. It's a characteristic of forming ice about this thick that occasionally a person's weight will start a fault line, or crack, streaking out from between their legs with a screaming sound that can make your hair stand on end until you come to realize it doesn't mean the ice is opening up under you or that you've seriously disturbed a banshee. Carol, Sally, and Jon had a couple of heart-stopping frights with that until I assured them it was okay. At Nerka it had snowed while the ice was forming, so they hadn't experienced this particular fright, though as the temperatures had dropped we'd listened in the darkness to the expanding ice groan and howl like some monstrous birthing happening.

The kids helped by carrying back the fluff items like a family pack of toilet paper or maybe a two-by-four. It was exciting and fun in its own way. A couple of days went into getting the stuff to the bay and up the hill to the site. As might be said today, it was good exercise—especially good because the weather was clear and brisk, our spirits high, and our bodies full of vitality. It sure beat the hell out of the exercise bike pedaled by grim determination or the jogger breathing exhaust fumes alongside a highway. We were all getting stronger in body and cleaner in mind—not so much clutter of things to attend to in there. It was all quite simple. Lao-tzu would have approved.

We were in the middle of the big channel the second afternoon pulling our gear along when an amphibian flew over low, circled over Pope-Vannoy and our knoll, buzzed us, and flew back the way it had come. We all looked up and waved, but the airplane didn't waggle its wings in return greeting, as is usual in the bush. We were soon to realize that the people in that plane had not flown out to welcome us into the country but to confirm the report that we were indeed there and in the process of settling in.

No one at Pope-Vannoy knew anything about the Bureau of Land Management and the legal status of the land in Intricate Bay. The word we had gotten from Pope was "Come on up, pick out a nice spot, and settle in. There's no end of good spots and just about no one living here." Swell, thought the Professor, wide-open wilderness! Anyone but an English professor would have taken the precaution to check carefully with the state and federal authorities to make sure. With Carol's urging, I did check, sort of. The responses I got were a little unsettling but, I was prone to think, rather ambiguous. When the authorities realized who I was and what we wanted to do, they'd cooperate with us. Yes, of course. Call my remission naivete or innocence or irrational exuberance, or just plain stupidity. They all apply. In any event, we were soon to receive a very official notice from the BLM that we were trespassers and should prepare to vacate the premises.

"They just don't know who we are and why we're here," I assured Carol out of my idealistic daydream. "We're not land-grabbers or businesspeople out to exploit the land or people in some way." Feeling confident about my credentials and social status as a tenured full professor from a prestigious university,

I smiled. "I'll write them a nice letter explaining everything, one colleague to another, and they'll give us the okay." As it turned out, they didn't give us the okay, despite our noble purpose for being there, our daring experiment in life and family values, which I thought they might actually offer to subsidize in some way or at least encourage. Instead, they gave us the boot. They couldn't kick us out with winter coming on, but with spring they could and would, despite my eloquent letters of appeal. Now if I had arrived with some kind of commercial scheme to develop (exploit) the country it might have been otherwise. As an American I was still idealistic (ignorant) about our national agenda and the people who established it.

So for the winter we'd be squatters; what spring would bring we'd find out when we got there. Pope again offered us a piece of his land to live on, but still it seemed too close an arrangement. We'd wait and see.

With two-by-fours leveled across the logs resting on the footings and the plywood floor fitted and nailed down, the dome's platform was ready to support our home. Buckminster Fuller had designed his structure not only for strength and economy but for ease of erection. Even with the necessity of gloves making the handling of nuts and bolts and wrenches a little clumsy, the building went up remarkably fast. The fair, sunny weather held. Bureaucracy didn't want us there, but maybe the Big Eskimo in the Sky did, recognizing us as his kind of folks, at least potentially, by intention. We not only revered the wild beautiful country but greatly admired its native peoples and traditions. Unfortunately, whoever had turned us in had apparently lumped us in with the generality of white exploiters. We understood that kind of resentment and hostility and held no grudge against whoever it might have been, no doubt someone or group from Kachonak. We never tried to find out.

It had been getting pretty cold living in the tent, even with the sheet-metal stove. So moving into the dome was a happy day. Gene had been on hand throughout, with his ready laugh constantly easing my sense of urgency. We had our small mishaps, like when I was at the top of the ladder trying to fit the last stovepipe into the chimney rig and reached too far and lost my balance. The column of shiny blue pipes buckled, collapsed, and flew in all directions, with me and the ladder about to follow suit. Gene steadied the ladder, and in the midst of the chaos of crashing pipes looked up and, seeing my wide-eyed expression of alarm, broke into a helpless belly laugh and almost lost hold of the ladder. We had all been a bit tense at the job, what with the Coldman prowling around, but Gene's laugh broke the tension and we all wound up laughing too, even Carol.

The clouds gathered and the snow came drifting down the day after a mild, sunny afternoon when, with some help from a blowtorch, we finished taping the seams. Photo finish. The handsome Franklin stove stood slightly off center of the hexagonal room about four feet in front of the four-by-eight plywood platform covered with bedding and pillows that was both couch and bed. It held the whole bunch of us, the kids on the floor on the hide from Steve's moose, or kneeling behind us with their arms around our necks and their faces between ours, gazing at the open fire and listening to all the talk of moose and trapping and the village of Kachonak.

The dome proved comfortable enough, though a bit on the cool side when temperatures dropped below zero. The Franklin stove, even with its doors closed for maximum output, wasn't quite up to the job. We wore long johns, wool socks, and sheepskin booties, and put on sweaters as needed. The hexagonal space was also short on furnishings. The couch-bed did fine for Carol and me. We partitioned off a room and put up bunk beds for Beth, Sally, and Jon. Steve chose to stay in the tent to sleep; he liked tent living, the wind fluttering the canvas, the soothing sound of rain or snow hitting against it, the fire popping quietly in the little stove. I made a rough table out of leftover plywood and two-by-fours, around which I placed log ends cut to the right size for everyone. The main bank of windows overlooked Intricate Bay. The first heavy wet snowfall streaking by those windows made the fire in the stove glow brighter and overnight painted the dome white. So now we were right in place, properly fitted into the landscape: a palatial igloo overlooking its kingdom of the wild.

I bought an Evinrude snowmobile. By the time we got word it had arrived at Iliamna there was more than the six inches of ice a Cessna 185 required to land on skis. Pope and I flew over on the mail plane with Trig Olson to pick up the machine. I had opted for a snowmobile rather than a dog team because I didn't want the hassle of feeding and tending the dogs year-round, not to mention all the barking and howling—and mindful of what happened to Marlene. But I have to confess there is nothing quite like riding the runners or sitting in the basket behind a good fast team, lulled by the quiet hiss of the runners over the snow (no engine noise, no exhaust). Dogs bred to the sled want to *go*. They love it. Getting them into harness, yelping, lunging, sometimes snarling and fighting and tying the lines into Gordian knots, with you in the midst of it, yelling, kicking, lifting the dogs over one another to untangle the mess while trying to stay clear of their teeth, and with this accomplished, when you pull the anchor you better be fast and agile getting onto the runners because they're *going* full tilt from ground zero.

And then if you happen to cross a moose, even if you don't see it they'll smell it and there's just about no way you can control or stop them. Hang on, Hannah!—and hope they don't run the moose down because then you've got a very bad situation on your hands. And another thing: You might be many miles from home with the team, and you stop and set the anchor, maybe place the sled on its side too, but it does happen that, say, they smell a moose or whatever, surge forward, rip the anchor loose, and are gone over hill and dale, dragging the sled bouncing behind them and leaving you stranded. This occurrence ranges from pain-in-the-ass to potentially fatal if the snow is deep and your snowshoes are tied in the basket now fast disappearing. Snow machines can't smell moose, and when you turn them off they stay put. They can get badly stuck, true, but with experience you learn to carry snowshoes and a snow shovel, and while it may be a sweat, you can get unstuck and backtrack. So I have never put together a dog team, though I like dogs and animals generally. With the wild animals it's more than liking.

Nevertheless, in the modern world, even in wilderness, you must learn to tinker with machines, figure out bit by bit what makes them tick, because you have to. At first, I knew almost nothing about machines beyond using the choke and starting them—and even using the choke right takes some learning regarding cold versus hot engine starts and, worse yet, the in-between state when you're not sure whether you should or should not use the choke, risking flooding. Both my fishing partners, VanDevere and Pope, had been in charge of engine maintenance and overhaul; to date I hadn't even learned how to adjust a carburetor. But over the winter, under Gene's tutelage, I learned a lot about two-cycle engines.

I got my first lesson in the course of my first ride on the Evinrude, with Pope seated behind me. A brand-new machine, and it's running rough, wanting to stall. We were about a mile out onto the lake when Pope said, "Cut the ignition. I think she's starving. Let's try richening it a little." Whatever that meant. He lifted the hood and started tinkering and I'm thinking, "A new machine. What good could he possibly do it? It's 'starving,' so 'richen' it? He thinks it's a dog. So much for my beautiful new snow machine." But it did run a little better after he "fed" it, good enough to get us back. Next day Gene went at it in earnest, reasoning like a mechanic. It turned out to be a freak engineering flaw. The in-line gas filter was too "tight," not letting enough gas through. Pope started pulling plastic tubing out, like disemboweling some beast, with my heart sinking. He got a drill and bit, inserted the bit into the protruding middle of a flying saucer thing (the in-line filter, villain of the episode), and started drilling. Voilà! Successful operation. Patient was up and running for the rest of the winter.

With machine maintenance, the manuals help, but there's nothing like experience. Now, some thirty-five years later, even the unschooled Professor would have figured that one out. Under Gene's tutelage I already had learned to tinker with the points and condenser on our water pump: Chopping the hole in the ice was okay, but lugging five-gallon jugs of water up the hill gave rise to feelings of regret as to my choice of home site; so I bought the pump and hose and every few days filled the two fifty-gallon garbage cans that served as our convenient in-house reservoir. For the kids' Saturday-night baths Carol now had a two-man inflatable raft, spacious enough to hold Jon, Sal, and Beth. About midwinter Jon decided it was an indignity for a warrior to be bathing with his little sisters, so he bathed alone like Steve and his mom and dad.

One night the darkness was scattered by multiple beams of light down on the lake below the dome, and the roar of engines shattered the silence. There was a party afoot. A bunch of wild and crazy guys were on the loose, Trig Olson the pilot and Big John Nielson among them. They had come down from Kachonak to round up Pope and the Professor and his wife (Steve would watch the kids) for what turned out to be a full-bore race across the lake to Walker's lodge and the booze, headlights slashing up and down and across, a scene that would have captured the attention of Stephen Spielberg.

At the lodge, Pope and I got pressed into service with guitars and songs. The big barroom filled with music and talk and laughter. Carol was by far the prettiest woman there, and the Kachonak Eskimos were after her for every dance. How green I was to the ways of these people was evidenced in the fact that I started getting uptight about it and after a certain number of drinks actually put down my guitar and grabbed this one guy I thought was coming on too strong and had my fist cocked, but Nielson and Walker, laughing, stepped between us and hustled me to the bar for a drink, making light of the incident and cooling me off. The native guy I had foolishly threatened with violence just stood there looking bewildered. Carol put her arm through mine and murmured that the guy wasn't hitting on her but simply having fun. I have regretted and been embarrassed about my behavior on that occasion many times in the years since. It was just John Wayne bullshit.

The ride back must have been at least as furious as the ride over, but I have no recollection of that. I think if I had been alone and on my own I might have wound up at Pile Bay instead of One Mile Bay. The lake was one big sheet of snow and ice, no land visible, and I couldn't navigate by the stars.

The snows deepened through November, obliterating the underbrush and opening the country to snowmobile cruising. It was just luck that before I set out cruising the territory—sans snowshoes or shovel—several days had passed since the last heavy snowfall, so that the snow had settled enough for my machine to stay on top. Which it would not have had I launched my ambition to explore too soon after new snow. Hopefully, in that case, I would have discovered the error of my ways, which is to say my innocence or ignorance, and gotten stuck not far from home, so that I could make it back on foot and go on living and learning. Gene advised me about all of that the evening of my first day's outing. He didn't own a snowmobile, but many of his friends did, who would tell him how and why they got stuck on occasion; and of course Gene knew about varying snow conditions and their varying effects on snowmobile travel. There were no long-track machines back then—but even they can get stuck if you're not careful.

Through the first years of wilderness living you are constantly learning. Consciously or, as I like to put it, by osmosis. It never really stops because there's nothing mechanical, machinelike about wild nature. She isn't composed of "parts" that can be assembled and disassembled by rote. She is an organic whole and isn't ruled by fixed laws and stone tablets that can be understood and memorized, and that's that. Like a great artist she is spontaneous, unpremeditated, various—better described by chaos theory than by Newtonian "laws of nature."

So you must keep your wits about you and pay attention to present circumstances. Yet once you've learned the basic patterns, even though you stay alert to the unexpected, your mind will be free to tune into the invisible dimensions of the natural world— yes, but in fact those dimensions, you come to realize, had been informative in you all along, coming through the visible dimensions, as body is the visible portion of spirit and spirit the invisible portion of body. The conditionings of your civilized life that had bent you out of shape are strong and tenacious, but nature wants to draw you back to herself. And now that the distorting influences of society are no longer omnipresent and pressing in, you begin to hear her voice, and all those elements composing your being that belong to her—all your natural, true self—will secretly, silently respond. You may not realize it's been happening until much later.

A scene I carried around in my head for years before leaving for the woods was like the memory of a bad dream. I'm in Manhattan and wanting to walk uptown to a concert in the park or maybe the Metropolitan Museum of Art, but the hordes of hominids are all coming the other way, knocking into me, spinning me around, pushing me downtown toward the sunless canyons of Wall Street.

Steve and I, with Jon our willing accomplice, had been putting a lot of time into getting wood. Fortunately the dome was insulated and held quite well what heat the stove put out, and winters in Iliamna country tended to be a good deal milder than in most of Alaska, except perhaps Southeast Alaska. So far, the Coldman had been treating us with kid gloves, temperatures between zero and twenty-five or thirty above. But that could quickly change. I wanted to stay ahead of the curve and bring in a lot of wood for when things got nasty.

Following Pope's advice, we snowshoed a trail into a good section of woods containing several standing dead spruce. The snowshoe "float," as it was called, would set up well overnight. In the morning I'd run the machine over the float a couple of times, then give it another night to harden. The Evinrude had a Santa Claus type of sled that hooked up behind. It was big enough to hold two or three people, so it could carry a lot of firewood. That system worked like the shoemaker's elves. The woodpile stacked around the dome seemed like a scarf against winter.

One of Steve's closest friends through high school was Kelly Ernst. Now if you're just out of high school and you've read some Jack London and your best pal is living in the Great North Woods, what options do you have? None. You're going north. Kelly arrived, looking overwhelmed by the actuality of this immense wilderness country. "Jesus Christ, Steve, is this real? Is all this still here—in the twentieth century?" Pretty soon, it was the quiet little convoluted town of Morrisville that was seeming unreal to him.

Kelly had to get in on a moose hunt. What? Be in the Alaskan wilds and not hunt the great Alaskan moose? Go back to Morrisville and hang your head in shame? Dreadful thought. But Kelly had lucked into it.

Fresh tracks had crossed our wood trail several times. We were talking about that, making plans, when, as the Eskimos would believe, that moose offered himself to us. Jonny and Sally, with Junior and Sharon, were playing on the slope across the bay, sliding down, when suddenly they came careening and tumbling down, trying to run. Breathless and wide-eyed, they looked up at us and said a huge bull moose had suddenly appeared and *growled* at them and clicked his teeth and with his ruff up and ears laid back had started for them. Carol came down when she heard the kids' excited voices. She took them back up with her for some hot chocolate.

I turned to Kelly and Steve standing there. "Okay, Big Kel. Here's your chance. Take my rifle." I paused. "You can't overtake him on snowshoes, but follow his tracks—quietly as you can—and maybe he'll stop to feed along the way and you can sneak up on him for a shot."

Kelly was so seriously hyped, he looked a little pale, as if he might faint from the excitement.

The two young men strapped on snowshoes and crossed the bay and climbed the hill to where the kids had encountered the big moose, picking up his trail.

Now I had a thought. With Kelly spending half his time face down in the snow, they wouldn't come up on the moose even if he did stop to browse. But if I was right about the pattern of tracks that big fellow—huge imprints—was laying down, and given the direction he was moving in, maybe I could cut straight across and head him off, turn him back to Kelly and Steve. It was worth a try. Kelly had my rifle so I strapped on the Ruger .44 Magnum, thinking I might need to fire a couple of shots in the air to turn him. Shad was jumping around, wanting to go. Okay, he might give me another chance of turning the moose, if he smelled him when I couldn't see him—might just chase him back into Kelly's and Steve's sights.

It was a beautiful clear day and the excitement of the hunt was in me too. I headed out briskly. I wore snowshoes but I'd make much better time along the firm wood trail than Kelly and Steve in the soft stuff. If my guess about the moose's direction was right, I should hit the general area where I hoped to run into him with time to spare. Kelly and Steve would be way behind.

And I was right about intercepting him. But very nearly dead wrong about his reaction. He was not about to turn around in fright and head back. That big bull had had enough of hominid harassment—first those kids yelling and jumping around disturbing the peace, then the two bigger ones charging up the hill at him and making him move out of the nice patch of willows he'd been munching on, and now his way blocked by another one. He knew I was there before I knew he was there. I didn't see him at first but I sure as hell heard his roar, sounding as big and bad as a bear's. He emerged into my view like a thousand pounds of fury about twenty yards off and coming directly at me. Even if I could have climbed a tree in snowshoes it wouldn't have done me any good because I was standing among a bunch of scrub spruce only a little taller than myself. The snow was deep enough to slow the bull's progress a little. I looked back for Shad, man's best friend. My rescue dog was fast disappearing back down the trail.

I had only one option and I took it. When you are sighting in a Magnum handgun such as the Ruger .44 the explosion sounds like the crack of doom and the recoil almost throws your arm out of joint. But when, using both hands, I started shooting at that enraged bull coming for me I was unaware of noise or recoil. He was charging at me directly; my target was only his heaving chest and lowered head. His ruff was up, his ears flat back, his eyes blood red. He wanted me bad. One well-placed blow of a hoof with a thousand pounds of rage behind it would lay me low, and he'd probably keep pounding me into a bloody mess.

After the fourth shot, he wobbled but kept closing the distance. The last two in the revolver brought him to his knees, blood coming out of his nose. He was struggling to get up and finish his mission. I said to my hands, "Steady now." I had to reload. Controlling the tendency to tremble, I got a couple of rounds loaded. He was maybe five yards from me now and trying to stand. I put those two rounds right into his head and he collapsed into the snow and lay still. Now I heard my heart pounding and my hands started trembling—but not during the previous couple of minutes, and that was what counted. Steve and Kelly heard the shots of course and came running, so to speak. They burst into the opening and looked at me and the moose lying dead so close to me.

"Holy shit!" said Kelly, looking from me to the moose with big eyes. Steve just grinned. I was his dad.

"Sorry, Big Kel," I said. "I wanted you to take him, but I didn't have much choice because he was out to take me."

The bull was an old one, lots of battle scars on his hide. But he turned out to be good tasting and tender. During the skinning and butchering we recovered seven of the eight bullets I had fired.

My efforts via letters to the BLM through the winter to persuade them to let us stay, buy maybe just an acre atop the knoll, failed. The area was closed to entry, period. Carol was dead set against living so close to the Popes on a piece of their land, mainly because of Teresa but also because she considered Gene a bad influence on me as responsible husband and father. I wasn't enthusiastic about the idea either—though I have to say that our time in Intricate Bay would have been a lot tougher without Gene's help and advice, not to mention his predominantly high spirits. Intellectuals tend to think too much, and when they think they fasten their hands upon their hearts. Pope's upbeat presence dispelled much of that tendency.

One such fastening upon the heart had to do with the thought that we had no money left, our home was about to be yanked out from under us, and what do we do, where do we go now? Well, something would turn up. The worst-case scenario, living shoulder to shoulder with the Popes and Grant Vannoy, wasn't really that bad as far as I was concerned. It might work out. Patience. Wait and see what Wakan-Tanka has in store for you. The you with your hand fastened on your heart doesn't run the show. Worry has no credentials in the universal scheme of things. What beats your heart and circulates your blood and shines the sun runs the show. That's the you that is before Abraham was. The wild country, *biblia naturae,* tells you that, wordlessly. Something the size of a grain of mustard seed was all that was required.

A letter came from Les VanDevere, wondering how we were doing and saying he'd like to drop in on us in his little Piper Cub kind of airplane. I wrote and said sure, come on over, this is great country. So one day he did, bringing with him an old friend, Wayne Byers, from Chinitna Bay, on the wild side of Cook Inlet, where they both ran set-net operations through the summer. Wayne was short and wiry, very friendly. He had a surprisingly deep, resonant voice and that air about him of a man seasoned in the ways of wild Alaska. I liked him right away, clearly a man you could trust in any situation.

They had brought a jug with them, and after introductions to Carol and looking the place over, we sat around passing it and talking. One thing led to another, and as the looming prospect of the Durr family's homeless predicament arose Les made us an offer we hadn't foreseen and were happy not to refuse. We could winter at his set-net site in Chinitna Bay.

The BLM in one of its negative responses to my petitions proposed that we might want to look into an Open to Entry Program the state was about to initiate in remote areas north of Anchorage. We could winter in Chinitna Bay; with our help, Les would insulate his little plywood house there. Throughout the winter months there would be no one in the bay except maybe Wayne if he decided to do a little trapping. Les would be back at his job on the Nikiski dock near his home north of the town of Kenai on the peninsula of the same name, but he said he could fly over now and then for a visit and bring the mail and some supplies. We could get the dope on the Open to Entry Program from there and chalk up another year in real wilderness.

New country! Les said it was a good area for moose and the grizzly bears loved it because of the spawning salmon. (That wasn't altogether a recommendation.) The salt waters of Cook Inlet in front, and in back a fringe of woods slowly rising into the mountains. Seals floated in and out of the bay on ice floes, and beluga whales often visited. I was lukewarm about trapping, but we were broke and would need a little money to get by, so I was glad to hear that Wayne occasionally made some good catches.

It was a short hop from Lake Iliamna to Chinitna Bay. "Come on, I'll show you the place," Les said. There wasn't room enough for Carol too in the little airplane, so she stayed behind and sat down with Wayne to ask him those questions about Chinitna Bay that would especially concern a wife and mother.

Les's plane took off fast after only a short run. Within a few minutes—we were moving as the crow flies—Les banked, pushing the stick forward, and we swooped down out of the clouds above the bay. He circled Wayne's place, an old-time sod-roofed cabin with the usual outbuildings situated at the head of the bay. Then, flying low, he followed the beach toward the mouth of the bay, and there was his site—a classical, calendar-art image of the backwoodsman's homestead. Not. His plywood cottage fronted the expanse of Cook Inlet in the brave colors of pink and blue—the result, probably, of Les's taking advantage of a big paint sale, color restricted. Or maybe Les, under sway of some untoward artistic impulse, chose those colors as symbolic or resonant of the curious phenomenon of the north country that the clearer and hence colder it became the sweeter and more pastel became the sky and landscape, innocently wearing the pink and blue colors of babyhood—or perhaps not innocently but perfidiously, inasmuch as the Coldman was by far the most dangerous presence in the north country. That his colors should be pink and baby-blue! What could that signify, beyond being a heavy irony? That death was different and luckier than anyone supposed, as Whitman wrote? That death was a kind of birth? Maybe we fearful and fearfully confused hominids of modern times have been giving the Coldman and his comical sidekick Death a bad rap.

While Pope and I were scratching for fish down in Bristol Bay the family was having an eventful summer back in Intricate Bay. It was an ancient pattern in that country for the men to leave for the fishing grounds in the spring, the women and kids generally re-

maining at home. I didn't worry about them. Carol was a remark-
able wilderness woman already, Jon was quickly becoming a good
hunter and fisherman, savvy about the woods, and Art, Patty,
Grant, and Teresa were nearby. Jon has written an account of that
summer back on the lake:

*The day that Dad and Gene left for the fishing grounds Mom, the
girls, and I sat on the bluff in front of the dome and watched the
Diane until it was out of sight. Understandably, Mom was a little
nervous about being alone with us kids at One Mile Bay, but she
knew our Pope-Vannoy neighbors were nearby in case of an emergency.*

*Springtime is the leanest period for bush dwellers, with the fall's
grubstake nearly gone, along with the winter's moose meat. Also,
during breakup it's often impossible to get supplies or mail in, sometimes for several weeks. Such was the case that spring at Iliamna.
Breakfast was cornmeal mush, and the other meals were whatever
we could come up with.*

*We went egg hunting often with the Popes. Everyone feasted on
wild-egg omelets for weeks. I had developed into a pretty good
hunter and fisherman and was able to bring back ducks and trout
for the pot. Earlier in the spring, before leaving for Dillingham,
when the lake was part open and part still ice, Dad had gone out
almost every day after ducks and trout. He never came back empty-
handed; some of the rainbows were trophy size, but we didn't take
their picture, we ate them.*

*One event of that summer worth telling about gave us a crash
course in wilderness first aid. The girls and I were playing around
and I jumped off the table and landed on a piss pot—a Crisco can
with a sharp rim. It sliced open my foot. Mom told Sally to go get
Art and Patty. Sal put on her sternest, most determined expression
and ran out the door. Along the beach to Pope-Vannoy she almost
bumped into a grizzly bear. From what she told us, the bear must
have been taken by surprise to see a little girl running alone along*

the shore with such a stern expression on her face. Maybe it was that expression that caused him to back off and let her go by.

Before long we heard the skiff. Art, Patty, and Grant entered the dome with Sally. Her expression had probably scared them too. Patty told Mom I couldn't be flown out because the weather was just too bad for flying. Fearing infection, she held my foot on her lap, with paper towels under it, and went right at cleaning the wound with rubbing alcohol—that got my attention—and then closing and dressing it.

We then took it day by day, changing the dressing and inspecting the wound for any sign of infection. After a few days of my staying in bed it became apparent that the cut was healing well. After about a week I wanted to get going again. I couldn't use the foot, but that didn't slow me down too much. Art made me a pair of crutches and the Pope kids hauled me around in an old wheelbarrow.

When the salmon started showing in the streams it was decided that the Durrs would move down to Pope-Vannoy and help put up the winter supply of fish. There was an easy rhythm to the days. In the morning, Art and Grant tended the nets. When they came back, we unloaded the skiff, and our little processing crew sprang into action, splitting the fish, putting them into the brines, and then hanging them in the smokehouse. During this period of intense harvesting, the smokehouse was kept going around the clock.

These were great days. I was living the life of my hero, Huckleberry Finn. The Pope boys and I had a camp on a small creek over the hill from Pope-Vannoy. Here we would roast trout, drink strong Labrador tea we brewed in an old coffee can and sweetened with smuggled sugar. We also roasted potatoes and turnips appropriated during nighttime commando raids on Grant's garden. When the berries got ripe, Billy Pope and I would spend entire afternoons lying on our backs in the middle of a salmonberry or blueberry patch eating our fill and staring at the sky. Yes, these were great days, and what a great place to be, right on a big mysterious lake filled with fish and the hills around filled with wonderful animals.

Alaskan summers are short and intense. August had hardly started when I began to notice the first faint signs that the seasons were about to change. The Coldman was still asleep but not for long.

After the season down in Bristol Bay (the BLM cut us that much slack) we would accept Les's offer and leave the Iliamna country for Chinitna Bay. Steve and Kelly had flown out of Intricate Bay with Trig in April. They hung out at Walker's lodge for a week, doing gigs (Kelly "played" the bongos) for their room and board. Then they flew Outside, Steve to pursue his music career and Kelly his predilections. I think we were all half expecting a last-minute reprieve from the BLM, which was not forthcoming.

We dismantled the dome and ran it around to Pope-Vannoy on the *Diane,* where we stacked and covered the sections. The Pope family was all sure that someone, or maybe the village itself, would buy it—at the right price, which of course would be at a considerable loss to us.

Everyone at Pope-Vannoy was woebegone that we were moving on, especially their kids, as well as our own. But the air of freedom that blows through bush Alaska fosters the attitude among the people there that you are free to do as you think best, a freewheeling tolerance even for what might be regarded as an act of folly or a dangerous enterprise. No one laid down heavy negatives or stern counsel. The attitude was: Go for it! and damn it, we wish you luck. That was the code of the north woods, the last frontier, as it had been the code of the original frontier, the Wild West. I went back to the East Coast a few times during my thirty-six years in the Alaska bush and never scented that air of freedom. Quite the opposite: a close, judgmental stuffiness. Eyes on you from every direction. Breathing Big Brother's secondhand breath. At first I thought my asthma might be acting up. But it wasn't my bronchioles that were uptight.

With the little money I had made fishing that year, a bum year,

I was able to make arrangements with Carl Williams to transport us, the Evinrude, and the twenty-four-foot skiff and kicker rig I had also bought out of Kachonak over the mountains to the Cook Inlet side, where an ex-G.I. landing craft out of Homer would run us up to Chinitna Bay.

Johnny Nielson was skeptical about the kicker. The skiff was an old-timer, built heavy and tough. But the kicker had only twenty-eight horses that gave every indication of being ready for the glue factory. Not only that but if we needed a little get-up-and-go, to run out of the way of a sudden blow and find shelter, for instance, I would open the throttle in vain. There weren't enough of those horses for the heavy and loaded skiff, and the horses were tired to start with.

"I got a forty-horse outboard I replaced with a new one," Johnny said. "I'll let you have the old one. It's got the power, and the last I used it it ran good. You can pay me whatever when you find the mother lode."

He hefted the huge engine onto his shoulder and started off. We were at the old Walker cabin, about a mile or two from the Pope-Vannoy side where I'd beached the skiff with the twenty-eight. I'm not sure I could have lifted that forty-horse motor, but I'm sure I couldn't have crossed hill and dale with it on my shoulder. Johnny set it down on the beach, waded in to the rear of the skiff, moved the small outboard to the side, to act as backup if needed, then grabbed the forty and fastened it to the transom.

"Now maybe you'll make it to Pile Bay." He grinned. "And maybe I'll be able to sleep better, not thinking of you guys depending on that worn-out nag."

He glanced at the old twenty-eight, dwarfed next to the gleaming white forty.

"Well, good luck, Professor." He stuck out his hand, into which mine disappeared, fearing for its life. "See you down around Naknek next summer." He turned and walked back down the trail, a big broad-shouldered man, high-liner fisherman, frontiersman, blond hair bright in the sunlight. Back at the university, they'd want to study him.

I hooked up the gas lines and shoved off. She started up on the second pull. I gave her a little throttle and actually lifted the bow some. All right! I got me an outboard that'll turn the trip up the lake into a pleasant sightseeing cruise.

Yes, of course, it didn't work out that way.

I was always good at interpreting literature but had no gift for interpreting engine trouble. We were among the islands inside Tommy Point—me, Carol, Jonny, Sally, Beth, and Shad—with all our worldly goods packed into the bow's "doghouse," when our pleasure cruise acquired a sharper edge. Why, I don't know, but our hefty marine recruit in starched whites collapsed as though from sunstroke or a sniper's bullet. I cranked over the old twenty-eight and pulled the forty forward so that its prop was out of the water and turned toward shallow water, so I could get out and diagnose the sudden malady. A hose come lose? The choke not fully open? Throttle cable defunct? None of those. Everything, to my ignorant eyes, looked shipshape. As far as I could tell, this marine had answered a call I couldn't hear and given up the ghost, in full dress whites.

"What is it?" Carol wanted to know, peering over the transom at me standing there in the crystal water in my boots. "What's the matter?"

I wanted to make light of it. "Can't be anything much. I just can't figure what the problem could be. Maybe we'd best go back to Pope-Vannoy and have Gene take a look at it. Leave tomorrow morning."

"No," said Carol. "We've started. Let's keep going. It'll just take a little longer."

Inwardly, I was astonished. I was sure that if I had said what she just said—the hell with it, let's keep going—this little lady abducted from the cloistered confines of Middle America would vigorously have objected that we were *not* going to run half the length of Lake Iliamna at the mercy of that derelict twenty-eight. —Too much, Bobby! We go back till everything's fixed. But there she stood, all five feet two inches of unexpected determination and grit, saying, "Let's go for it."

So that's what we did. And a couple of miles farther along I misjudged the depth of a rock and sheared off the prop pin. No sweat. I found a nail of the right diameter and pinned the prop back on, cranked her over, and off we went, a little farther out from shore. I was feeling strong for the journey, up to it, confident if the worse came to the worst and we broke down I could get us to shore and we could set up a camp and build a fire and wait for someone to find us, maybe in the meantime having to catch some fish or shoot a duck or whatever. We were in the country, on our own. We weren't expecting to be ushered from one spectacle to another in guaranteed safety and comfort.

So on we sailed under clear blue skies, a light wind in our faces. Mile after mile of beautiful, untouched shoreline. We had space aplenty. No one to help us out of a jam, true, but I thought it a good exchange, the freedom of this great unconstrained land for the security of a rubber room.

We were a couple of miles from Pile Bay at the northern end of the lake when, like *Tyrannosaurus rex* rising from behind a hill, dark and threatening, the sky ahead turned the color of a bruise. Just as suddenly the wind picked up, blowing toward us, quickly white-capping the water, and driving a heavy rainfall. You could see the rain coming, machine-gun bullets striking the water. Before the first of the waves hit, Carol was hustling the kids into their rain gear and life vests. This would be a lot more than a little exposure to the elements. They crouched at the opening of the dog-house, holding on. The heavy skiff half rose with and half plowed through the bigger waves, coming down hard. There was spray aplenty now, and the dense rain, driven by the wind, pelted down hard, nearly blinding me. Carol turned to me and pointed to the land.

"Get to shore! Get to shore!" she cried.

Yes indeed, yes indeed. But if I turned in abruptly, the waves would hit us broadside and we'd likely swamp.

"It's okay," I called. "We're all right. I'll have to ease over, so the waves don't hit us broadside. Hang on to the kids."

I was cautiously quartering in toward shore, throttled down to where I could just maintain control, and scanning ahead for some kind of half-sheltered cove to pull into. But sudden squalls like that rarely last long. Within maybe ten or fifteen minutes, the rain stopped, the wind died down, and the sky turned blue again. I had to stay at the tiller of course, so I was drenched. But the sun had come back out and we were all right. I gave the old twenty-eight an appreciative pat and throttled up.

Carl Williams wasn't at Pile Bay. His little old-fashioned wife said he should return next day and invited us in for cookies and milk or tea, which were welcome. We'd had only a sandwich since starting out. Besides some smoked salmon and rice our cupboard was bare. Art and Patty had given us the sandwiches and probably assumed we'd have dinner with the Williamses, but the invitation wasn't forthcoming, for whatever reason.

To supplement our lean cuisine, I took Jon with me and headed down the road with the twenty-gauge shotgun after some spruce chickens. The spruce woods at Pile Bay were dense and abundant with those "fool hens." Within the hour we had eight, enough for supper and breakfast. At this time, late August, they were full grown, tender and tasty, feeding on berries. Later in the year they toughened up some and tasted more like the spruce needles they fed on.

The trip across the mountains next day was uneventful, other than that the country as we climbed up from Pile Bay became open mountainous terrain, beautiful and wild as the first day of creation. Carol and Beth rode up in the cab of the big flatbed truck with Carl, who remembered me from '64, when Les and I first made the trip with *Port N Storm*, coming the other way from the

Cook Inlet side. I was glad Carol and Beth were in the reassuring cab with Carl, because the high pass was more than a little scary— the road narrow, the drop into the valley below precipitous. It wouldn't seem so awful from up in the cab. I sat in the skiff with my arms around Jon and Sal, smiling as I told them not to look down.

On the descent to Iliamna Bay I saw that the "barge"—the surplus landing craft from World War II—was docked there. We were about to start another chapter of our Alaska adventure. We'd winter in Chinitna Bay and in the spring I'd check out the state's Open to Entry Program and maybe find a piece of land of our own. All the state's offerings would be "remote," which meant in the bush, and that suited us. In the bush was where we wanted to be.

5

Chinitna Bay

Family portrait, November.

(August 1969–May 1970)

The strange dark craft looked like a huge prehistoric beetle crouched there in the little bay; the hard-edged metal thing seemed so out of place—black, unyielding, hostile, while all around were the warm colors of early autumn, soft breezes swaying the treetops. The metal boat recalled the world of perpetual aggression and war. For a moment it darkened my mind. But it wasn't there to open its maw on a beach of bunkers and machine-gun fire. It was waiting to transport us to another marvelous landscape of wild Alaska.

Carl Williams backed his long bed into the water. His helper in hip boots undid the straps fastening down our skiff and threw the bowline to a guy on board, who cinched it down on a stern cleat. We retrieved our duffel bags and stowed them in the cabin. The helper then shoved our skiff into the water. She would follow behind in the wake. Pope and I had made an uneventful trip to Pile Bay earlier, freighting the Evinrude snowmobile and sled, which we now lashed down in the skiff.

The man on board was the captain, or pilot, a middle-aged native with iron-gray hair and twinkling eyes. There was nothing grim or warlike about him. His round face was creased with permanent smile lines above his short, stocky body. He looked hale and hearty, very much like those original peoples of the far north the famous photographer Curtis had recorded with his camera. The early explorers of the northland and, later, the anthropologists all attested to the great good humor of these hardy, intelligent people. This man appeared to be a living remnant. Somehow he had made it through intact, while so many of his people, unable or unwilling to cope with the white man's world, had succumbed to depression, alcohol, and the wish to die.

"Come! Come!" he said to Carol, smiling broadly and extending a hand to help her and the kids up the ramp and into the enlarged cabin. I shook hands and smiled at this obviously good-natured and probably happy man. Carol and the kids sat on a long bench on the port side, while I elected to stand beside the captain and look ahead. The engine sounds, the oil and gas smells, and the tang of the salty air were all reminiscent of my time commercial fishing.

Out in the inlet a chop was white-capping the waves, but the craft was big and heavy enough to iron them flat with hardly any perturbation. I smiled over at my family. Carol's eyes were fixed on me, and I saw relief come into them at my smile. No one would be getting seasick. We were off to a good start. Shad, our well-behaved rescue dog, stretched out at their feet.

Down this far, Cook Inlet was miles wide, a large body of water ships as well as fish boats traversed with caution. Les's set-net site fronted the whole southern portion of the inlet opening into the Gulf of Alaska, and I wondered about that kind of exposure should a big blow coincide with a high tide. But Les had been set-netting there for years and didn't mention ever having been washed out to sea. I was assuming he would if he had. To the extent that Pope was careless, Les was careful.

I asked the captain, "About how long before we reach Chinitna?"

The captain never spoke unless spoken to but replied readily enough, the smile lines crinkling.

"Oh, we're making good time." He glanced at me, his eyes merry and bright. "An hour or so. Yeah. Maybe."

Good enough. We plowed ahead steadily, and soon I spotted the gay incongruity Les had erected on the beach of the bay. When we were closer, I motioned Carol over and pointed.

"Home sweet home for the winter." I grinned.

She stared, then smiled, almost breaking into a laugh. "Pink and blue! You weren't kidding. Our rugged Alaskan set-net site is pink and blue—like baby bunting!"

Les's pastel palace in that rugged setting was actually a perfect statement about Alaska, a land of outlandish incongruities, not toeing the line, doing its own thing, a so-what? chip on its shoulder.

As we entered the mouth of the bay, Les was hauling on some kind of mooring rig with pulleys, bringing his skiff and kicker in to him. In my peripheral vision I saw another rig bouncing along toward us. That would be Wayne coming to lend a hand. Les pulled alongside, smiling. He waved. The captain nosed the craft right up to the beach, onto the sand, then cut our skiff loose for Wayne and Les to handle. They were both standing by their kickers, wheeling and dealing with the waves and the skiff. Then Wayne had her in tow, heading back up the bay to park her in a protected slough.

I shook hands with my old partner, and Carol gave him a hug. Les and I carried the duffel bags containing our worldly goods ashore. When we had landed at Iliamna we had been affluent Americans, sort of. Stepping onto the sands of Chinitna Bay a short year later, after having bought the dome, the snow machine and skiff and kicker, the stove and miscellaneous gear, plus the grubstake, and then the cost of getting us and our stuff from Pile Bay to Chinitna Bay, we had only clothing enough to keep us warm and bucks enough from fishing to buy some staples to go with the fish and game we expected to harvest. I planned on setting out a trapline too, the fur hopefully to bring in more of the cash we'd need come spring and our next move—to wherever. The state's Open to Entry Program looked like our best bet. I'd be finding out about that through the winter. But in the meantime we had this beckoning new world to explore and savor. We wouldn't let money spoil that.

Steve was still Outside doing his music thing, not in Morrisville but in New York City. He wrote us, of course, and the word was he was doing well. At eighteen, he had a band, performed nightly at the Cafe Bizarre in the Village, and had cut a single that had made the charts. But reading between the lines Carol and I detected that he was missing the family pretty bad and was nostalgic for the bush life. We put no pressure on him, leaving him free to go with his inclinations, though we all missed him being with us. I felt almost handicapped not having him by my side. We suspected we'd be seeing him in Chinitna Bay before long, but we couldn't anticipate that he would be able to relieve a lot of our money concerns when he returned to Alaska by landing a good gig through Les at the Forelands Bar on the Kenai.

Les was a good carpenter, and the plywood house appeared sturdy enough to withstand the storms typical of the region. The main room downstairs held a kitchen table and chairs, a cupboard for dishes, with drawers below for the cutlery, a small sheet-metal stove for heating, and a small propane stove for cooking. In a corner against the wall stood a big double bed. There were two single beds and a cot upstairs. We were all set for sleeping. The "toilet" of course was outside behind the house. Sitting at the kitchen table looking out I could imagine we were on a houseboat, because the short apron of beach didn't show, only the inlet stretching away to the horizon. Seeing nothing but big water out the window, I wondered if Les should have built his house up away from the beach a little farther. The tides in Cook Inlet weren't as big as those in Bristol Bay, but they were big enough.

Wayne showed up smiling and greeted Carol and each of the

kids and shook hands with me. A bachelor, he was very courteous, almost formal, almost bowing to Carol. Les produced a jug, as usual, and we all sat around the table passing the whiskey, chasing it with cold water from the creek running close by the house. We talked about the bay and its wildlife—some moose, quite a few bears when the salmon were spawning, a healthy population of spruce chickens up the valleys at the end of the bay, ducks in the sloughs through the fall, a few pockets of snowshoe hares, and foxes and some lynx attracted by the hares, seals floating in and out of the bay on ice floes, and beluga whales visiting often (they were plentiful in Cook Inlet in those days). Another pristine wilderness area. Roads and towns, people and civilization were on the other side of the inlet, on the Kenai Peninsula.

Jon and his sisters were eager to go out and run around, taking in the feel of this new place of salt water, sand, and surf. I told them not to wander off too far or go into the woods and to keep an eye on little Beth. Above the high-water line the sand was dry and loose, but below that it was hard-packed and great for walking or running. The barge was now a small dot in the distance riding the ebb back to Homer. I was relieved to see my kids running around. They had been pretty badly bummed out at having to leave Iliamna and their close friends. But our wilderness adventure seemed to be always opening onto new and exciting vistas to occupy their minds, precluding too much brooding, and they were young, flexible, and basically happy. "The busy bee has no time for sorrow," wrote Blake.

Carol and I liked the funky little place, and as we passed the jug the usually taciturn VanDevere loosened up and it became obvious that he was pleased to have us there, not only because he wouldn't now have to transport a lot of his gear to the Kenai side out of the reach of possible opportunistic thieves, but because he had a reason to fly in with our mail and various provisions and hang out with us for a visit. Wayne too seemed glad about the prospect of our living there all winter; if he chose to trap, he'd have neighbors to visit. I hoped he would decide to trap and be in the bay at least most of the winter. He was a good guy, a pleasant, unpretentious man, experienced, skillful, and amazingly strong for someone of his small stature and wiry frame. I was to see him tote a hundred-pound hindquarter of moose a couple of miles down the far valley to his cabin. And he knew this area like . . . like the back of his hand. I was always glad to hear his basso-profundo voice call out as he came down the beach to our Pink and Blue Apparition (as we sometimes referred to Les's creation).

In anticipation of our coming, Les had brought over insulation for under the floor, the roof being already insulated. Occasionally through the summer when he was there set-netting, sometimes with his family, a raw, cold spell would settle in. The completed insulation would hold the heat from the small stove. Les and I went at it next day, with Jonny happy to be our gofer.

One mild, sunny morning after the insulating job was finished and Les had flown back to the peninsula I decided Jon and I had best hike down to Middle Valley and investigate its population of spruce hens. I carried the over-and-under (a .22 long rifle atop a twenty-gauge shotgun barrel—for the ones that flew off instead of sitting). Jon marched along with the Remington single-shot .22. I had strapped on the .44 Magnum, just in case. I wasn't sure the revolver could do the job on a bear, but I was sure it was a better bet than a punch in the nose. If you're not actually stalking one, or vice versa, bears will typically hear you coming and just melt away into the underbrush. I was sure that would be the case with the two of us walking along through the dry leaves and talking.

I felt fine this morning, cool air, warm sun, blue sky overhead, and a wind rustling through the leaves. It was good to have Jon trudging along beside me. It was good for a father and son to be out like this in such a place, on such a morning. This was the sort of thing I had always wanted. I didn't care if my kids never became president of anything, never got to be a big shot with lots of loot.

If they came to *see* the land as Indians had, as sacred, that would be my best legacy for them.

We hadn't gone a mile into the woods up the valley when we put up a big flock of spruce chickens, at least two dozen birds exploding off the ground all around us. A few flew straight off, and I got one of them with the shotgun, but most landed in the branches of nearby trees. It's a mistake to shoot several in your excitement and then run around trying to find them in the underbrush. Shoot one at a time and go directly to where you saw it fall. And if you see a gang of them tiered in a tree pick off the lowest one first and then the next lowest, and so on up. Amazingly, they generally won't spook. But if you take the top one, his crashing down will send the others flying. We started back with eight birds, all cleaned out on the spot. They'd be good eating. Jon had bagged a couple of them for the pot himself. I could see he felt more like a young warrior than a little boy, marching along with his gun, toting his birds back to the family. He had matured a lot that way back in Intricate Bay when Pope and I had been down in Bristol Bay fishing, with Steve in New York. Big Jon had assumed the role of provider, getting ducks and trout for the table.

That night Carol and I lay together in bed listening to the soft pounding of the surf along the beach. A half moon cut through the scattered clouds and caste its light across the floor and onto the bed. At first, the kids had been whispering, but now the house was silent. The long day and the rhythmic surf had lulled their excited minds to sleep. Soon Carol was asleep, with her head in the crook of my shoulder and her arm across my chest. I lay there for a while thinking about this new place and the wilderness country all around waiting for us to embrace it, and the thought came to me, "All things are waiting to be loved." That was our job as humans. Soon I went to sleep too.

The morning's silence was shattered by Shad's furious barking, followed by Les yelling, "Get that dog!" as he came rushing down the stairs in his long johns. "Moose! Right in the creek! Call in the goddamned dog!" He darted out the door with his rifle.

I jumped into my pants and grabbed my Winchester, yelling for Shad to "Come! Come!" When I rounded the corner of the house, Les was standing barefoot in the creek, his rifle at the ready, peering upstream for a possible shot. Shad's barking seemed a long ways off but stopped at my call, and I felt proud that he was coming back. I wondered briefly if the moose had turned on him, hastening his return. Did he remember the big bad bull back at Iliamna?

Les looked at me. "Fuck! A nice bull. And right at our doorstep. No packing out!" He shook his head. But then he grinned. "Let's shoot the goddamned dog instead."

A line of red drifted out behind his feet. He had cut a foot on a sharp rock. We went in, Les leaning on me, hopping on one foot, leaving red drops in the sand. Carol was up, the kids too, sitting front row center on the bed, taking it all in. I bandaged his foot; it wasn't a bad cut. Ah well, I was thinking, at least we knew there were moose around. There'd be other opportunities. We'd bag our winter meat for sure. . . . Maybe. Nothing's for sure, not even death and taxes. Let's say I felt optimistic about our winter meat. (It's not a good idea to come on cocky in Wakan-Tanka country.)

Les, however, wasn't thinking about future opportunities. We'd just had a nice young bull standing in our backyard. He shouldn't be too far off. The cut foot wasn't bothering Les. He pulled on his clothes, slipped into his boots, strapped on his skinning knife, and picked up his rifle.

"Let's go after him," he said as he dressed. "We'll go up opposite sides of the creek. We can shoot ahead but not across the creek. Okay?"

Okay! I hustled into my clothes, grabbed my rifle and some extra shells, slipped my hunting knife onto my belt, and out the door we went.

"Be careful," Carol called after us, "and good luck." Jon, Sal, and Beth stood by the stove in their pajamas.

We moved fast at first, figuring he was too far ahead to hear us, but soon settled into a still-hunt pace. After maybe half an hour I lost sight of Les but then *Bam!*—a shot from up ahead a little ways, and then another. I picked up my pace but kept to my side of the creek in case he had missed and the bull crossed my path.

"Yo! Bob!" Les called. He hadn't missed. It was a young bull, and fairly small as moose go. We spent the rest of the day gutting, skinning, and packing him out. Hunting and all it entails were a main focus in bush living, for us as well as for our forefathers.

We didn't have any game bags, but Les had a box of pepper from the year before, and we rubbed it into the raw, exposed ends of the meat and any crevices to discourage the blowflies. The pepper worked pretty well. We inspected the meat every day, finding only a couple of pockets where the flies had blown. We cleaned them out with vinegar and smeared on more pepper. Les would take some choice portions with him when he flew out but left the bulk of the moose for us.

The days passed uneventful and peaceful—except for one morning when we woke up with the house shaking from the gusts of wind driving up the inlet right at us. I looked out. The inlet was cresting with white caps on pretty big waves. I fished out Les's tide book: a big tide and still flooding. The breakers were pounding in close and reaching up toward the house. While my nose was in the tide book, Carol, who was at the front window wide-eyed, gave a yell.

"Bob! The propane! The surf's grabbing at it!"

I dashed over, the kids right behind me, and sure enough, the wash of the breakers had reached our spare propane tank standing in the sand a few yards from the door. It was on its side now, the undertow rolling it toward the breakers. I ran outside, Carol following, and I was thinking, "Maybe Les didn't altogether know what he was doing."

Carol and I each grabbed an end of the tank, the salt water swirling around our ankles, and heaved against the pull of the undertow, hollows forming around our feet. We dropped to our knees, the better to push and roll the tank up to the house. The water was icy cold. It took all our combined effort, but we got the tank onto the dry sand and continued rolling it till it was up against the house. Three small heads were at the window watching. The sizzling foam of the breakers reached to about ten or fifteen feet of the front door. But the tide had turned, the ebb under way.

The blow had pushed the flood tide as close to the house as it had ever done, Les assured us next time he flew in. That was a comfort, of sorts. Carol and I exchanged glances, each thinking the same grim thought: What if a *really* big storm, a perfect storm, coincided with a really high tide, the wind again out of the south?

Les noted our exchange of glances and guessed our thoughts. "I've been at this site a dozen years"—he half smiled—"and you won't find any water line on the house. If you want to worry about that sort of thing, why not worry about a comet hitting us?"

"Or," I put in, getting his point, "what if Moby-Dick gets lost and mistakes your place for the *Pequod* in drag?"

We all laughed. "What ifs" were a waste of time. Just being in the Alaska wilds didn't validate the syndrome. You had to be alert and watch what you were doing. Sure. But going around with "what ifs" buzzing like flies about your head was a very different number. Better to just stick with what's right at hand instead of always looking for trouble. Take it as it comes. How did Shakespeare put it? "Present fears are less than horrible imaginings." Or as they put it in Tierra del Fuego (stealing from Dylan): "Things that look large from a distance up close are never that big."

The wind died down overnight. Next morning after breakfast Wayne showed up. "That was a close one," he said, grinning and nodding toward the high-water line outside our door.

"Hey, don't go scaring my guests," Les returned. He had flown in earlier that morning to check on things. Then, knowing his longtime friend and neighbor and noting a little excitement in his demeanor, "What's up?" he asked.

"Ducks!" Wayne replied with a wide smile. "A couple of flocks must have landed in the big slough across from my place. Kept me awake half the night with their quacking. Sounded like a dinner invitation to me. Duck soup anyone?"

Les looked at me. "What say, Professor? Duck soup or maybe roast duck sound good to you?"

"Ducky," said I. "Sounds just ducky. Let's go shopping."

"It would be a nice change from all the moose meat," Carol said from her perch on the bed, Beth and Sally by her side, interested as always in everything that was going on. It was swell having the whole family in on everything. I glanced over at Jon. I didn't have to be a mind reader to know he was itching to go along. He always wanted to go with us, on any and every expedition. And no reason he shouldn't. Never a drag, he was able to keep up on his tireless legs. And he was fast learning what the wilderness had to teach. Carol continued with correspondence school for him and Sally, which was necessary and good—he went on to earn a master's in archaeology from the University of Wyoming, and Sally got a degree from the University of Alaska— but the lessons they learned outdoors were those they absorbed most readily and happily. The wild and wooly beluga chase that would ensue was something unanticipated when I told Jon to dress warmly and grab his rifle.

Carol was always a little apprehensive on these occasions, but she agreed with me that it was good for him to go along, within reason. She wouldn't have considered chasing beluga whales all over the bay at top speed to be within reason.

Besides our shotguns for the ducks, Les, Wayne, and I brought along our rifles in case we spooked a grizzly in the tall marsh grass bordering the slough. We were heading across the bay with Wayne at the tiller when Les let out a whoop and jumped to his feet pointing off the starboard bow. I looked in the direction he was pointing and saw the rolling white backs of some half-dozen beluga whales. "Look there, Jonny," I said, pointing. But Wayne had looked too and without any consultation or hesitation he opened the throttle and swerved toward them.

It was crazy. I knew nothing about hunting—or chasing—beluga whales. What would we do if we got one? Would it float or sink? How would we get it back? And what would we do with all that blubber? —Not eat it. Not me. One time down in Bristol Bay I was shooting off my educated mouth, assuring my white friends that eating preferences and dislikes were "all in your head." A couple of our native pals put me to the test. It just so happened that they were boiling up some muktuk (blubber) on their boat. Down the ladder we all went to the boats tied off the dock pilings and crowded into the little cabin of their double-ender. At the first whiff of the boiling blubber I knew my habitual stomach had parted company with my liberated mind. I was not about to try the taste of muktuk. I and my white friends promptly exited into the fresh salt air topside, much to the amusement of the two native fishermen and the ribbing of the other guys. "All in the head you say, Professor?"

But however uncertain the proceeds of the chase, should we be successful, we roared out across the bay, Les standing ready in the bow with his rifle. I sat with Jon amidships, holding on to the seat and him. The water was not altogether calm, and the whales were fast, sleek white forms streaking away just below the surface, then rising to blow. We were moving equally fast, bouncing hard, getting dowsed with spray. The whales didn't just swim straight off; they swerved, dove, and looped around, with us swerving and looping after the one we'd cut out of the "herd," turning sharp, tilting almost down to the gunwale. Why the whales didn't simply swim on out of the bay I don't know. Could they have thought we were playing with them? Les got off a shot each time the whale rose to the surface to blow, but the target was fairly small at six to eight feet, and tricky, fast, and agile, the skiff equally fast and bouncing and turning sharply in pursuit, and I'm sure all he hit was the broad back of the salt sea. Finally one of them, and then the others, perhaps tiring of the game, headed for the open inlet and were gone.

The chase had been exciting, the close contact with those fabled creatures exhilarating, but frankly I was relieved that it had ended without the skiff flipping over and also that I wouldn't have to confront any muktuk.

It had been a typical backwoods enterprise. Men in those days living outside the pale of society and its strictures were apt to be possessed of a latent hair-trigger wildness. Les and Wayne had been letting out whoops like Indians riding hard after the buffalo. I knew some of that wild spirit was seeping into my kids—and surely into myself as well. After all the years fishing and cavorting in Bristol Bay and now into my third year of wilderness life I knew I was no longer the same man I had been back in academia. Parameters had been broached, forces released that had lain dormant since childhood. I was opening up.

After the whales swam off we continued on our way to the slough and the ducks, a little damp from the spray but heated by the excitement. We parked the skiff against a cut-bank, tied up to some willows, and moved cautiously through the tall grass to the slough. We didn't surprise any bears but we did bushwhack the ducks. They took off in twos and threes and sevens and eights when we reared up out of the grass. There were probably a hundred or more of them strung out along the winding slough. *Bam! Bam! Bam!* went our guns as we moved up the slough, dropping a dozen of them, mostly mallards. As expected, they were delicious. Wild ducks, unlike the domestic variety, are lean, as are the spruce chickens and most moose. You don't have to worry about cholesterol or getting fat when living off the land. You don't see any fat Indians among Curtis's photos, taken before the advent of the white man's diet. The same with the Eskimos back then: short and broad but solid muscle.

Jon bagged a couple of sitting ducks with his .22. What a day it had been for a twelve-year-old boy. Back on Iliamna I had done a lot of duck hunting in the fall and spring, always with Jon, who played the part of retriever and sometimes dispatcher when one was wounded. But we had never run into a flock so large. Not many stateside boys ever experienced anything like it. Well-to-do hunters paid good bucks for the opportunity. On a subsistence basis, we enjoyed the kind of hunting and fishing city and suburb fellows only dream or read of, some of them scrimping hard to afford a once-in-a-lifetime trip into game country like this. The popular notion that our hunting and gathering ancestors led hard lives—"nasty, brutish, and short"—seemed to me perversely absurd. For us, love and need were one, and the work was play for mortal stakes (to cite Frost).

Before Wayne left for the Kenai Peninsula, which he did every year after the set-netting season, a big-game guide made arrangements with him to use his place as the base for two Outside sportsmen in quest of moose—more exactly moose antlers, the bigger the better. They got their moose, or rather their antlers, a nice rack of maybe sixty inches, but weren't interested in the meat, which they gave to Wayne, a hindquarter of which he gave to me for helping to pack it out.

The sportsmen had connected about three miles up Middle Valley. There was no trail through the blowdowns, devil's club, and tangled underbrush, which made those three miles a tough haul for Wayne and me (Les was back on the peninsula). Wayne stood about five feet five and weighed maybe a hundred and forty pounds when soaked with sweat. A hundred and forty pounds of hard, experienced muscle. The hindquarter on his pack-board weighed probably about a hundred pounds or more. I helped him heave it onto his shoulders, and he in turn helped me get the other hindquarter on my back. Then he turned and started out, with me grunting and wobbling behind. My years in the bush, with several other pack-outs behind me, together with the vigor of salmon fishing during the summers, had me in pretty good shape, so I was able to keep up. But I was amazed at the strength manifest in Wayne's lean frame.

The first time we stopped for a breather Wayne sat on the ground, the pack-board still on his back but resting on a downed tree trunk so most of the weight was off his shoulders. That was the way to do it, as I quickly learned when I sat down heavily on the log and went ass-over-head backward with the weight of the hindquarter and lay there helplessly gazing up through the trees at the sky.

Wayne had to chuckle. "Don't worry," he said in that voice you'd think was issuing from a frame of *six* feet five, "we'll come back for your bones in the spring." Then he slipped out of the harness and helped get me to my feet. We were both laughing. I slept especially sound that night, waking in the same position I had fallen asleep in, my muscles unwilling to exert themselves in so much as a turn over.

We were doing fine as regards meat, but we needed staples like flour, potatoes, carrots, powdered milk, and so forth. We had the money from the dome someone in Kachonak had bought, plus some fishing bucks, so we thought it best that I fly out with Les and do some serious shopping for the winter before the snows came. Les didn't have a root cellar, but there were cold corners on the floor of the house capable of keeping our produce preserved. I was to be gone only a few days, Carol bravely agreeing it was a good idea, and then I'd hire a Widgeon to fly me and the load of produce back in. But the weather turned sour, heavy winds and mixed rain and snow. The Widgeon stayed on the ground, and I paced the floor at Les's Kenai house, worrying about my family alone over there. It was more than a week before I made it back. I'll let Jon tell you how it was for them while Steve and I were both away:

For the first few days we had a blast. The weather was great, a real Alaskan Indian summer. The girls and I played on the beach, splashed in the creek, and just had fun running around our new neighborhood. We didn't have to worry about cars and trucks or someone telling us to quiet down or get off their lawn. We didn't worry much about bears either, because we stuck pretty close to the house and were making plenty of noise. We had learned enough about bears to know that it was very rare that one would stalk a human, though it does happen. So we did sort of keep alert in a relaxed way, about like city kids do with the traffic. Dad and Steve, and Les and Wayne too, were away, but we knew Mom could handle the shotgun in a pinch. She kept pretty close watch on us.

We also got into splitting wood. We were determined to have a nice stack of split wood by the house when Dad got back, and we did.

A bummer was when Shad got into a porcupine and was real sick for a while. There wasn't much we could do for him.

Then the weather turned ugly, as it often does on the Alaska Peninsula in the fall. It was day after day of cold, wind, and rain. We stayed close to the stove and played games at the table, glad to be warm and dry, with the cold wind and rain whipping around outside and the sky and water just shades of gray. It wouldn't let up, and Dad became overdue. To make matters worse, the battery that ran the radio was low, and we couldn't get the generator going to charge it. We could get a little reception but couldn't transmit at all. That made us all, except maybe Beth, feel a little uneasy, like we were really cut off. There were no other people anywhere around. But Dad got a message through in the blind ("in the blind" means sending a message without knowing whether it would be received). We all leaned close to the radio. The message was simply that he would be back as soon as the weather let up and not to worry. That made us feel better, just hearing from him.

One morning the weather had improved, and we started listening for a plane. I was outside and heard it first and yelled in to everyone. Soon a Widgeon came into view and we all cheered because we knew Dad would be coming in a Widgeon. The plane banked hard *and landed out front, bouncing off a few tops of the waves. It settled down into the water, and the pilot drove right up onto the beach. The door opened and Dad came out smiling. We all ran down to meet him. It was such a relief to see him back.*

So now we had food for the winter but no money. Trapping was the only way I could think of to get some. I had begun trapping in the area around the Pink and Blue Apparition, being careful not to wander into Wayne's trapping territory. I caught very little, a couple of mink and a red fox. Then we got a few inches of snow and my explorations revealed a half-mile stretch between the base of the mountains and the big slough that was pockmarked with the prints of fox and, excitingly, lynx and even wolverine. It was a confined passage between the mountain and the slough that looped back from the end of the bay. At high tide especially, any animals traveling between East and Middle valleys would have to traverse this passage. I turned it into a kind of minefield of traps and started making catches.

Most significant and valuable was the lynx. I remember the first one vividly. As I approached the set, in a hollow stump, I saw light fur about a foot long in the trap. I stared, my heart picking up speed. What kind of critter was that? And then, instantaneously, I was looking into the awesome eyes of a large lynx, whose head was above its trapped foreleg. I don't mind telling you that those pale, intense eyes looking straight into mine shook me up. As I drew my pistol I realized that my hands were trembling, partly no doubt from fear—could that great cat pull free and in one leap have its jaws at my throat?—and partly from the shock of the unexpected sight.

I caught five of them that first week, possibly a family traveling that route. I recall I was both proud and upset, regretful. I took my time skinning them out very carefully so as not to mar the pelts in any way. Carol and the kids were astonished at the size and beauty of those wild cats. Beth ran her hand wonderingly over the soft fur. Yes, we ate the choice parts of the cats, as a matter of principle, and yes, they tasted just like chicken.

We knew that Steve was back in Alaska and had landed a good gig, through a friend of Les's, in the Forelands Bar on the Kenai, making pretty good bucks. Then one day in November, a couple of days before Thanksgiving, we heard Les's plane entering the bay, flying low along the beach. We dashed outside to wave, and there was a strange light in the airplane, like a small sun. It was Steve's face, beaming at us.

Steve's arrival initiated a new phase of our winter in Chinitna Bay. Evenings before he burst upon the scene were generally pretty quiet, Carol and I reading by the light of the kerosene lamps, sometimes Jon or Sal too, or Carol or I reading to Beth. Sometimes we played a simple card game like "Go Fish." At bedtime for the kids we continued the practice, almost a tradition, of me picking up the guitar and singing them to sleep with folk songs. Afterward the silence was deepened by the soft swishing of the surf and the softer fluttering of the lamps, whose light too on the wood walls and ceiling was soft and restful. It was easy going to bed early and easier still falling asleep, a pleasure so simple and elemental we almost failed to recognize it. I think of those multitudes Outside who have never experienced perfect silence (the surf and wind were really the sound of silence) as severely deprived.

But besides the Thanksgiving turkey and trimmings, Steve had brought in a Monopoly board, which turned the kitchen table into a war zone every evening. We got caught up in the game, transformed into rabid capitalists. Gone were the quiet family evenings. There was a lot of chatter; voices were sometimes raised. Trades especially were fiercely argued. "The three railroads for the three blues? No way! You'll have to throw in the utilities and five hundred dollars cash." "But you'll control the whole side of the board, except for the one railroad!" Or "Park Place and the Boardwalk aren't really that good. They're too expensive in the first place, and houses cost too much—*and nobody ever lands on them; they're jinxed.* I want the three tans or no deal."

There was no such thing as being loaned some money to get out of a tight spot. No quarter was given the loser. This was capitalism. Hands reaching for the Chance or Community Chest cards were seen to tremble. Winners gloated, losers complained about a trade or the prejudiced dice. We played the long version, right to the bitter or triumphant end, sometimes going way past bedtime. Every night we gathered around the table and the Monopoly board. It was almost like being back in the real world, except that we knew this was a game.

A rule of thumb in bush living is that little things get big. In the Outside world they're throwing thrills and extravaganzas at you constantly, such that you get numbed down (yes, and dumbed down) as tolerance is reached, and then the horrors, explosions, killings, and sex have to get ratcheted up higher and higher to elicit any reaction at all. When you're no longer shooting up all that junk the quiet world emerges into being, the wind says things, a bird's warble plucks the strings of your heart, a family enjoys one another around a simple game at the kitchen table, and crawling tired into bed is lovely.

As regards our heated games of Monopoly, to make matters worse, or better (depending on your point of view), Wayne had brought over his old pal Dick Rusk to trap with him, but then, for reasons unexplained, returned to the Kenai, leaving Dick to tend the trapline, which bummed Dick out because he was definitely not a loner. He walked down the beach to the Durr household almost every evening, often enough arriving at suppertime, and enthusiastically joined our game, making a fifth (Carol and Beth made up one player, as did Jon and Sal).

Dick was a rare entity, even for Alaska. About the same height as Wayne, Dick however was husky instead of slim, a little rotund. And like Wayne, he had a full-bodied voice, though unlike

Wayne's mellifluous basso profundo his was simply loud and raspy—and unconstrained, especially when projecting a laugh. With Dick on hand, the tempo and timbre of the game were cranked up a notch or two. He had spiked hair, bulging eyes, and crooked, protruding teeth of dubious color. We all liked him, for he was jolly and, appearances notwithstanding, gentle and good-hearted. A bachelor, he took to Jon, Sal, and Beth, talking to them, enjoying everything they had to say. Kids can read character, regardless of looks, and little Beth liked to climb up onto his lap, which obviously delighted him. It was a downer for all of us when after a month or so he flew out with Les. But we would see Dick Rusk again some years later in the Susitna Valley. "Trails cross" is an old Alaskan saying.

The winter passed slowly and quietly. The kids did their correspondence schoolwork without complaint, played outside, got excited when some ice floes drifted into the bay with seals resting on top, now and then lifting their heads to look around or sniff the air. We lay just off the beach among some brush watching them glide by so close. Back in Syracuse we'd go to the zoo fairly regularly to see the animals, but it was nothing like this. These animals were wild, doing their natural thing in the wilderness that was their natural home. If a killer whale suddenly hurled itself out of the water and picked one of them off, that would be natural and all right too, however much it might be a shocking event for us.

We got a few good snowfalls, deep enough to warrant snowshoes. I rode the Evinrude down the beach to where my trapline started, but one day after a snowfall rested in soft billows over the land, without thinking I swerved the machine to take a shortcut to the line and felt my heart skip as the front end of the machine slowly started sinking into the smooth white snow. I should have known better. On a really big tide, salt water could reach undetected under the snow up to the spot where I had been able to cross during lesser tides.

Adrenaline to the rescue. With a couple of extraordinary heaves I got the track back onto solid ground. But that was it for the engine, despite the couple of buckets of fresh water I rushed from the house to flush away some of the salt. Too much had seeped into the engine, which was a goner. I brought it with us on the barge in the spring and on the Kenai managed to trade it for a square-stern aluminum canoe, which turned out to be so well made we use it on our lake to this day. I don't know if the guy I traded with wanted the machine for parts or if he figured he could get it going again. Alaskans tend to be good at fixing up things, often in unorthodox ways, which some of us call "Alaskan ingenuity."

I almost lost my other large piece of equipment, the skiff and kicker, in Chinitna Bay that winter. Les had flown in with mail and some supplies, among which were a couple of jugs. Well, in outback Alaska bottles of booze are never stored in liquor cabinets to be nipped at on occasion. Once they are opened, it's a foregone conclusion that they will be drained of their life force and given an honorable burial. With Les's visit, we were taking the afternoon off, sitting around the table passing the jug and waxing jolly. Finally, somebody noticed that it had started blowing. I looked out and saw white caps driving at our beach. Thanks to the jolly jug time, Les and I had been asleep at the switch. My skiff was taking a beating, swinging on its tether to the pulley line, broaching to the oncoming waves, and taking on some water. Whoa! I was thinking, what do we do about that? Les's experience in the bay came to the rescue. After surveying the situation, he pulled on his hip boots and gloves and headed for the door.

"Come on"—he turned to me—"it might take two of us."

I had no idea what he had in mind. Outside, he picked up a small four-pronged anchor on a long line. He went into the surf as far as he could without water pouring into his boots, me right behind him, both of us getting drenched. He whirled the anchor overhead like a cowboy with a lasso and hurled it out toward the bounding skiff. His first throw was short because a wave lifted the skiff out of its reach. But his next toss caught the stern, which straightened the bow so it could ride the surf, and we were able to pull it in till we got it onto the log rollers Les had situated at the edge of the beach, and we pulled it up out of the reach of the sea.

I clapped him on the back. "You and John Wayne," I said, laughing. "Well, that's got to call for a little firewater."

We went back in flushed and wet and quietly triumphant. We went upstairs and changed into dry clothes, then resumed our places at the table and opened up the second jug, which was doomed. The storm raged against the house, but inside was warm and lit with laughter and spirits.

Spring came and breakup was fast, again because of all the surrounding waters. We had followed up the lead from the BLM about an Open to Entry Program conducted by the state in the Susitna Valley making available five-acre plots of land in certain remote areas, supposedly for recreational use. Five acres per adult, which meant that Carol and I could get ten between us and Steve another five. Steve's gig at the Forelands Bar on the Kenai paid well, counting the tips, and he was able to rent a trailer for us near the bar. Our plan was to use the trailer as a base of operations from which I would go to the state building in Anchorage to get the detailed information on the program, papers of application, and study the maps. I would be looking for a lake or at least a creek to file on—one that no one else thus far had filed on.

Steve was on hand to help us make the move from Chinitna Bay to Homer and then somehow up the peninsula to the trailer. Our oldest son was our breadwinner now, and we figured we should be able to hire a small truck to get us and our gear from Homer to the trailer. The furs from trapping should be worth a pretty penny too.

The landing craft arrived on schedule, the same skipper at the helm. We greeted each other like old friends. During those seasons fishing down in Bristol Bay, as mentioned, I had formed a quiet affection for the native people, especially the older ones from the villages upriver, a gentle, soft-spoken, good-natured people. Some of the younger ones, no longer embedded in their ancient culture and influenced by the modern world of the white man, had assumed macho stances and tended to drink too much, often becoming violent. I saw them as confused between two divergent cultures.

The trip across the inlet was uneventful, and we did find a guy in Homer with a truck whom we hired to take us and our gear up to the trailer Steve had rented near the Forelands Bar.

Les was back at work on the Nikiski dock but would soon return to Chinitna Bay to get ready for the start of the Cook Inlet salmon run. We visited with him and his family, wife Betty and son Dyer, at their little house off the North Kenai Road. Before we left the Kenai for the Susitna Valley Les and I bought each other a few rounds at the Forelands Bar while taking in Steve's gig. I've mentioned the Alaskan saying that "trails cross," and we did see Wayne and Dick again briefly in the Susitna Valley, at which time they said, "Yeah, VanDevere's doing his usual." But I never did see or hear from Les again, nor from Wayne or Dick after the Susitna visit. I heard a rumor that Les and Betty had divorced but not a word about Wayne and Dick. The Alaska bush can be a dangerous place, swallow you up, and of course commercial fishing is even more dangerous. I doubt that any of them just went back to the States.

It seemed that once again a chapter of my bush life had firmly closed while another was about to open on vistas of the unknown. But that's what adventuring upon life is all about.

6

The Susitna Valley: Open to Entry

Framing a window.

(May 1970)

The Kenai house trailer at first seemed luxurious: comfortably furnished like a regular house, central heat, hot and cold running water, shower and bath and indoor toilet, electric lights. All the amenities, all the "creature comforts" required—as *necessities*—by Americans, even though such "necessities" had been unknown to all those generations enduring life without them right up to the twentieth century and then available mainly only in the industrialized West. We played with it like kids with a new toy at first, taking long hot showers, turning on lights with a twist of the fingers. But then quite quickly it all became boring. The creature comforts were taken for granted and thus whited out for lack of contrast. The trailer started feeling bloodless, in some sense dead. The "wood" on the walls wasn't really wood, the table and chairs were vinyl and chromium, the ceiling some kind of sprayed-on plastic, the featureless furnishings what you would find in Everyman's Motel. It had no character, no personal presence. It wasn't really there. It was a cutout from a slick magazine pasted on a "quiet side street." But its robotic servants weren't quiet; they whirred, hummed, and clicked on and off all day and night with tireless insistence. When Steve came in from his gig at the Forelands, hours after we had all gone to bed, he'd often have trouble getting to sleep because of the racket.

In a cabin, the various fluttering of flames in the stove, mixed with the random crackling of the firewood, and the occasional crick or groan as the logs shifted ever so slightly with a temperature change—these things were just part of the basic drone of silence. They were like a quiet conversation with your consciousness. At the time we inhabited the trailer, we weren't really aware of all this; it hadn't formed into an idea. But we felt it as a subtle uneasy vacuity in our lives. We didn't belong there. The thought of getting a job and living in such a place hit me like nausea. I think that trailer probably represented civilization for me, unconsciously. Materially Convenient (always capitalized, like God), spiritually dead.

"You know," I said to Carol over breakfast, "I think I'll borrow Steve's wagon—he'll be able to catch rides for his gigs—drive up to the state building and pick up the survey maps, head right on up to Talkeetna and Trapper Creek, look the area over."

Much of the Open to Entry lands lay north of Talkeetna east of the Alaska Railroad, a remote area with only one road and almost no people. I'd check out the Trapper Creek area too, on the west side of the Susitna and Chulitna Rivers, because the Parks Highway, dirt and gravel then, ran that far north at the time, which would make access easier. I was doubtful about the Trapper Creek lands though, because the maps showed a lot of swamp and bog. Worth a look-see nevertheless because of the road. Settling in was going to be hard enough any way you looked at it. A road would surely be a help. But on the other hand roads bring in people, sooner or later—and there goes the neighborhood.

"Today?" Carol asked, looking up, sensing my restlessness. She looked over at Jon, Sal, and Beth playing some game on the floor. I knew she was apprehensive about this new move, into wilderness on our own, with everything uncertain. But she was a special woman, capable of a special kind of love, whose rarity in the modern world I've come to appreciate increasingly through the years since she died. Her love for her family was her strength. But also, she understood where I was coming from and believed it was right, in her own estimation. She never mentioned going back. But that doesn't mean she didn't think about it at times, prompted by a mother's concern for her children.

"Sure. Why not? It'll take only a couple of days. The longer we delay, the more likely someone will file on a spot we would have liked. We're just treading water here. I can at least get the feel of the country up there and look over the towns." I paused. "That's important, right?"

We'd passed through some disappointing junky "towns" traveling the north country: half a dozen run-down buildings, a one-pump filling station with a corrugated metal shop, tar paper shacks, abandoned cars, mangy sled dogs, no trees—blotches on the land around them, evidence, to me, of the crazy white man's determined degeneration, doing to the last frontier what he had done to the first frontier. Sometimes my cynical part would accuse me of a kind of childish romanticism: to be expecting villages and towns with golden log cabins amid tall spruce and birch, like in a Hollywood movie. Well, the "golden" part might be a bit much—except if you're looking at a new cabin glowing in the afternoon sun—but Talkeetna when I first saw it came surprisingly close to my ideal.

The highway north out of Wasilla in 1970 was under construction. The town of Wasilla was small and rustic and okay, not even a supermarket in evidence. Until this new highway, now with big machines pushing gravel and dirt around to support the asphalt or concrete, Talkeetna and any settlement north of Wasilla formerly could be reached only by railroad or airplane. Talkeetna was the main point of supply for the trappers and miners who worked the surrounding wilderness, returning to the town to work the Fairview Inn, its one bar and focus of its social life, which is to say the site of the week- or month-long binges the men went on to recuperate from the solitude and hardship of the trades they plied in the woods, until they were broke again and went back "out." In the early days, I've been told, there had been one other hot spot in town, the whorehouse at the end of town, known, for reasons unexplained, as "The Bucket of Blood." I have stood outside its roofless, broken-down walls and let my imagination fill in the gaps.

Before driving the spur road into Talkeetna on that first exploratory trip, I followed the half-done highway up to the Trapper Creek area. I parked alongside the road, pulled on my boots, and since there were no houses or people anywhere around to launch a search and rescue mission should I get turned around, I stuffed map, compass, waterproof matches, knife, rope, and some jerky into a small day pack, grabbed my rifle, and then set off into the woods. I walked or splashed around for an hour or so and concluded it was as the geological survey map had indicated—wet. So much for the road and its easy access.

I returned to the Plymouth wagon and drove back to the Talkeetna spur road. It was too late by then—about 3:00 A.M.—to expect anyone to be up and around, even though there was daylight, so I pulled over by a little creek, rolled out my pad and sleeping bag in the back, and stretched out with a sandwich and soda. I listened to the creek and breathed the cool, sweet air of this new country, too excited to sleep right off. Unless Talkeetna turned out to be a complete bust, I felt it would be somewhere in the woods north of town that we would settle in and make a life.

The creek gave voice to the silence. It didn't babble or sing any lullabies. It spoke, but what it spoke lay too deep for any of that Disney stuff, too deep for words. Beneath my anticipatory excitement, I felt very alone, a stranger in a strange land, and when a loon let loose one of its cosmic-loneliness calls on a lake nearby I sensed the padding about of the metaphysical horrors. They didn't get to me, not quite, but it was a while before sleep finally came. I was a man stretched out and dreaming fitful dreams in the back of a Plymouth wagon on the side of an empty road surrounded by endless miles of dusky woods dreaming their own dreams.

Some hours later, the sun on the sleeping bag was hot and bright on my closed eyes. I opened them and gazed up out the window. The overcast of the earlier hours had cleared away. The sky was now a flawless blue, almost metallic, the sun already high. I raised up on an elbow and looked out and there was the Alaska Range, Denali itself and Foraker and all the mountains of the range, spread out across the sky only a stone's throw away. Gleaming, still, and silent in their grandeur, the mountains seemed so close. But from the little hilltop I'd parked on I could look down and see the blue-gray water winding its way around the small islands of cottonwood and willow, the braided lines of the Susitna River stretching out into the distance before reaching the foothills.

In 1970 there wasn't even a tourist pullout with a plaque describing what they were seeing. The mountain range had yet to attain the status of being an "attraction." Nor was there yet any garbage on its slopes from the hundreds of climbers who later came to conquer one or another of its peaks. —In fairness I should add that a significant number of those climbers came not to conquer but to admire and, perhaps also, to prove themselves capable. A few of them whom I came to know located in Talkeetna and on memorable occasions, which others have described, performed heroic feats of courage and endurance. (I'm thinking of climbers like Ray Genet, who met his end on Mt. Everest, and Brian McCullough, who participated in the daring rescue of the survivors of a plane crash on Denali, and of glacier pilots like Don Sheldon, already a legend when I met him, and Cliff Hudson, retired now, and his son Jay, still operating Hudson's Air Service, who was the youngest pilot ever licensed in Alaska.)

I drove down the gentle hill that led directly into the center of town. "Whoever loved who loved not at first sight," wrote Shakespeare, and that's how it was with me. Spare, open, seeming almost uninhabited, I saw at once that Talkeetna possessed the rare charm of authenticity, while at the same time it could have served as a Hollywood set. The post office was in the general store, the B&K Trading Post, a large log building painted maroon, now weathered. Across the road, set on a scant fringe of scrub grass, was a square frame two-story building painted white, also weathered, whose plain sign over the entrance read "Fairview Inn, 1920." I half expected John Wayne to stride out the door with his crooked grin: "Howdy, stranger."

I cruised the rest of "main street," about the length of two or three city blocks ending at the hard-packed bank of a bend in the Susitna River. About midway was another old-timer of a building, low-slung, made of squared logs, also painted white, and also weathered, bearing a sign that read "Roadhouse. Rooms and Meals." A couple of log cabins set back among trees also breasted the main drag. The railroad ran down the east side of town, one small building constituting the station. Here it was that the trappers and miners first disembarked to seek their fortunes in the woods. So far I had seen only a couple of people walking down the road, which had no sidewalks (and still doesn't).

I turned back to the Fairview Inn and sat awhile looking at it. Square and altogether unadorned, free of any kind of architectural attitude or pretense, it was unself-consciously what it was— but I realized at once that that was its charm, its claim to my regard. It was the real thing. It wasn't playing around, acting up, attracting clientele. The wilderness was serious business for the people of a frontier town. The building spoke of a time and way of life immersed in rain, snow, wind, cold, hard traveling, periodic "sweats," and trappers and miners who didn't make it back out of the bush. The Fairview Inn was where you went to find some comfort, especially in the winter, and where you'd likely find some human warmth as well, a few friends to have a drink or two or ten with, swapping lies. I saw that no modern lodge or inn could duplicate or rival its authenticity. It wasn't picturesque in any ordinary sense of the word. It was warm and dry, had rooms with beds, and served booze to the rough men who craved it.

This formed my first impression—of course there was more to the town down side streets—but it was enough. I was a goner for Talkeetna. And now, more than thirty years later, it's still a marriage, despite all the changes and all the newcomers. Shakespeare was right.

I entered "the View," as we've come to call it. A few men were already at the bar at just a little past noon (I hadn't gotten to sleep till maybe about 4:00 A.M.). There were the usual gigantic moose and caribou racks on the walls, about a dozen "true to life" paintings of old-timers now in the happy hunting grounds, and above the bar a large painting, very well done, of a grizzly confronting the Alaska Range. The men swung around to see who it was, and not recognizing me, turned back to the bar, minding their own business. But of course they were curious; not many strangers found their way into Talkeetna. The bartender came over and nodded.

"What'll it be?" he asked in classic bartender form. I ordered a beer, and when he brought it over, "Looking for someone?" he asked, probably by way of starting a conversation, which I welcomed because I wanted to ask these men some things about the country north of town. I knew they were all listening in. They had that same lean, alert but unconcerned look about them I'd noticed invariably when encountering woodsmen.

Yes, it was good country north of town. Plenty of moose and bear, caribou in the northern hills, some fur, almost no people—a few trappers in season, a family homesteading about five miles out of town, right off the tracks, one of the last of the "Fifty-niners" the government had brought in to start up some agriculture but who hadn't, except for a family vegetable garden, and farther north, up around Gold Creek and the hills above Curry, some miners through the summer. Real good fishing for rainbows and graylings in Clear Creek, especially where it enters the Talkeetna River—and of course the spawning salmon in late summer and early fall. Big country, good woods, plenty of tall straight spruce for building mixed in with the birch.

They answered my questions readily enough but asked none of their own. I was planning on staking out some land up there, and that was enough to know. I didn't look or act entirely green. My business was my own. Go for it!

I reported all this, obviously hyped about it, to the family around the kitchen table. Not only Carol and Steve but Jon, Sal, and even little Beth gave me their full attention. They all sensed that this could be it, our final push into life in the Alaska bush.

"There's a small lake on the survey map that no one has filed on yet. It's about ten miles north of town and maybe a couple of miles east of Chase on the Alaska Railroad, which I'm told is a whistle stop. No trails showing anywhere and only a few cabin indicators right at the tracks at Chase, which the guys at the Fairview told me are all fallen down and decayed, since Chase has been abandoned for years—apparently once used by the railroad for something or other. There's another little lake close to the tracks with two five-acre plots marked off. So I'm figuring we'll go for the lake back in. Have it all to ourselves. Miles and miles of woods around us and a town only ten miles away . . ."

"Only ten miles away," Carol repeated. "Can ten miles be reasonably referred to as *only?* How do we get ourselves and supplies over those ten miles from the town to the lake?"

"Well, the railroad to Chase. They take freight. Then two miles, about, overland by trail to the lake."

"Are there trails?"

"Well, no. Not yet. We'll make them."

"And what about the things we'll need for a cabin—like stoves for heating and cooking?"

"We'll pack them in from Chase on our backs, I guess."

Carol sat still and gazed at me. Not fiercely, as might have been the case, but wonderingly. She was beginning to think that Nerka, Iliamna, and Chinitna Bay had been vacation spots compared with what was shaping up in her mind about the Susitna Valley. Those first locations had been trial runs really. Ready-mades. This would be starting from scratch. On our own. No cabin or shack to move into, no trails, no one around who knew the country, no one to help if we got into trouble or hurt. Now some fear went through her, and she thought of the farm back in New York and me coming home from the university in the evening.

"First, of course," I went on, "we'll have to find the lake. If the weather's fair, Steve and I could go tomorrow. You know what they say in Tierra del Fuego: Time's a-wastin'! We'll get our packs together this evening. —Don't let me forget the map and compass. It's obvious, studying the map, that there's damn few landmarks to go by. The ground cover will be dense. We can hope for a little sun to steer by, but we're going to need the compass and map. Otherwise in new country like that, you know, you could get turned around and walk in circles till your legs dropped off. —Though one 'landmark' that could save our asses if we were hopelessly lost is the railroad: I'm sure we would hear a train sooner or later, and we'd know that was west."

I grinned at Carol. "I know you'd love to come along"—she grimaced at me—"but we'll need you here so that if we're not back by, say, five days, you can call out the marines to go looking for us somewhere east and south of Chase. Actually, we should be back the third or fourth day—one day in, one to stake the land, then one out, and the drive down to north Kenai. If the crick don't rise."

Steve and I swung down from the train at Chase, having properly notified the conductor that we wished to disembark there. Otherwise the train would have rumbled right on by. Chase was no longer a scheduled stop; it was a "whistle" stop, though if you wanted the train to stop so you could board you had to do more than stand there whistling Dixie. You had to step between the rails

when you saw it coming and wave—arms, a jacket, a handkerchief—until the engineer acknowledged your presence with two
toots of his whistle.

We hurried back to the baggage car, where the baggage man
handed down our packs. Then he gave the engineer the go-ahead
signal. The train pulled away and soon got small in the distance
between the receding walls of green. We saw no buildings, only
the unbroken front of the forest, leaves bristling in the wind. We
knew someone had staked a claim on the first lake in from the
tracks about a mile, so we shouldered our packs and started walking along the siding looking for some sign of a trail. You had to
look close, but yes, there it was heading in. Not much of a trail—
just one or two men doing maybe a dozen round-trips, but we followed it, heading in the generally right direction for the back-in
lake we wanted to find.

We were pushing through the brush and tall grass, thirty-foot
spruce and birch overhead, when among the tops of the trees we
saw peeled golden poles forming the peak of an A-frame taller
than any I ever thought possible. We reached the small clearing in
front, which was facing away from the lake below. The building
looked like it had been designed as a four-story structure, with
only the ground and top floors closed in with logs at this time.
Hardly a "ground" floor: the sill, or bottom, logs were set on
eight-foot posts. The ripped-log door was at that level, but there
was no stairs or even a ladder up to it, just a thick manila rope
hanging down within reach. Was that the way in?

Steve and I looked at each other and grinned. Were we getting a
whiff of our first neighbor? What? A giant? Had we recited the
"men to match my mountains" mantra too earnestly—and here
was one of them?

"Have to take a peek inside," said Steve. He doffed his pack and
grabbed the rope, going up hand over hand, with some help from
his boots on the logs. He pushed, and the door swung inward.

"Hey, Dad, you'll want to take a look at this."

Okay. I was sure it would be worth the effort. Up the rope I went.

The inside was cavernous, barnlike. Three tall windows looked down at the lake. To the left of the doorway stood a gigantic cast-iron cook stove, and midway into the cavern loomed an equally gigantic wood-burning stove with a firebox that could swallow three-foot chunks of wood. Who got those stoves to the site? And how? Queries reinforcing the giant theory. Or extraterrestrial? But there was more to wonder about. The top three floors at the present stage of construction were just plywood platforms open to the cavernous space. There were no stairs. But there were ropes dangling from beams. Maybe our neighbor was an outsized orangutan. That would explain a lot. In any event, that A-frame was a sign we had chosen the right neck of the woods to settle in. Whoever or whatever was at work on it clearly had size and was no ordinary citizen. Suburbia could never contain or tolerate such an outlandish structure nor its architect and sometime inhabitant, one Denny Dougherty.

As we came to know him, we saw that Denny Dougherty was as outlandish as his A-frame home. He showed up at Back Lake one day to meet his new neighbors, or perhaps more to the point, to present himself to our regard. We were impressed. Sally and Beth kind of shrunk back at sight of him. For here was the cartoonist's conception of the wild man of folklore, somewhat along the lines of the fabled Bigfoot. His gangly frame stood well over six feet, and on top of that frame was a tangled mass of long auburn hair and full bristly beard punctuated by two intense, cobalt-blue eyes. This was a man you couldn't fit into a gray flannel suit.

He started talking right away, shaking hands and offering to pick up the girls, who demurred with wide eyes. He had gotten blown up in Vietnam and been pinned and stitched back together in such fashion that his stance and walk seemed angular and somewhat akimbo. "I'm dying," were the first words out of his mouth, followed by volley upon volley of unpremeditated speech, accompanied by oddly awkward, vigorous arm gestures. He was glad to meet us, glad we had come, we looked like great folks, the cabin looked great, had we seen his place yet? He and his brother had put it up and when completed it would have a full basement with a shop and workout room; he liked First Lake better, but this was a great lake too, what a spot! and so on and so forth. He displayed unusual energy and gusto for a dying man. We saw quite a lot of Denny and his tall, attractive lady Edie through the months and years following and became good friends.

Steve and I shouldered our packs, checked the map and compass, and headed out, hoping to make a beeline to the back-in lake. No trail, no obvious landmarks, dense woods. Beelines, under such conditions, are hard to come by. There was a creek we couldn't cross without a long detour, a swamp and marshy ground we had to circumnavigate. It wasn't raining, but within the hour we were soaked in our own sweat and more than a little confused, having had to make too many navigational adjustments. We found ourselves back at the tracks, invested with a lot less energy than we had started with. The bush stood by silently, impassive, enclosed into itself. Big woods, it came to me . . . and definitely still wild.

We laid out a different route down the other side of the first lake and then along a ridge that curved toward the unclaimed lake of our desires. We overshot it, not having glimpsed it from the ridge. Where was it? Which way should we turn? We descended the ridge and pushed ahead through the brush a couple of hundred yards. We stood on a patch of grassy land that looked like it had been rutted by running water. Runoff from a lake? I turned around, looking back up the swath. Between the trees, a patch of blue that wasn't sky!

It was a little oblong lake, but not a pond: a lake, maybe half a mile long, a couple of hundred yards across at the middle. The water was very low; we could tell from where the waterweeds started.

We walked around the edge, a bit revved up of course: that we were actually there on the lake where we might live! And that there was no sign of anyone else.

The day was clear and sunny, a light breeze dallying among the treetops. The first big hatch of mosquitoes had not yet appeared, only a few of the big ones from the summer before on hand, no doubt to remind us that even Eden had its serpent. It was a great day to be out in the woods. It smelled so good, aromatic and clean, a smell you only find in deep forest. Moose and bear tracks were everywhere. A flock of mallards took off, climbing the air steeply. Now and then as we walked, we heard explosions of spruce chickens taking off in the woods near the shoreline. The loons suddenly started an excited kind of calling, and we looked up to see a bald eagle gliding past the trees on the far shore. All we needed now was for Natty Bumppo and Chingachgook to stride out of the woods to welcome us.

I raised my arms and swung around in a circle. "Lafayette," I shouted with all the joyous absurdity I could muster, "we are here!"

We set up camp on a grassy spit a little north of the lake's center that was high and dry, though normally it would be underwater. It gave us a panoramic view of the whole lake. About midway of the lake on the east side the shoreline bulged out a bit, and I knew right away that would be the site of our cabin. That small projection would catch all the breezes, which would help with the mosquitoes, especially after we whacked the bushes and grasses where the little beasts of prey hung out.

That night around midnight, the sun still above the trees (Land of the Midnight Sun), we were awakened by splashing at the south end of the lake. We thought bear first and reached for our rifles, but it was moose—two of them feeding and cavorting in the shallows. In the late sunshine they gleamed darkly against the warmly lit-up brush and grasses. It was a scene of primal peace and beauty, and I had to wonder why, starting some ten thousand years ago, it had become insufficient for human happiness. The trees, the sky, clean waters, magnificent wild animals, wind, rain, and snow, men for women, women for men, song and dance, children and games, delight upon delight, and all freely given. And yet not enough. Clearly, the fall into history had been a precipitous descent into the snake pit of insanity. It seems greed and unhappiness arose coincidentally with the rise of civilization on agriculture's back and have been gaining strength ever since.

The initial approximate stakeout was done with measured lengths of rope and rough-cut stakes pounded into the ground at the four corners. Before the state would grant title the plot would have to be surveyed and recorded professionally within the first ten years of occupancy in a reasonable dwelling.

We were fairly sure of the route back to the tracks and blazed both sides of trees as we went, to establish a trail. We left plenty of time to reach the tracks before the evening southbound passenger train would arrive at Chase, in case we got turned around again.

It seemed somewhat doubtful that the great big train would actually stop for just the two of us standing there. But it did. It was only about a fifteen-minute run by rail into Talkeetna. As the train pulled away from Chase we gazed out the window at the unbroken forest. We had a foothold in that country. With the exception of a couple of guys in suits, businessmen from Fairbanks probably, the scattering of other passengers all wore the bushy look. Steve and I blended right in. They would not think it, looking at me, but I had been famous long ago for penning papers in the halls of academia.

When we got back from the lake with the exciting news of its many splendors and perfections, we were met with other exciting news. Several of Steve's freshly graduated high school friends, having gotten the glowing word about Alaska from Kelly (who naturally had been prone to exaggerate and embellish, since he had made the scene), had decided that the most attractive prospect in their immediate future was not pumping gas or bagging groceries, not when their old pal Stevie Durr was up in the wilds of Alaska shooting moose and building log cabins and camping out at fifty below. Back to nature had been the word all the while they had been growing up. The Durrs being willing, maybe as many as half a dozen of Steve's pals were raring to drive up and lend a hand.

"Lend a hand!" The phrase resonated with good omens. Four to six young bloods: enthusiasm backed with energy. Settling on the back-in lake suddenly became quite doable. If in fact those hands arrived, it would be a sure thing. (Oh, yes, I had had my doubts, bad sleep-disturbing doubts.) But many hands make light—and fast—work. By the time the Coldman started breathing down our necks we would have one, probably two cabins up and at the ready. Let the hoarfrost of his breath whiten the land and freeze the lake. Let the winter winds howl. Who's afraid of the big bad Coldman? We got *hands*. Ask and it shall be given unto thee. I didn't know it then, but I had been asking for this, life in the wild woods, since I was a kid, and something had been listening and had liked the sincere ring of those inarticulate yearnings. And now the helping hands were being offered. All things come to him who waits, if his desire is true.

They sat on the floor before me like disciples of some sacred order, so shining with trust were their eyes. Paul Simon's very blue eyes were especially bright. A new life. A better life. No more working for the pharaoh, no more respectable drudgery. A life of adventure, and of *meaning:* to be building a new life according to nature's plan. That's what they wanted, knowingly or not. I wanted that too, and I was their point man, leading the way. Hence their shining young eyes.

But I didn't want them thinking it would be like going to the movies. So I spoke of blood, sweat, and tears: the hard work of clearing land, the hard weight of a log on your shoulder, rubbing and bearing down as you stepped over deadfalls carrying it out; the aggravating, wearisome work of draw-shaving the bark off a half-dead spruce; the long trek packing heavy loads in from the tracks. But there would be this too: the smooth luster of the shaved logs, the incense of pine pitch on the clean air; the sense of muscles strengthening, of becoming capable; the delight at night as those muscles soak up rest while you listen to the frogs' drone periodically pierced by the primordial calls of the loons, and the cool breeze wafting over the water as the sun sinks behind the trees; and seeing the cabin rising under the work of your hands. This and so much more subsumed in the aboriginal satisfaction of building your own home.

Besides Paul Simon, the others from Morrisville, New York, were Steve Cross, Phil Pugh, Paul Crandall, John Gourley and his girlfriend Maggie Resnick, with Buddy Kobell and his wife Linda to arrive shortly. They were, as mentioned, counterculture hippies out of the sixties, young people who envisioned something more to life than making money and being important. The thing was sweeping across America, and we happened to have been in the vanguard.

We set up our tents along the east shore of the lake, near the slight promontory I had chosen as the site of our cabin. The first day or so I gave over to making camp, exploring, and fun. We had carried my sixteen-foot aluminum canoe in, and there were always two or three of "the kids," as I was wont to refer to them, out paddling around. In the late evening hours after supper, everyone gathered around a big campfire at the site, in high spirits, talking, kidding around, laughing, and somewhere along the line singing behind Steve's guitar, with the sweet scent of pot on the air. They were high just being there; the pot was merely an adjunct. It was basically an all-American scene. Norman Rockwell could have painted it, except for the joints.

I was careful to tell them what I knew about bears, how best to deal with them—like "Don't just start shooting if one comes nosing around at night, because they can usually be scared off by yelling or banging pots or, in extreme cases, a shot in the air.

Killing bears is not what we're here for, unless you have no choice—like if a sow with cubs is charging: probably the most dangerous bear situation." They were all fascinated. This was exciting stuff. Bears! Real wild bears—not in a zoo or movie but maybe in your face! We talked bears and moose and woods lore late into the night around the fire. After all the bear talk, I was wondering how sound they'd sleep with one eye open and both ears akimbo.

Every night by the light of the midnight sun I sat on my bag in the tent and read up on cabin building. Carol would usually be asleep, with Beth's little head next to hers. Carol had plenty to do throughout the day and lay down gladly at night. It was a big enough tent for Jon and Sal to have their own space in a corner. Steve had his own tent. Nobody had any difficulty sleeping soundly.

I had two old, dog-eared books. What they described was the methods old-timers used, mainly trappers and gold-panners, so what I was learning and attempting to apply the following day was really quite primitive compared with the skilled craftsmanship of today's builders, who scribe-fit the logs and use Perma-Chink caulking, resulting in very tight-fitting logs needing only a narrow bead of the caulking to keep out the weather and retain the heat. The old methods tutoring me typically resulted in gaps between the logs, often as large as an inch or two, which had to be chinked.

Old-timers often used sphagnum moss for the chinking, plentiful in most woodlands, and that was my choice. I liked the look and smell of the moss, which was abundant here and there around the lake. It was Jon's and Sally's job, sometimes with Beth tagging along, to bring back large plastic bags of it, not only for the chinking but also for the roof, since ours would be a pole-and-sod roof: continuous spruce-pole rafters covered with plastic sheeting and topped with sod and moss. These kinds of old-time cabins looked like they had grown right out of the woods.

Smart trappers in the old days, putting up small one-man cabins, laid flattened birch bark sections over the roof poles. Removing the sections of bark from the trunk, each maybe three or four feet long, took time and effort but was worth it because the natural oils in birch bark rendered it impervious to the elements and, almost, to time. Many such cabins have been found with walls rotted and caved whose bark covering was still sound. Actually, of course, the early trappers or miners had no choice. They were too far from any kind of store, and there was no such thing as rolls of plastic. They had to use what the woods supplied. Even their window opening, if any, would likely be covered with the stomach casement of an animal, scraped thin and clean enough to let in some light.

Our circumstances were similar, although we had the railroad, and plastic had been invented. Still, all but the floorboards, secondhand windows, and plastic covering came from the surrounding woods—and the plastic would rot under the sod after a few years, wouldn't you know. Nor did we have a chain saw, considered essential nowadays for building and cutting firewood. We had only axes and a rusty two-man saw we found in a secondhand store in Anchorage. But we had *hands*—and good muscles and willing hearts—and it was sheer adventure to be in the deep woods building a log home. Each log we brought in and shaved or peeled was a satisfaction, each tier that went up a triumph. We worked through hot sunny days and through cool rainy days. We became creatures of the elements. Our spirits and energies never flagged. When completed, golden and green, with the flowers and berries of the moss decorating the roof and winking out between the logs, that first cabin was a thing of beauty and pride to all of us.

We didn't expect a cabin to be like a house, didn't even want it to be. We regarded it as a shelter, like a wigwam or tepee, a beaver lodge or eagle's nest, a bit of the woods gathered together to keep out the rain and snow, keep in the heat. The difference between this kind of cabin and a house is comparable to the difference between an open fire before a lean-to and a Winnebago. With the former, you're immersed in nature, in the latter walled off. Our cabin blended right into the woods, as though it had grown there. Which would have pleased Frank Lloyd Wright, our sod-roofed, moss-chinked cabin or Mr. and Mrs. Whitebread's Winnebago? The shiny white house on wheels might (or might not) be more Comfortable and Convenient, but man doesn't live by Comfort and Convenience alone. The Winnebago had Comfort and Convenience, let's say, but lacked spirit. Our cabin was short on Comfort and Convenience by ordinary measurements, but long on spirit, which is to say life. How come those people in the grandest mansions on the grandest estates seem to spend their lives scheming and murdering to get yet more Comfort and Convenience— oh, yes, and power. What's their problem? What are they lacking?

When our sweaty bodies got covered with sawdust and bits of shaved bark and we needed a break, there was the lake, and after our swim we sat or lounged around drying off in the sun and breeze. It was the intense summer sun pouring into our open site and the lake breezes that kept the mosquitoes away—most of the time. Because of the unusually dry spring, that summer of '70 was "not a bad mosquito year." Nevertheless, on some still, mucky days, especially if we were working in the woods away from the lake, we had to resort to bug dope. I for one wondered how the Indians and old-timers managed without it. True, it dribbles into your eyes with your sweat and burns—there's a down side to everything—but bug dope is one bit of modern technology I'm grateful to have. And there was this: When we were able to swim and lounge in the sun and breeze bug free it was a luxury we didn't take for granted. We *appreciated* it, and appreciation is at least half the constitution of good fortune.

Furniture too was homemade from spruce poles and, for the table's top and benches along two sides, leftover floorboards. Seats at first were log sections cut to size and set on end, as we had done at Iliamna. We sectioned off a room for the kids' bunk beds, also fashioned out of poles and floorboards, with foam "mattresses" we packed in. Sleeping bags were our bedding. Even after a hot day, in the Susitna Valley it cooled down to where you needed some covers. Carol and I slept in "the cubbyhole"—something like an oversized bay window projecting from the east side of the main living area of the sixteen-by-twenty cabin. The cubbyhole was cozy; you felt like you were sleeping both inside and outside, warmth from the cabin on the inside and outside the woods and stars close up to the big window.

Packing in the twenty-inch propane cook stove and the "Airtight" sheet-metal heating stove over the two-mile trail from the tracks was hard work but also a great accomplishment strengthening more than our muscles. It was even fun in a way. All hands on deck, every man jack of us pitched in, taking turns with the loads, each man carrying for maybe fifty to a hundred yards before the next guy took over. Some of the fun happened when someone carrying tilted too much around an obstacle and the weight took him ass-over-head into the bushes. The joking was nonstop the whole two miles. Then out of harness and our clothes, dripping sweat, and into the cool, clean water.

Everyone had brought some food in, which we supplemented from the land. The fiddlehead ferns were a staple. Picked early and stored in a cool mossy spot they kept well for a long time. They were rich in vitamins and minerals and could be prepared in a number of ways. Everyone living in the woods values the fiddlehead fern. In the spring there are also the fireweed and "watermelon berry" shoots—the latter so named because the red succulent berries in the fall tasted like watermelon. The shoots went well in salads, soups, and stews. To this day every spring finds me out picking these wild vegetables, just as every fall I'm out after the berries and mushrooms. As hunting is exciting, gathering is fun. I don't think our hunter-gatherer forerunners had it so bad, lacking supermarkets. Anthropologists tell us, from studying their bones and teeth, that they were a lot healthier, eating a wider variety of organic, fresh foods, than we agricultural peoples are.

Chunilna Creek—"Clear Creek"—flows into the Talkeetna

River about five miles east of our lake. When the spring runoff is over, and if the summer isn't too rainy, Clear Creek looks like a classic calendar trout stream—riffles, foaming gray rocks, smooth muscular runs, deep promising pools. At least a couple of times a week a few of the hands would grab their fishing gear and head out for Clear Creek, their mission to enjoy themselves and to return with rainbow trout and arctic grayling for everyone. That summer the creek was perfect, low and clear, the fish concentrated. We ate a lot of fresh trout and grayling, usually cooked over an open fire.

Our lake, I learned from the old-timers, used to be full of fish, innocent fish, unlearned in the tricky ways of humans, easily caught. Sheldon used to take his hurry-up clients on the short hop to this lake. They would stand on a pontoon and have their limit in half an hour. But either the 1964 earthquake or beavers rerouted the stream that used to come into the lake, the running water making it possible for trout to reproduce; and then also the outlet emptied into the Talkeetna River, some of whose abundant population would surely wander up into our lake. So, without running water, there no longer were fish in the lake. All right then, Clear Creek it is.

On one of the first days exploring the woods around, following the low ridge that ran south above a marsh, we had come upon the old "Fifty-niner" dirt cat trail they had carved out of the brush with a bulldozer, running from their homestead by the tracks at Mile 232 to Clear Creek. This cat trail was about a mile south of the lake, and we soon had a rough trail going to it, our highway to the fish. Besides their fishing gear the fishermen carried rifles, because bears like easy going too, and also, where the road stopped was high above the creek, a steep climb down, and then along the bottom you had to push your way through dense fern forests, over your head, and it was evident that you could surprise a bear or vice versa in very close quarters. Hence the rifles and all the loud talking, whistling, and singing. "Here come we, Brer Bear. We be a jolly crew and means you no harm—you can see, or hear, we be not trying to sneak up on you. Okay?"

In the course of that summer of hard work and fun we got my cabin up and most of Steve's, across the lake on the ridge; Steve Cross managed to build himself a small place; and Phil Pugh started a cleverly constructed tree house in the branches of three stout birches on the ridge a ways down from Steve's. (Phil, in partnership with John Gorley, went on after he left the lake to become a very successful contractor in the Wasilla area.)

One day another Morrisville couple, Buddy and Linda Kobel, friends of Steve's, arrived at my cabin. Who could forget the moment Buddy stepped into the clearing sweaty and wide-eyed— *wild*-eyed—and gazed at the new, golden cabin. He turned to me as to someone he knew well (we'd just met). "Bob," he said, placing his hands on one of the corner logs, "I'm having an *orgasm*. This is an orgasm!"

Well, I knew what he meant despite his odd way of putting it. We all felt that way—elated, which is to say, high. What we were doing was not something incidental, like establishing a vacation retreat or having a swell experience. What we were about seemed important, to our lives personally and to America. For the kids it was an expression of the values of the sixties counterculture: This was where it was at, the center of the movement, what it was all about, the return to nature and the elemental life, the rejection of the world of crass consumerism and ego bloating.

Buddy was very glad to be there with us, and he immediately became one of the hands. Moreover, he and Linda stayed on the lake for the first years, as did Paul Simon and Steve Cross. The following summer we built small, twelve-by-fourteen one-room cabins for Paul and Buddy and Linda, the idea being that they then could add on rooms and in the meantime have a dry, warm shelter as a base of operations. Phil inhabited his tree house for a couple of years, accompanied the second year by a lovely young lady named Romona. Phil was tall and well built, and his dark hair fell to his shoulders, so how could I resist thinking of him and his lady as Tarzan and Jane? Crandall and John and Maggie left at the end of the summer. Which, it turned out, was a good move, because that winter the Coldman was in a bad mood and had determined not to fool around with us intruders into his silence. He would show us what winter in the great north woods was all about.

7

That First Winter: The Coldman Cometh

That first winter.

(1970–1971)

As early as August you could sense it, a certain feeling in the air on cloudy days, a different kind of chill when the wind came out of the north. You paused and looked up into the wind coming down through those dark clouds. By the end of the month that year the first hard frosts hit, which was early, like a forecast of things to come. We hadn't had time to plant the garden plot the girls and my kids had worked on so hard, chopping down the brush, pulling up the long tenacious roots, tossing the rocks into the lake, but the dark, moist soil early on those first frosty mornings would be laced with a filigree of ice crystals that could be read more certainly than tea leaves, and the bushes and grasses were spattered with twinkling diamonds and opals. We donned sweaters or jackets and wore light gloves until the sun was well up and the work had warmed us.

The Coldman came on not as a marauder but slyly, secretly, with the lengthening nights when the stars shone brighter than ever and the air was still and clear as the temperature silently fell.

In September the shallow inlets along the shore began to show ice. The old-timers in Talkeetna all agreed it would be an early freeze-up. The gold-panners were already coming in, the trappers readying their traps. The fireweed had blossomed at least a week or so earlier than normal and was now going to silvery seed blown on the wind. The birch too were prematurely turning from the greens and limes of late summer to the gold of mature autumn. When the wind blew, the air was awhirl with golden flakes, as soon it would be with white ones, the mottled yellow and umber of the ground turning to all the nuances of white.

As the lake began settling into its winter silence, and with so few humans on hand, it seemed the wildlife moved in closer. Earlier we had heard wolves now and then, off in the distance, but now one night we heard their howls much closer, maybe just in the hills rising northeast of the lake. Jon has a short story to tell:

One October day I went hunting with my little husky Rigby. We had wandered down to the north end of the lake when all of a sudden wolves started howling, all together. It seemed they were real close and all around us. Rigby was terrified. She crawled under a blowdown and lay there shaking. I knelt and pleaded with her to come out, but she wouldn't budge. The howling rose and fell and so did my heart. Wild wolves can stir up a boy's imagination. I didn't exactly panic but I ran home to get help, afraid they were maybe after Rigby. Wolves will kill a dog every chance. Rigby knew that instinctively. I told Dad and he grabbed his 30.06 and followed me to Rigby. She was still frozen there under the tree shivering with fright. We had to drag her out and carry her home quivering in my arms.

We knew that wolves rarely if ever attack people, but there was something unsettling as well as exciting about their being close by. They and their howl came through as the very soul of the wild. We were glad, thrilled (if a little intimidated), to have them in our area, just knowing that they were there alive and well, wild and free—though it's true they would kill any of our dogs or cats that happened to stray into their vicinity, and not necessarily to eat them. Did they harbor an instinctive hostility toward the tamed and domesticated? Perhaps. What concerned us wasn't the wolves but the Coldman, he of the deadly embrace.

By October as the lake was freezing over tent living had become a hardship. All construction work was suspended. The diehards, son Steve, Paul Simon, Steve Cross, and Phil Pugh (whose tree house was not yet ready for winter), pulled up stakes and moved into a tight little trapper's cabin we had discovered back off the tracks a ways at Chase. It appeared to have been lived in fairly recently, for although a weathered old-timer it was in good repair, the chinking and sod roof sound, double-decker bunks ready for occupancy, even a stack of firewood next to a thirty-gallon barrel stove, which would be more than adequate for heating, since the place measured only about twelve by fourteen.

Our guess was that it was available to anyone passing through who needed shelter for the night or possibly longer, its original owner and builder having left it for that purpose perhaps—not unheard-of in the north country, where people away from their cabins typically left them unlocked in case someone had to get out of the weather. So the boys moved in and were probably snugger and warmer that winter than the Durr family in their drafty cabin back on the lake. Bud and Linda moved to town, having found a low-rent one-room cabin on a side street. They planned on building a place of their own on the lake the following summer.

We've all heard or read how insects and other animals are able to attract the opposite sex uncannily from long distances. It would seem that ability may be part of the human animal's makeup as well, for one day when I was over at Chase and walked up to the boys' trapper cabin I was amazed to find two pretty girls there having tea with them. They were sisters, one blond, one brunette, Anna and Mona. I recalled having met Anna briefly the past summer when she and her husband, Darrel, whom she was about to divorce, had visited at our lake. I remembered that son Steve and Paul Simon had somehow met them all in Anchorage previously. Making their

short story even shorter, Steve and Anna, the older sister, paired off
and so did Paul and Mona, who was new to my acquaintance. The
four of them about midwinter rented a small apartment in Anchorage, to get jobs and hopefully save money to put into their cabins
next year. The following summer when we had indeed completed
Steve's and Paul's cabins the girls moved in with the boys and became welcome additions to our little community.

Nevertheless, I never believed the tales about woods nymphs.

The only ones left then on the lake that winter were Carol and
me and the three smaller kids, though son Steve and Steve Cross
came over frequently from the trapper's cabin, eating up the two-
mile snowshoe hike as though it were all downhill on skis. Steve
Cross seemed to take to the woods life naturally, being tempera-
mentally suited to its low-key, slow pace. He was the strong silent
type, good-natured, always willing to lend a hand when he visited,
and always welcome. He seemed to like the family atmosphere. He
obviously liked the kids, and they liked him, regarding him really
as a big brother, just as they had Wayne and Dick at Chinitna Bay.
Actually, our community was a kind of extended family or infor-
mal commune. I felt that was beneficial for my kids, something
like the ancient tribal life.

I especially appreciated the two Steves' help with the firewood,
at which we had to spend hours every day, given the fact of the
porous cabin, the Coldman's relentless assaults, and that we had
only a thirty-inch band saw and axes to work with—no chain
saw! So the lake was quiet, with so few people on hand and no
chain saw.

Freeze-up at Nerka, Iliamna, and Chinitna Bay had been much
more gradual. True, we had had a taste of the Coldman's power at
all three locations—a few nights of thirty to fifty below—but each
cold snap had been short-lived, a night or two followed by moderation. During the winter of '70–'71 in the Upper Susitna Valley,
however, the Coldman was in no mood for moderation. The hard
frosts came early, the lake froze early, before mid-October, even

the first snowfalls stuck, and through the darkening month of November the Coldman really bared his teeth: night after night down to thirty, forty, fifty below, "rising" to about twenty to thirty below by high noon. If our cabin had been a submarine helplessly descending below its maximum depth, bolts would have been popping out at us. The Coldman was putting the squeeze on.

Throughout that first winter on our lake the severe temperatures hung in there for solid weeks at a time, interrupted by brief intervals when clouds came rolling in, the temperatures climbed to ten to twenty above zero, and the dark clouds opened like huge dump trucks, unloading heavy snows that almost buried the cabin and plugged our wood trails. But there was no snuggling up to the stove watching the flakes fall during those respites. The wood trails had to be reopened, and the fire god had to be served or at fifty below his displeasure could mean our discomfort, or worse.

We kept one eye on our shrinking wood pile and one eye on the outside thermometer. At first light every morning we checked the temperature and scanned the sky looking for any sign of clouds coming, bringing warmer air (air a little less frigid, that is). But when the wood pile looked like it was getting low we had to go out after firewood no matter what the temperature.

Thoreau remarked that firewood warmed you twice, once while you're getting it and once when you're burning it. And that was true enough. Even after it had "warmed up" to only twenty below or so the wood detail brought out the bodily BTUs. It was hard work and took hours every day. We had frosted eyebrows and eyelashes and very rosy cheeks, which we needed to check now and then for the white spots of frostbite.

Our Mickey Mouse sheet-metal "Airtight" stove was rumbling full-bore through most of the day and evening, glowing cherry-red at times. When we bundled into our sleeping bags at night I partially banked the stove but had to stoke it through the night to keep the indoor temperatures—at least above the floor—from hitting the freezing mark. We didn't need a refrigerator indoors, and outdoors was a huge deep freeze. I look back now and marvel that we got through that winter without a cabin fire, because our "chimney" passing through the roof was a five-gallon can insulated with fiberglass, at best adequate for mild fires in the poor overworked stove.

We wore long johns and woolen socks day and night, put on sweaters as needed, and mainly sat up close around the stove. One or another of us periodically scraped the frost off the window to check the outdoor thermometer. "Thirty below already! It's going to be another rough night." It was exciting. I made sure there was a big stack of night wood handy by the stove.

When someone came in, a mist of cold air rolled in across the floor with them. The logs in the "kids' room" turned white with frost as they slept. The heads of spikes through logs from the outside were also white with frost: the Coldman's probing fingers. Northern lights tended to be very bright and colorful at these temperatures, ghostly figures shimmering across the sky. Some nights we were sure they made a crackling sound as they undulated, and some nights we would just have to step outside briefly and look and wonder at the awesome display. The colder it got, the brighter shone the night sky. Bad-ass as he might be, we had to admit the Coldman was outfitted in splendor.

And on top of all that we needed a moose. All the Eskimos and old-timers agreed you needed meat to fend off fanged cold. Pancakes and rice won't do it. Our catered honeymoon with the far north was over. We were up against it. Carol's anxieties about this new phase of our venture hadn't been unfounded.

Nevertheless, there were special pleasures attendant upon this extreme winter. The kids were glad to get into their warm beds early—nothing exciting going on to rev them up. Their bunks were piled a foot high with blankets and sleeping bags, and they wore their long johns like a second skin. Crawling under those covers in the still darkness and being tucked in by their mother was as cozy as it gets, a deep pleasure deepened by the fine old folk songs I sang them just about every night.

When it's really cold like that, it becomes the main feature of your awareness. It has presence. You hear the cabin logs creak as they expand with the dropping temperature through the night, and outside in the blue starlight the lake groans and growls and sometimes "shrieks," a sound something like whale calls, as a fault line streaks across to the other side, and the trees pop as the ice expands in their veins. Windows become forests of ice ferns. Icicles grow down into the snow. They shine in the sun and glint in the starlight.

That it got dark early, by 4:00 P.M., was not altogether unwelcome. For one thing it meant we had to come in out of the cold; outdoor work was over for the day. For another it meant we lit the kerosene lamps, four to six of them, and they helped bring the cabin to a more uniform warmth than the stove alone could supply. Even their soft yellow light seemed to warm the cabin.

On those nights when the Coldman was prowling around, pressing his advantage against us, the family would draw closer not only to the stove but to one another . . . and in the quiet of the crackling stove, reading or coloring or repairing something and looking up when the lake groaned, eyes wandering to the starlight on the filigreed windowpanes, we didn't feel grim or heroic. We felt cozy and close together against the Coldman.

Steve had a funny way of describing the deep cold: It was like in the morning the Coldman stood flattened against the wall by the door, and when you stepped out of the cabin he hit you in the face with a snow pie.

In the deep cold every hair on your face becomes white with frost. Men with beards try to avoid smiling because it hurts as the frozen hairs pull away. I'm talking about outside; it never got that bad indoors.

Mornings I would be up first as always, stoking the stove, opening the draft. As the cabin warmed they began to stir, and then after first light—about 9:00 A.M.—they would pop out of the back room in their sheepskin slippers and huddle around the stove, Carol right there among them, and I would tell them the news: forty-five below again! To them, it was exhilarating, not scary, not even uncomfortable. If you live in a modern house or apartment that is always warm you don't know what warm is. They had been warm and slept long and deep. Even today, so many years later, after so many changes, they tell me they remember that first severe winter in our own cabin, the magic and wonder of it, with nostalgia.

I knew what they meant. I had experienced that kind of magic and wonder myself as a boy in the old house in Brooklyn. No central heat, just the big cast-iron stove in the kitchen and some kind of gas heater in the living room. Very little heat seeped into the bedrooms upstairs. My sister and I slept in a feather bed in flannel pajamas, with flannel robes and sheepskin slippers handy for the dash downstairs to the kitchen. When it snowed, and a wind was blowing, a drift of snow would form on the windowsill inside and a dust of snow lie without melting on the floor. I remember one morning after it had snowed like that all night, the first big snow of the winter, my father squatted with my sister and me by the window, as gleeful as any kid, pointing out how deep the snow was down on the street, up to your knees, covering the curbs, the trees all white and heavy with it, and still coming down, the sky still leaden with snow, and not a car moving, my sister and I feeling with him something of the fascination and delight of it.

But really—in that adult reality that is always referred to as hard—it was tough going on the lake that winter. Firewood was the most serious demand. At forty to fifty below you cannot run out of wood because everything freezes quickly at those temperatures, including human beings. You can't just bank the stove and then open her up in the morning. You had to keep the fire going all through the night. And even that wasn't as bad as it may sound. The night silence in the still cabin was profound, and when a full moon shone in the clean sky its light laced the gleaming snow with a filigree of shadows, a mysterious beauty fraught with inexpressible meanings.

We went through a lot of wood that first winter. It was a big job for me and my two sons. As mentioned, Steve Cross helped get that firewood in and stacked by the stove. Phil Pugh was in Talkeetna or Anchorage frequently but would show up with Cross now and then and lend his hand to meeting the firewood challenge. Most often, as is usual in the bush, they stayed the night (fixed a pallet down on the floor). Carol always managed to come up with good meals for them, appreciative of their help.

People helping one another, anthropologists tell us, was universal among our kind through all the hunter-gatherer ages and was one of the secrets of our success as a species: cooperation, not competitiveness. It's only since civilization that hominids have systematically preyed upon one another, typically the rich and powerful preying upon the poor and powerless, even in America, the richest country the world has ever seen, with wealth enough for all to have a decent life were the rich not so rapacious. But apparently they can't get no satisfaction, because they're always wanting more.

In the egalitarian hunter-gatherer times there were no rich or poor, no ruling oligarchies, no hierarchical states. Everything was shared, everyone was equal. "Head men," or chiefs, had no coercive power. They had simply proved worthy of respect. They were the chief givers, not the chief takers. Some scholars believe that subliminal memory of those times is the cause of our undying nostalgia for a paradise lost and our yen to answer the call of the wild, to get back there. Certainly I believed that modern culture, especially Western culture, was bad for human beings and their home on earth.

Potatoes, onions, carrots, beans, rice, and lentils were nutritious, inexpensive foods and were our staples. Carol baked loaves of whole-wheat bread. But as has been noted there's no food like meat to help fend off the cold. So once again, as at Nerka, Iliamna, and Chinitna Bay, I felt a strong responsibility to bag a moose: our winter meat. It had been easier done at those other locations mainly because the cold hadn't been so relentlessly severe, and in all three places I had had help. After midwinter, with Steve in town earning some bucks, Jon and I would have to keep the home fires burning and bring back the bacon—though I was sure I could call on Cross for help with the skinning, butchering, and packing back once I connected. He was subsisting on ptarmigan—flocks of them feeding on the willows along the tracks and river—and trout fished through the ice on First Lake (which had springs big enough to sustain the fish population, as our lake did not). And of course he had a store of the usual staples. But I knew he'd welcome a haunch of moose meat.

This is not to sell ptarmigan short as food. They're about the size of the spruce chicken, but unlike that near relative they turn color in the winter, becoming pure white except for their eyes and beak and the tip of their tail feathers, which makes them hard to spot among the hummocks and clusters of willow where they feed. It's only after some heavy snows that they are forced down from the high country, their grubstake having been buried under the white stuff. Notice of their arrival in our neighborhood is their tracks, mainly along the railroad and the river, where willows are abundant.

We'd snowshoe to the tracks and then move ahead slowly. In those days there wasn't much snowmobile or dog-team traffic along the tracks to scatter the flocks, and it wouldn't be long before we'd run across the sharp indentations of their fresh prints. Sometimes we'd spot a few hunkered down motionless, depending on their near-perfect camouflage. Those would be fair game for the .22. But more often than not, especially when the flock was large, the birds would start running through the underbrush and among the hummocks—difficult targets for the .22. We were meat hunters, so we weren't above ground-sluicing with a shotgun if we could line up three or four in a bunch. Carol complained a little about the occasional pellet in the meat but was always glad to have the change in diet.

That we were meat hunters didn't mean the hunt was without zest. On the contrary it compounded our pleasure. Bringing back a dozen birds or more for the pot was significant to more than our egos. But they weren't a sure thing, weren't easy to bag, and didn't sustain our larder long. We loved going after them on those brisk, sunny afternoons, but for the homesteader "winter meat" means moose or, if present, caribou.

I had put as much time as I could spare into hunting earlier through September and October, but to no avail. But in November after we had enough snow to read tracks I would be out at first light regardless of the temperature. Besides my Winchester 30.06 I carried a small pack with the gear I'd need to gut a moose—sharp knives and sharpening stone, a meat saw and ax, and plenty of rope. The moose in our part of the valley didn't follow established trails but wandered where they would—hence the benefit of snow for reading their whereabouts. You couldn't just sit on a high spot overlooking a good trail. You had to still-hunt, and the best place to try was the low land south about a mile from the cabin, because that area had a goodly growth of willow, the moose's main food supply. To feed your family go where the game feeds.

I would hunt doggedly, moving slowly and deliberately, stopping to look and listen every few yards. It would be easy to miss spotting a moose standing still among the snow-laden trees and willows. There were tracks aplenty among the willows in that low-lying area. And I had devised a strategy. Where the old homesteader's cat trail made a sharp turn to the east off its northerly course I discovered an old trail, snow-covered but discernible and open enough for easy, quiet snowshoeing, that cut across the bend of the cat trail. The willows and small scrub spruce were dense within that bend: a likely spot for moose to feed or bed down. When the wind was right, blowing north, as I went down the old trail my scent would be carried into the loop area and would likely drive any moose away from me and up onto the cat trail. I would keep going down the old trail in its easterly direction and emerge at its end where it meets the cat trail. If my scent had moved moose out, they wouldn't be alarmed and would be pushing through the snow slowly, so that I could reach the cat trail and turn and watch for them.

I had been hunting like this every day for maybe a week when the strategy worked. I was standing still up on the cat trail watching when two moose climbed from the dense cover just twenty or thirty yards down from me. They stopped and stood broadside, perhaps sensing something wrong or just checking things out, since they had caught my human scent a few minutes ago.

My heart started beating its drum and my breath came sharp. I quickly brushed the ice crystals from my eyelashes and eyebrows to see better, doffed my outer mitts (attached to a cord around my neck), and tried to work the bolt to jack a shell into the chamber. It wouldn't budge. Frozen stiff. I hit it with the heel of my hand to no avail. The moose stood still, but the nearer one turned its head my way, ears forward. They were alerted. I had to move fast. I pulled my belt knife out of its sheath. Its handle was wooden and wouldn't be too loud. I whacked the bolt's knob, breaking the ice seal. When I looked up a second later the moose were gone.

Despite their dark coloring, they can disappear into the snow-laden foliage like ghosts. And there's no use of a man on snowshoes trying to run them down. They may look ungainly moving out fast, but they are powerful and can cover ground unless the snow is up to their chests and hard to push through. I cursed myself for not anticipating the possibility, in those temperatures, of the gun oil and/or some condensation freezing the bolt in place within ten or fifteen minutes of leaving the house. I should have wiped the moving parts clean, left the rifle outside, and checked the bolt action before heading out. I wouldn't make that mistake again. There was a lot to learn.

I did connect in roughly the same spot the day before Thanksgiving. It had been snowing heavily and was still coming down hard, but I had a kind of hunch. Carol was surprised when she saw me getting ready for the hunt.

"You won't be able to see a moose through this stuff unless you're right on top of him, Bob. And speaking of 'on top,' your snowshoes won't stay on top of this soft new snow. Right?" Carol was learning fast. "Why not take a couple of days off? Take a rest. You've been pushing yourself hard, what with the firewood and trapping. We're not about to starve."

"Right on all counts, wilderness woman. But I'm going to mosey on down there anyway—on a hunch. —And consider this: They won't be able to hear or see me coming. And also, the wind will be in my face, which takes out their noses. And look: We're into a warm spell. It's already warmed up to twenty above. The snow levels the playing field for me."

Snowshoeing was harder all right. Each step sank through the fluff almost a foot, which then had to be hefted back on top again. But I wasn't in a hurry, and in my peripheral mind the woods on such a day seemed more magical than ever, every tree and bush an incredibly beautiful sculpted form, each contour perfect, each tree and bush a masterpiece. The silence too was perfect, muffled, this deep snow and the densely falling soft flakes like a thick wool blanket drawn over the land's winter sleep, so peaceful I could imagine myself just letting go, dropping into it, and drifting off into bliss. But I too had promises to keep, a family to care for, a life to be lived out. And yet my focused attention all the while was alert to the possibility of moose.

I reached the cat trail and voilà! there they were: the dark forms of three moose not twenty yards in front of me. I didn't worry about snow covering the lens of my scope; I didn't need a scope at that range. They started moving out, away from me, long, powerful strides. I dropped the largest one, most likely to be a bull. The other two disappeared into the whiteness.

Steve Cross and son Steve were due at the cabin that afternoon for Thanksgiving and of course my reliable sidekick Jonny was on hand, so after making sure the moose, a medium-sized bull, was dead I hurried back over my float to enlist their help in the gutting.

There weren't any trees near the downed moose that I could tie to in order to pull the legs away from the torso so I could work on the gut area by myself. Two pairs of helping hands holding the legs away would make the job very much easier and faster.

Before dark we had the animal cleaned out and most of the hide off. I cut out the back straps to take back with us for the Thanksgiving dinner—a big improvement over the frozen spruce hens we had planned on, since we had no turkey.

That first winter was the most unrelentingly cold of all the thirty-some winters I've lived through here in the Susitna Valley. We thought it must be normal: The north country was what we had wanted, and this was it. Every winter will treat you to a stretch of forty to fifty below for a few nights a few times over the winter months, these on top of a lot of "milder" subzero days and the frequent "January thaw" when temperatures go above freezing and it may even rain. —It's a compensatory treat after such a thaw, by the way, that when it turns cold again branches of every size and bent are turned into fantastic clusters of ice jewelry, especially with the low sun shining through them, the likes of which neither Queen Elizabeth nor Elizabeth Taylor ever beheld and could ever possess.

I don't know where the money came from, possibly from selling the fur I somehow found the time and energy to trap, but about midwinter I was able to buy a small chain saw. That was a saving grace, if you can refer to a machine in those terms. I was very glad to have it. It cut my firewood time in half. Yet it must be said that at ten, twenty, or more below zero a chain saw is not altogether an asset. It's hard to start, the chain tends to freeze to the bar, and when that happens, or anything else goes wrong, it's difficult to make repairs with mittens on your hands (which get cold anyway) and impossible without them. You try, your hands freeze, you place them inside your jacket, in your armpits, to thaw, which invites the Coldman to apply the pliers to your fingertips and squeeze hard.

The saw, however, was helpful with firewood most of the time, but perhaps surprisingly it was helpful with water too. We got our water through a hole in the lake ice. In a winter like this the hole froze over again quickly after each time we reopened it, despite our covering it with a piece of plywood and shoveling a couple of feet of insulating snow on top. With just an ax and a six-foot ice spud, getting down to water through the three feet of ice we had by midwinter was time-consuming and exhausting. With the chain saw it was faster and easier.

We emptied the chain oil reservoir, cleaned it out, and put in some vegetable oil. The cuts into the ice, the length of the chain saw's bar and just a few inches apart, first across one way and then at right angles, made it possible to chip out large chunks of ice with the spud. Then, kneeling and holding the small saw in one hand, we leaned into the hole and made another series of cuts, which brought us to or near to water. If the saw tip made it into the water we would get sprayed. The sprayed water froze almost instantly on our clothes and hair. The man working the chain saw would hurry back into the cabin looking like the Tin Man with a red face. We tried to keep the hole open wide enough to be able to dip buckets out, which we emptied into the large plastic garbage-can reservoir inside.

Breakup came slowly. The Coldman hung tough before the advancing sun, though he knew his days were numbered. By February, the daylight hours were clearly lengthening, the sun definitely growing stronger. On a still day you could feel its warmth on your back, like a friendly arm around your shoulders. Trappers pulled their sets; with the sun now too strong, the fur was losing its prime.

But the advance toward spring wasn't steady. The Coldman wasn't knocked out; he had some punch yet. Nevertheless, he was staggering, his punches losing their wallop. In February and especially in March he might take vengeance for his waning ability to inflict severe cold upon us by dumping deep snows on us. It was like the Battle of the Bulge, the defeated enemy showing a last insistent defiance and taking his toll of our endurance. The winter was long, but in February, and more so in March, you could believe the poet who assures us, "If winter comes, can spring be far behind?" Well, yes, that's true, but how far is far? Winters in Alaska are long.

But then in April the snow starts going. You notice it first around the base of the trees; a kind of bowl forms. The trees gather in the sun's warmth and it melts the snow around their bases, as though they were as eager for summer as we were. It's in those basins that you first see ground and dead grass. It's a welcome sight, seeing the earth again. In a way much too subdued for a Hollywood portrayal it's like a reunion with a friend or relative or lover. From that start the bare ground spreads, and only patches, islands, of snow remain in May.

But there's enough of them and deep enough in their centers to make it tough trying to go anywhere during breakup. To traverse the two miles to the tracks at Chase, for instance, you have to carry snowshoes, strapping them on to cross an especially big island of snow in your way, then taking them off and carrying them again until the next big island. There'll be a lot of wet ground too, wet ground and big puddles; so you need a pair of "breakup boots," which that first year we didn't have. What we had instead were wet feet. There would be patches of snow on the ground in places well into May, even as green shoots and grasses were coming up and the birches were getting fuzzy with tiny buds. The woods were special at that time, open and bare, with a certain tentative tenderness to the look of the land, like a naked woman.

This was a time of bountiful fresh vegetables, free for the picking. We had learned back at Iliamna to make good use of them, spears of delicate green life pushing up through the earth toward the sun. We all went out gathering the young plants. Fiddlehead ferns were everyone's favorite and were even sold in supermarkets. They could be prepared any number of ways: sautéed in extra virgin olive oil and chopped garlic, added to stews and salads, or— a favorite of mine—dipped in beer batter and deep fried. Delicious! The shoots of fireweed and the watermelon berry plant, together with the young leaves of the dandelion, were all excellent in salads—and their freshness was chock-full of vitamins and minerals, plus roughage. We were eating along the lines of our hunting and gathering ancestors, who, as mentioned previously, ate much more nutritiously than agricultural peoples do. And what do you suppose was easier and more fun, hunting and gathering for a few hours a day or rising before dawn to tend to your domesticated, penned animals and the watering and cultivation of your crops from dawn to dusk?

Finally, in late May, the leaves of the forest unfurl, the lake ice turns to sparkling blue water, the ducks, loons, grebes, swans, and gulls appear like magic even before all the ice is gone, the frogs go on like the drone of a raga, the birds send forth their mating songs, the Coldman is gone, the green world is back, and it's summertime.

And back also are the bears. Every spring the hungry bruins, just out of hibernation, find our dump, a hole we dug about a stone's throw back of the cabin. Typically, we'd hear the cans and bottles being rattled and clanked sometime during the hours of dim light. The kids would rush to the windows to watch them. But I would grab the 30.06, not to shoot them but hopefully to put a good scare into them with shouts and shots over their heads, to discourage their coming back, when maybe I would have to shoot them. The bears worried Carol considerably, because of the kids.

Chasing them away usually worked, but not always. There's a saying in the bush: "Watch out for the ninth bear." Eight out of nine would be "pesky," but the ninth could be dangerous. He keeps returning after being chased off. With the shouting and shooting, he runs off, moving through the brush and tall grasses.

But then the grass and brush stop moving maybe fifty yards off, and you know he has stopped and will return. The ninth bear. Early one morning there was a whack on the window of the cubbyhole where Carol and I slept, and I opened my eyes to see a big black bear's head looking in about six inches from my head. He dropped to the ground and bounded off when I yelled (very loud), waking the rest of the cabin.

Later that day I was about to step outside but pulled up short. The bear was out front with his snout in a can of white dog gruel. (Shad was inside, and I thought it best to leave him safe in ignorance of the bear out front.) He stood there. Slurp, slurp. He ignored me, though of course he was aware of me, about six paces from him. This was no good. The ninth bear, making himself at home. I spoke to him in a normal voice. "And what do you suppose you're doing?" He pulled his long snout out of the can and looked up at me, nonplussed, then went right back at the dog gruel.

I had to be concerned, for the kids especially. He wasn't stalking us, just doing a little opportunistic scrounging. But he was big and if surprised in the brush by one of us he would very likely attack. That was an unacceptable possibility. I waited a couple of days to give him a chance, keeping an eye out for him and keeping track of the kids. But he kept coming back, up at the dump and even in the garden. Carol and I agreed he had to go.

We skinned him out and sent the haunches in to a friend's freezer in town. "Bears is damn fine chewing." We buried the head and after a year or two retrieved the teeth; one of the "eye" teeth, with a couple of trade beads on each side, was made into my favorite necklace.

In all the years here at Back Lake we encountered only two more editions of the ninth bear, with similar consequences. Paul Simon had to shoot a charging grizzly from his front door, and another neighbor was forced to kill one that charged him on the trail to his cabin. If we have to kill a bear, we eat it. (The exception being a bear that has been gorging on salmon—they reek. But a happy, well-fed bear is rarely interested in our meager pickin's, so that all evens out.) The haunches make into a good stew, and the rendered fat is the lightest in the world. It's the best fat for pemmican.

Bears have broken into every cabin in the area when people were away—every cabin except ours. I don't think that was just luck. I think the word was out in the bush: "Don't mess with Jungle Bob's place. They're good folks. They really like us so long as we behave. Make sure the ninth bears get the message."

So all of this was the seasonal round in which our lives were immersed. Year after year, the same pattern, the same returns, and it never gets old. Spring is wonderful, summer is wonderful, autumn is wonderful, winter is wonderful. Nature never makes a wrong move. She is *always* beautiful, good, and true. Call me a man for all seasons.

8

Hippies, Old-Timers, and Redneck Raiders

Bob, all frosted up.

That spring after breakup, at about the time the loons, grebes, and gulls returned, so did Steve and Anna, Paul and Mona, Buddy and Linda, and Phil and Romona. Steve Cross had never left the Chase area. All hands were back on deck.

The good folks of Talkeetna—old-timers and regular Middle Americans—weren't sure what to make of us. We were in Talkeetna fairly often, one or a few of us, for supplies mostly, so there was contact. They had heard a lot about hippies, most of it bad—drugs, free sex, un-American notions, long hair, and weird outfits sporting feathers and beads: "Flower Children . . ." What the hell was that? In their minds it was the same as *pussy*. We were the first specimens they had actually seen and talked to. They weren't hostile toward us, just cool, regarding us with a slight upward tilt of their eyebrows and a slight lowering of their eyelids. But they had to reckon with the fact that we had actually moved into the woods around Chase, some actually wintering up there. And what a winter it had been! This confused them. Pioneering was part of their movie; they couldn't feature hippies in it, even as extras—well, maybe playing Indians.

We got wind of some whopping rumors about us: I was the mad professor, despotic leader of the clan, taking their food stamps and conducting orgies every Saturday night in the one big cabin we all lived in. A Freudian would have fun with that—it's called "projection" or maybe "wishful thinking." Some of those old-timers had wild streaks in them wide enough to accommodate that sort of thing. Inwardly they might have chuckled when the rumors reached their ears. "I don't know . . . but sounds like the Professor's got a good thing going."

Jim Beaver and Rocky Cummings were two of the town's old-timers we all liked and admired. They were both bachelors—though there was this fiery redheaded ex-wife ("fiery" referring more to her temperament than her hair) who stormed into town on occasion apparently for the express purpose of giving Beaver some grief, or maybe to bully a few bucks out of him. If you happened then to be within a hundred yards or so of the House of Beaver (Jim's place, so named) when she was there you would know that while the cabin might be insulated it wasn't sound-proofed.

When Mary (an alias?) was riled, which was usually, her voice carried. A couple of times a day, an airplane would come in low, roaring over the Fairview, and touch down a stone's throw from Jim's cabin alongside the village airstrip. Now that noise he was used to and didn't much mind, but Mary in a tirade he couldn't handle. He was as tough as they come, but this woman could drive him out to seek sanctuary at the bar, also conveniently only a stone's throw away. And if Rocky happened to be there, which was not unlikely, Jim would have found shelter from the storm. He now had her outnumbered and in a public place—although that circumstance alone would not protect him were she really riled.

"You look like you could use a drink, Jim," Rocky would offer, his shoulders bouncing in a chuckle. Mary's voice could reach the Fairview, so Rocky knew why his friend looked so woebegone. Fortunately, she rarely charged in there after him. A bar was kind of off-limits to women of their generation; it was like a church or sanctuary for men. Women generally respected the arrangement. When they entered the premises it would be on the arm of a northern gentleman. (That's no longer true of the younger, liberated generations.)

Talkeetna had been Beaver's base of operations from the start. He had sallied forth at one time or another into most of the pursuits typical of the Alaska sourdough—trapping, mining, and in Jim's case, punching through some of the first roads in the trackless bush.

A story I heard about Jim involves a guy who shall remain nameless. Jim had a daughter, of whom he was very fond. She lived in Anchorage but visited him often. One evening after Jim had been out in the bush and was wearing a .357 Colt on his hip, he was relaxing with a drink or two at the View when the fellow came over and sat down at his table. He had been drinking and was feeling cocky. The story wasn't clear on the details, but the gist of it was that this guy started talking about Jim's daughter in terms and with implications unfavorable to her and her reputation. Maybe he thought he was being funny or wanted to give the impression he was on easy terms with this renowned old-timer.

Beaver, however, was neither amused nor impressed. He looked over at this wise guy who obviously had no sense, drunk or not. He drew the Colt revolver and laid it on the table. "Your move, sonny." You can only imagine how fast sonny sobered and backtracked. Talkeetna in 1972 wasn't the Wild West but it wasn't the New York Public Library either.

Rocky was a man of the world. He had been a sailor in his youth, traveling the globe, but in his middle years had found rumrunning more lucrative, and maybe more exciting. The story goes that once when the Coast Guard was drawing down on his ship, which was loaded with the contraband at the time, he opened the petcocks and sank her. But not before he had affixed buoys to the crates of rum and tied blocks of salt to them, so that they sank out of sight with the ship but eventually bobbed up to the surface as the salt dissolved. After being rescued, in due time he and his crew returned to the scene of the crime, collected the evidence, and went on a week-long bender. Whenever the story was brought up Rocky would just sit there chuckling, his shoulders bouncing. He never said whether it was true or not.

Rocky was about eighty when I knew him back in the early seventies. He was tall and still slim, a little stooped, his complexion pale, his hands huge. Neither his eyesight nor his wit had dimmed. An unusually good-looking girl came into the View one evening when I was sitting having a drink with him. She was a stranger, probably up from Anchorage and visiting someone, and probably curious about the fabled Fairview Inn. I checked the girl out and nudged him. "Now there's one you might go for, Rocky." He glanced over at her. "How old would you say she is, Bob?" "Oh," I replied, "nineteen or twenty probably." "Well," said Rocky, "that's a little too old for me." And his shoulders started bouncing.

Men to match my mountains.

That phrase would describe most of the town's old-timers, women as well as men (I'm thinking of the late Dorothy Jones, for example, or Mary Carey and Roberta Sheldon, among others). Certainly it fit the two longtime bush and glacier pilots in Talkeetna, Cliff Hudson and Don Sheldon. They had been plying their trade since the town's earliest days, flying trappers, miners, homesteaders, and mountain climbers, plus their gear, to wherever they needed to go, landing their Cessna 180 or Super Cub on glaciers, gravel bars, lakes, rivers, and postage stamps. Feats of derring-do were their daily fare.

Sheldon was already famous for his incredible rescues when I hit town. (You can read about his exploits in a book called *Wager with the Wind* by James Greiner.) Sheldon became my pilot by default, as it were, because I had located Hudson first, wanting to be flown into the lake with a load of supplies, but he had looked at the day, which was seriously socked in and blustery, sized up the load in my station wagon, scratched his head, and finally demurred: a bit marginal, don't you know, heh heh, woof woof (Cliff had his own way with the English language, including the expression just cited). He was much more cautious than Sheldon, which in part explains the marvelous record he compiled over the decades of never having lost a plane or a passenger; the other part of the explanation is that he was a very skilled pilot. Sheldon also never lost a passenger, but he went through a number of planes and bunged up his legs pretty bad, which was evident when he walked.

I had total confidence in both pilots, but having started with Sheldon, I stuck with him. Many times I sat cramped and unable to move behind him in his Cessna with baggage, two-by-fours, and whatever packed in around me so tight I couldn't even turn my head. He didn't want to have to charge me for two trips if we could make it in one.

Both pilots were always friendly and helpful to us "Back Lake hippies." I remember Don cautioning me when we had just started on my cabin, "Lots of windows, Bob! Make sure you plan for lots of windows." No doubt he had in mind the scarcity of windows in the old cabins—one or two and in some cases none. A sure recipe for cabin fever: the long, dark winters and almost no light coming in! Even into the time of the midnight sun, you want the rays coming inside and stretching out along the floor, making the cabin glow.

The two men had their personal differences, however. It all came to a head one day in the B&K Trading Post. They tore the place up pretty good going at each other. Don's risky business flying never did him in, but cancer did, many years ago. His widow, Roberta, still lives in their modest house across from the Fairview and is a staunch defender of Talkeetna's character and charm against the forces of change that would cheapen it.

Doc Thompson was another old-timer. I heard he had gotten into a feud with Jim Beaver that heated up to the point where Beaver chased him down the airstrip with his .357. Fortunately,

Jim missed—fortunately, because in those earlier days Doc liked to sit at the bar with his old F-hole guitar and sing country and western numbers, which we all enjoyed, even those of us who weren't fans of country and western. He'd just walk in, order a beer, and have at it without preamble. He had a good voice and played a simple but competent guitar.

Of course many of the townsfolk were straight arrows, and their points were sometimes directed at us. Generally speaking, however, in Talkeetna there was less suspicion or animosity toward us and the other settlement of hippies above MacKenzie Creek north of us than there was toward the counterculture movement down in the States. We had earned some credit for having settled in the woods and also because, rumors aside, we didn't come on as weirdos or troublemakers but in fact seemed fairly normal. As time went on we got along better and better with most of the townspeople. Mainly because of our making a life in the bush it had to be allowed that despite the "Flower Children" label applied to hippies Outside, we also apparently were not pussies. Pussies couldn't have made it in the bush. The town knew that.

A contingent of hippie bashers found that out the hard way. Some half-dozen burly redneck types from Anchorage had heard about the hippie invasion up around Talkeetna and decided to conduct a little paramilitary operation on behalf of the town. They planned their raid to coincide with one of the community's festive occasions, since they'd heard the hippies liked to come to town and party at such times. And indeed there were several on hand in and around the Fairview, not just from our lake but from MacKenzie Creek and the few scattered cabins in our general area—people we knew a little or at least had heard of, counterculture, back-to-nature people like ourselves. We were always able to recognize one another.

Several of those hippie guys not only had long hair, they had long bodies with hard muscles as well. You see, these were "woods hippies," a breed apart from the stereotyped hippie lying around smoking dope all the time, getting soft. These backwoods hippies were in very good shape, and they had all accrued, somewhat unconsciously perhaps, a certain pride of self-confidence, a quality of independence, a "Don't tread on me" attitude, from living in the woods. In a way that had nothing to do with macho, they were tough—along the lines of those woodsmen and fishermen we had known in Bristol Bay, at Nerka and Iliamna, and in Chinitna Bay.

It's true they liked to party, and smoke pot and drink wine or tequila while doing so. They liked to make merry. They had this idea that life was to be enjoyed. So probably they didn't *look* tough to the redneck vigilantes when they swaggered into the Fairview and noted a few longhairs at the bar. (They failed to note a few more outside standing in a circle behind a couple of cars, passing a joint.)

I wasn't there, but this is the story as I heard it afterward: One of the Anchorage gang sat down next to a guy with hair long enough for his ponytail to reach halfway down his back. This was Kevin Wyatt, an old friend of the MacKenzie Creek people. Kevin turned out to be a bad choice for the burly redneck to harass. For one thing, Kevin's size wasn't apparent at the moment because he was hunched over his drink. What followed was classic; you've seen it in a dozen movies: the fellow who consternates his cocky antagonist when he unfolds from his seat to his full height. Even the redneck's provocation was classic, a stereotype. "Say, can I buy you a drink? Strikes me you're not a bad-looking chick. I especially like your long ponytail."

Kevin turned to the dude. "What did you say?" The dude, still unaware of the mistake he was making, repeated what he had said, looking surly. Now Kevin was not given to lengthy verbalizations when he understood that he had just been deliberately insulted. He stood up (his head now far above his feet) and knocked the guy off his stool. The other rednecks, who had been paying close attention, dashed over and started swinging at Kevin, who swung back. This alerted the two other longhairs at the bar, who immediately entered the fray. One of them was Kevin's longtime friend Rick Shears, from the MacKenzie Creek contingent. He was built strong and wore a derby hat atop his long hair. He and I were good friends. When we ran into each other, Rick would come right up to me: "Come on, Jungle Bob, let's get *shit-faced!*" Anyway, the melee also roused the hippies outside from their pleasant stupor, and they walked in, sized up the situation, and evened the odds.

Emily, a commanding presence, was tending bar. "Outside!" she roared. "Take it outside! I'm calling the troopers right now."

There was shoving, shouting, and swinging as the conflagration bumped its way out the door onto the road. It's been reported that Rick ripped the antenna from one of the rednecks' trucks and proceeded to whip them into shape with it. I don't have all the details, but the long and the short of it was that the Anchorage gang got badly shellacked and retreated to their trucks, eager to leave the town to its fate.

I have to confess that the following winter a sometime neighbor at First Lake, Mike Sheehan, suckered me into a costly snowmachine race—costly because my machine got wrecked, I got injured, and I came out of it feeling and probably looking like an asshole. I had just bought a little secondhand Ski-Doo Elan with money from the sale of the *Diane*. Its owner had beefed up the engine and created a wider stance for the skis. My thinking was that I had an ideal combination—power and lightness (for when I got stuck). An ordinary one-lung Elan is not a fast machine. Mike had a fairly new Arctic Cat. The outcome of the race seemed a foregone conclusion. We had been drinking, which had something to do with my accepting his challenge. He didn't know about the adjustments that had been made on my Elan, so I was snickering up my sleeve: He'd be eating my dust (snow dust, that is).

The race was to be from in front of the cabin, down to the beaver dam, and back, the winner to take possession of the second, unopened jug. Carol was apprehensive, but the rest of the community on hand were all smiles: They knew about the Elan.

We lined up shoulder to shoulder outside, and at the shot from Simon's gun we took off with a roar. I was out in front immediately, tear-assing toward the end of the lake. I think if I had not been drinking I would have sidestepped Sheehan's challenge, and certainly I would have remembered the hard-packed snow hummocks the wind had sculpted across the raceway about two-thirds of the way down. It was whiteout conditions, so I didn't even see the hummocks. But I felt them.

I hit and flew at least ten feet into the air and came down in a high-speed nosedive. My thigh caught the handlebar and bent it out of shape. In retaliation, the handlebar turned my thigh black and blue and green. I was also bleeding from my nose and mouth and right hand, from which the mitten had been scraped. Other muscles started complaining the next day. As I lay tangled up with the Elan in the snow Sheehan roared by laughing. He didn't stop then nor on his return trip from the dam, laughing all the way.

The super-Elan never performed well after that, partly because of the abuse it had sustained and partly because my calculations about its superior properties had been mistaken: I had been asking a racehorse to do the jobs of a truck horse, and more often than not it refused, resentful. Lessons learned the hard way.

Introducing Old-Timer Whitey Rudder

We completed three small cabins that summer and early fall of 1971—for Steve and Anna, Paul and Mona, and Bud and Linda. They went up fairly fast because we now knew what we were doing, mostly, and we had a chain saw. Also, we used the faster and easier "Hudson Bay," or "hog trough," corner construction. Each log was cut to size and butted against a vertical quarter-round log at the corner, through which we drove ten-inch spikes into the butt ends of the logs to hold them in place. For the superior notched-corner cabin the logs would have had to be about four feet longer than the cabin's dimension on each side to accommodate the notch and overhang. The notched corner is superior because the logs interlock for strength, but the Hudson Bay method will serve so long as the cabin isn't too big, which ours were not. Once again we used moss chinking and a pole-and-sod roof.

Humble dwellings, but home sweet home to "the kids," as I persisted in calling our hippie friends. Their own place, built with their own hands out of materials nature provided for free—not even any rent or mortgage attached—and located on their own lake, with a backyard that if you traveled east would reach as unbroken wilderness all the way to Hudson Bay itself. What could Morrisville offer them to compete with all that?

"The kids" were frequently at our place—for holidays like Thanksgiving and Christmas, even for a Halloween costume party, plus whenever someone's birthday arrived or whenever anyone arrived with a jug of wine—any excuse for a party. Gatherings were always potluck, invariably tasty dishes, and often enough the luck part was complemented by someone's contribution of pot.

We were a world unto ourselves, a merry little kingdom. I should have mentioned that by virtue of frequent reference to its location, "Back Lake" became the name of our virginal bit of water, although as hippies the kids had toyed with other names like "Monkberry Moon Delight Lake," which lost out to common usage.

Inasmuch as cash was always in short supply, birthday and Christmas gifts were homemade—something knitted or crocheted or carved out of wood. On the important occasions like Thanksgiving, Christmas, and birthdays a gift enjoyed by everyone was that the girls, including Carol and even little Beth, wore their best, most colorful dresses, in those days in hippiedom usually long ones, adorned themselves with the necklaces and bracelets they made by the light of kerosene lamps out of seeds, dried berries, and maybe a few glass beads, and did their hair up in lovely fashion. The guys too sported colorful headbands and shirts and multiple necklaces. By the soft light of the lamps and candles it was all quite splendid, like a three-dimensional Renoir. Given a little pot—even the mild ragweed of those days—these parties had magic. True enjoyment, not acting up. Very good times, very simply human. We didn't have to connive or lie or rip anyone off or kill lots of people to conjure up those good times. They were on the house.

The guys formed a singing group, "The Bannock Brothers," with Steve and Phil on guitars and every man jack of them, shy or not, standing in front of the stove and singing the songs they had made up about their lives in the woods. They were such a hit the girls quickly came up with their own group, "The Snowflakes," which included diminutive Beth all dressed up as lead singer, holding a slotted spoon before her mouth as microphone. They were also a great hit. So pretty and feminine in their long dresses, jewelry, and done-up hair, their voices so charmingly feminine, their songs so clever and humorous. Frontier women performing their daily tasks wore what men wore, as a practicality. So in accordance with the principle that contrasts are necessary for the drama of life, these dress-up parties were real treats, each one a taste of something fine.

On these occasions, no matter how dark and bitterly cold the night, I would scrape away some of the frost glazing on a window and look out and see their lights coming across the lake toward our cabin, and in my mind I could hear their chattering and laughter ringing on the air, the crunch of their boots on the flawless snow.

On one of those clear, cold nights everyone was gathered at our place getting it together to hike over to the A-frame on First Lake for a big party. I'm referring to Mike and Linda Sheehan's small A-frame; we had not yet run into the builder of "The Bird House," which is what we called the gigantic structure we had come across that first day searching for Back Lake.

The occasion for the party was the return of Whitey Rudder, one of Talkeetna's premier old-timers. I had met Whitey earlier, during the summer, and we had liked each other right off. This

winter he had been working his trapline farther north in the remote Lake Minchumina region and now was back. Mike and
Linda had offered him a berth in the A-frame's loft. It was well
known that if Whitey hung out in town he would be ossified most
of the time, which would be injurious to his well-being. Everyone
except the very straight Christian moralists liked and admired
Whitey. He was good-humored and a natural gentleman, though it
was clear somehow that he was not a man you would want to
cross.

Like most genuine old-time bushmen Whitey was freewheeling
about life, including his own. He played the hand dealt him, good,
bad, or indifferent, with neither dread of loss nor expectations of
gain. The game wasn't all that serious to him, generally speaking.
Life mostly struck him as humorous, because it was mostly crazy.
You had to keep a sharp eye on what was happening, of course,
but in a wry way. Jesus Christ! What next?

He wasn't burdened with attitude or ego. In fact, he was sort of
invisible to himself, like a cat that, coming upon a mirror, bristles
at the unknown creature therein. He had no image or ideal of himself to live up to. Stereotypes, like "the old-timer," never stuck to
him. I would see him getting off the train totally out of uniform,
wearing not a ten-gallon broad-brimmed hat rakishly cocked but
some dopey red vinyl cap set square on his head, and on his feet
not cowboy boots or even leather boots but rubber-soled nylon
things with bright yellow tops. No self-respecting frontiersman
would be caught dead in such incongruous gear. Whitey never noticed; he wasn't at all self-conscious. When he told a story about
something that happened to him or something he'd done or seen it
was as though he weren't talking about himself at all but only
about something interesting and funny that had occurred.

He never related "his story" as a set piece. It came out haphaz-
ardly bit by bit apropos a subject of our conversation or in matter-
of-fact answers to my questions. It seems he was raised as a cowboy
on a ranch out west—horses and cattle, boots and Stetsons. His

father worked his sons hard but was a fair man. Whitey grew up lean and wiry and a little wild, often smoking pot with the local Indian boys when he should have been mending fences. He got into rodeo, breaking broncos and bones, and was good at it, making the big time, all the way to Madison Square Garden.

Anyone whose head was screwed on right knew that Whitey just naturally spoke the truth, but his life had been so fabulous sometimes you had to wonder. I found out accidentally that everything he'd mentioned about his rodeo days was bona fide. *Playboy* ran an article on "The World's Best Cowboy," or something to that effect, and the next time I saw Whitey I asked him if he happened to have known the champion, since he would have been contemporary with Whitey's rodeo days. At first I mispronounced the star's name, and Whitey shook his head. Then I tried again and came closer to it. Whitey brightened. "Oh, you mean ————." Yes, he'd known him very well; they'd rode the same circuits for years. He went on, smiling at the memory of those days, to tell me some things about the champion that were in the article and some that weren't, like how the bronco and steer riders would toke up before settling into the chute on the animal's back. He laughed. "We'd be so stoned, everything was happening in slow motion and we knew what the horse was going to do before he did."

When the Depression hit, Whitey ran with a union along the lines of the "Wobblies," the IWW (Industrial Workers of the World), the most radical and effective union of the early twentieth century. They fought the capitalist establishment tooth and nail, and the moneyed bosses who owned the federal and state governments pressured the police and courts to come down heavy on them. But the union workers struck again and again for a living wage and tolerable working conditions. They were jailed, tortured, beat up, and on many occasions, murdered, their women and children included (read Howard Zinn's *A People's History of the United States*).

Like Woody Guthrie or Bob Dylan, Whitey didn't have to read

books to learn what the capitalist system was all about. He knew it firsthand. He knew America wasn't a democracy but a plutocracy owned and run by superrich greedheads skillfully mismanaging the people's minds with the lies propagated by thousands of hired media spin doctors. He had been in the trenches of social and economic injustice.

Nevertheless, Whitey was anything but a bitter man. He rarely spoke of all this unless prodded, and when he did it was usually in terms of some personal anecdote rather than of political ideology. He would chuckle when he told how he and his union buddies raided trains and tossed the goods or food out of the boxcars to be picked up and distributed among the needy families in the area. About the nation's wealthy rulers he would say, "No use *asking* them bastards for anything. They don't give. They take."

In the next glimpse of him he's telling a lieutenant during World War II that if he thinks that hill is so fucking important he ought to go check it out himself. He saw combat aplenty but once again was reluctant to talk about it except from his humorous—I almost said "cosmic"—perspective. "You think a gopher can dig a hole fast? You should've seen them marines on a beachhead making the dirt fly with their little shovels and the bullets whizzing past their ears!" But it came out somewhere along the line that he had lost some good buddies in the war and inwardly bore the scars of that.

After the war he returned with a Sicilian wife and settled in San Francisco. Somehow he had the wherewithal to open a couple of bars that became very successful enterprises, I have no doubt because Whitey was a very likable regular guy, and honest to boot. One of the bars was called something like "The Submarine Lounge." It catered exclusively to sailors from submarines and had the approval of the Navy brass because Whitey never took the boys but on the contrary took care of them. There was, for instance, a "Sailor in Need" jar full of money on the bar that any kid in trouble or just needing some dollars could dip into and pay back when he could. Whitey didn't keep records, and maybe that was part of the reason the boys always paid back in spades. Also, if a sailor put down change for a drink Whitey wouldn't take it. "You don't take his money because the kid is probably short. You just see to it that his glass is kept filled."

In the Renaissance it was understood that the essential prerequisite to the name of gentleman, the sine qua non, was generosity, largesse of heart and spirit. Whitey, this alcoholic outlaw, was to the manner born, a natural gentleman.

The outlaw part, as I pieced the story together, came about like a Hollywood movie. Because of the bars, Whitey was worth (as they say in the United States) a million bucks or more. But he got into heavy gambling. With evil companions. It seems he took some of the local mafia for a large sum of money, and they wanted it back. They appeared at his house one night in belligerent mode, and a shoot-out transpired. The cops arrived, unbeknown to Whitey, who was leveling down at anything that moved out there, and as luck would have it he wound up shooting a cop.

His lawyer got him out on bail and advised him to disappear. What was left of his million bucks after the bail money he put in his wife's name, keeping a few thousand for himself, and took the next boat heading north to Alaska. He wound up in Talkeetna not entirely by chance. In 1949 Talkeetna was little more than an isolated point of supply for trappers and miners working the bush. It was connected to the rest of the state and the Outside world only by the Alaska Railroad and the ubiquitous bush plane. Just what he needed. He disappeared into the bush. "Where the lawmen can't find you and the wild wolves don't care / What you did in that other world out there" (son Steve's lyrics).

Whitey was the real McCoy, an authentic Alaskan sourdough: a seasoned woodsman, big-time trapper, sometime bull cook, miner, big-game guide, and a man who had lived with the polar Eskimos for two years, about whom he spoke always with respect and admiration.

I had a glimpse of Whitey in that world one night when he and

I were on the town, in this instance Anchorage, tying one on in the orthodox fashion of the frontiersman everywhere. It was around three in the morning of the second night running. We were sitting at the bar of "Papa Joe's," a topless go-go joint still in full swing. Whitey knew the owner and wanted to stop by for one or two before calling it a night. So there we were. I had been ready to call it quits, but Whitey as usual was still going strong despite, or maybe because of, the quart or two he already had under his belt.

He sat on the stool to my right. Someone moved onto the stool to my left. I glanced that way and found myself gazing at a very curious thing, even for a Fourth Avenue bar at three in the morning. It was a definitively Eskimo face, of a woman probably in her thirties. She was bent forward and looking up at me with her eyes crossed and her tongue twisted and stuck out from a smiling mouth. I turned away quickly, a little startled, not knowing what to make of it. Then I looked again, a little longer, to make sure (after all, I too was under the influence). Her expression, or grimace, intensified, and she leaned farther toward me. I nudged Whitey and asked him to check this out, nodding to my left. Whitey leaned forward and I leaned back and swung around halfway toward the woman. She "smiled" even harder and uttered something in an Eskimo dialect. Then she changed her expression to what I'd call a beseeching look, almost sorrowful, tilting her head from side to side as she gazed at me. I swung back to Whitey with raised eyebrows and a grin. He had taken the whole thing in.

"Bob," he said, "she's just down from an arctic village, probably around Kotzebue. She's the real thing. Mustn't have been in Anchorage more than a couple of days. She can't locate any of her people. And she's lonely and horny." He looked at her again and smiled. "She's telling you she likes you. That's what that look means. Trying to make friends."

When I swung around toward her with fresh interest because she was a polar Eskimo she said something more to me in her dialect, leaning to look right into my eyes and at the same time placing her hand right between my legs, smiling broadly. "Whoa! Wait a minute," said I, and swung back toward Whitey. He continued quite serious about it and told me she would be a wonderful lover and a good woman, stick with me through hellfire and brimstone, and she was feeling very lonely and lost and had liked my looks and picked me out.

In his compassion for this lost lamb, and being loaded, Whitey had forgotten for the moment that I was already married to a good woman. When I shook my head and said I wasn't into it and wanted to go crash, Whitey said something to her in an Eskimo dialect, but she either didn't understand or had made up her mind, because she muttered something in a low voice, put her arm around my neck, and kissed me. On the mouth.

"Go on, Bob, take her," Whitey urged. "You won't regret it. They're wonderful women."

Well, I thought, maybe if I were single and not so burned out, for I did like her. She was so childlike and genuine. I'd probably never have another chance to know, in every sense of the word, another woman like her, a polar Eskimo. Their days of authenticity were numbered in the white man's world. Ah well. I bought her a drink and slipped away feeling very sorry about her plight and wishing I could have helped her. Whitey stayed behind. He would help her. She couldn't have fallen into better hands.

Whitey was an hombre second to none. He was the man movie actors like Gary Cooper tried to portray (in their better movies). It's easy to picture him because he was a dead ringer for the Walter Huston of *Treasure of the Sierra Madre,* with a touch of Cooper around the eyes. He was, he would declare on occasion, "a Hebe from the tribe of Joshua."

We didn't need snowshoes the night of the party because there had been quite a bit of traffic back and forth between the tracks and Back Lake, with the spur to the A-frame also well traveled, and the cold weather had set the float up like a sidewalk.

Carol decided to stay home with Jon, Sal, and Beth. It was in the air that this party might run a bit to the wild side. The presence of Dirty Dave Gonzales, Whitey's friend and a Hell's Angel, was enough to dissuade her from going, plus she was aware that we were bearing with us two gallons of wine, one of them "electric" (laced with LSD), for the adventurous, the other unadulterated, for general consumption along with the pot, the gentler psychedelic.

We strung out in single file—me, Steve and Anna, Paul and Mona, Bud and Linda, Steve Cross, and Phil and Romona. It was a clear night, brilliant stars and a full moon so bright it threw shadows of the trees out onto the lake. We didn't need flashlights. Even our breaths were like lit-up plumes. About every hundred yards we stopped and passed the jug of wine along the line, each of us taking a swig. We had all toked up before leaving my cabin. The walk was part of the party, a lot of fun, a mystical promenade across the moonlit lake and through the wondrous woods of luminous snow laced with the shadows of the trees. We talked and shouted back and forth and laughed at whatever. We were alive and on a great adventure. We were where it was at.

The A-frame had acquired an old sofa, several folding chairs, and right in the middle a counter of rough wood. The counter of course was really the bar. "Counter," as in kitchen counter, didn't fit—too everyday. So we placed our jugs on the bar, each clearly labeled as to its contents. Several other bottles, donated by Whitey, glittered on the bar in the lamplight. Whitey always came, as he put it, "highly recommended." He had some money from the fur, and what you did with money was spend it.

Hippies on pot will drink too given the opportunity. The general understanding of this, that they nevertheless never got nasty or violent, was true in my experience. Their objective was to feel good, get high, loose enough to let it all hang out, and stoned enough to be here now. As they smoked and drank they just got heavy-lidded, looked a little dopey, and laughed more, talking about whatever and losing track of whatever it had been that they had just said. Gone with the wind. And there was always a laugh in that.

Everything is known in the mode of the knower. We knew that where your head's at is more important to the quality of the moment than what is or isn't going on. Not only beauty but magic too is in the eye—or mind—of the beholder.

I should mention here that Dirty Dave was indeed an Anchorage biker whose club was affiliated with or was a chapter of the Hell's Angels. "Dirt," as he was affectionately known to his comrades in arms, was a husky, formidable-looking (scary) man: long black unkempt hair and beard, swarthy complexion, dark eyes. Black as the ace I am, black as the ace. Call it an oxymoron or paradox, but the fact was that he had a sunny hippie streak in him, something good-natured and generous.

Over the years of our acquaintance we formed a strange friendship, liking each other, the liking implying respect. There was a time to come when I and my family were up against it, and Dave was there for us as a friend. His life as a biker was of no concern to me, what he had done or not done as an outlaw rider. In a sense we were all outlaws, outside the law, if the law was the Man, the Pharaoh, the Establishment. I took Dave at face value, how he was with me, my family, and friends. He had linked up with Whitey, who seemed not to have any misgivings about him. Whitey had been around most of the blocks and could tell what was in a man. So if Dirty Dave Gonzales was okay in Whitey's book, you could say he came to us highly recommended. At the party he was simply one of us, white teeth glinting in his black beard as he laughed along with the rest. Even our psychedelic eyes saw him as all right.

A lot of the talking and laughing was centered on Whitey. He had his own way of saying things, peculiar, unique little expressions, something like Bob Dylan. You couldn't quite put your finger on it. He could tell tall tales with the best of them, and the odd thing was, the height of those tales was completely accurate. They were fabulous, but they were all true. He was unusually voluble that night (for reasons that became evident later). It was the first time he told us freely of certain parts of his life.

The expressions passing over his face ranged from merry to wry to concentrated, as though he were seeing his life as a play in which he was not only author, actor, and producer but audience as well: both in and out of the game and watching and wondering at it (Whitman). While he didn't take himself or his life seriously, it was, nevertheless, endlessly entertaining to him—especially when he was potted, which was most of the time. He *could* come down now and then with the cold sober blues infecting the general population. But he knew the cure. He drank.

I came upon him one day the summer before passed out on the gravel alongside the tracks at Chase. His nose was running down his cheek and the bugs were feasting on him. I was concerned he might be hurt or had had a heart attack or something. It was drizzling, and he was damp but oblivious. His white hair stuck up like a Mohawk warlock. The white stubble on his face was about three days long. Even passed out, he was muttering.

When he got drunk, he got high, not just drunk. Words flowed from him without let or hindrance and without regard for that fussy distinction between sense and nonsense. It was pure spontaneity, a stream of consciousness somewhat similar to many rock and roll lyrics and modern poetry in general. The sense it made was of an order other than the rational. It was the most colorful, unpremeditated, unpredictable, witty, absurd, and ultimately mind-blowing talk I've ever heard. And just when you thought he was lost in his own haphazard spiel he would grin, his eyes would twinkle, and he would come full cycle to a conclusion you couldn't have anticipated but that somehow brought it all together, as though he never had been lost in psychobabble.

I sat on my heels beside him, wiped his face with my handkerchief, and patted bug dope on his face and hands. This roused him. He opened a puffy eye and lifted a big hand in greeting. "Well, howdy, Sheriff," he said. "Where'd everybody go? How's about a little taste of Lady Luck."

"Don't have any, Whitey. The party's over and it's raining. Might as well head on back to the ranch."

I made a move to help him to his feet. He pulled away and told me to just sit down for a minute and take it easy. So I sat on the damp gravel and grinned.

Then he said, "I got drunk today, Jungle Bob. I been drunk before. And I seriously believe I might get drunk again. But let me tell you, Sheriff, these years here in Alaska have been the happiest years of my life. I've never been happier. I always wanted to live in the north woods and hunt and fish and trap, and that's just what I did. I did everything I ever wanted to do and enjoyed every minute of it. So let's you and me head for the Fairview and have a little drink to celebrate our luck."

The look in his eyes—like the young Gary Cooper, with the dark lashes curling up—was at once gay and earnest and something more. He was saying more than he spoke and he knew it but wasn't sure I knew it. But I did. He was telling me how to die without any unlived lines in my body. I grinned, patted his arm, and left him to his own devices. He didn't need any help. He knew what he was doing.

It was clear to him that those fits of sobriety and common sense he suffered through occasionally were cruel and unusual punishments, and since he wasn't worried about health, longevity, or conventional wisdom of the moral kind he did what he could to avoid them. As a poet once observed, "Malt can do more than Milton can to justify God's ways to man." Whitey would have been of one accord with Noah when the patriarch reputedly remarked, "I don't care where the water goes, so long as it doesn't get into the wine."

An English poet, A. E. Housman, wrote the following lines about a hundred years ago. Whitey never read the poem, but he would have understood it.

Could man be drunk for ever
With liquor, love, or fights,
Lief should I rise at morning
And lief lie down at nights.

But men at whiles are sober
And think by fits and starts.
And if they think, they fasten
Their hands upon their hearts.

Before the party wound down some hours later we noticed that Whitey had disappeared. Lying low up in the loft under the effects of pot and booze, so we thought. But in fact, as we learned some days later, Whitey wasn't asleep up there enjoying pot dreams. He was tripping out. Far out. He was involved in scenes more realistic than dreams, as present as virtual reality.

He's standing in the open door of this cabin watching the bears march by, mostly grizzly bears, with a sprinkling of blacks and polar bears. They're trudging along out there, rank upon rank.

"Well, I'll be damned," thinks Whitey, "I never did see nothing like that before." He turns to the guy at the table behind him, a man he doesn't know. "Say, pardner, where's all them bears going?" The guy comes over and looks out the door. "Oh, they're migrating. Yup. They're on their migration."

"Migrating! I never heard of nothing like that before," Whitey's thinking. Something weird is going on. "Yeah," the guy says, "they're polar bears heading back north." "Polar bears?" Whitey turns to the guy. "They're mostly all grizzlies and blacks." "Oh, that's all right," the guy says. "They'll all be polar bears when they get there."

Whitey looks back out. And there they are, marching along. Some are on all fours, some on hind legs. But now he notices that a couple of them are looking his way. They have blood on them and look like they're into bad attitudes. And sure enough, here they come down on all fours and right at him. As soon as he slams the door shut he's on the beach at Iwo Jima on his knees shoveling sand like a gopher, only faster, with bullets and shells whizzing and exploding all around him.

This much he told us when we finally caught up with him some three days later. But there had been other things from the war that had come back to him that night—and for a couple of nights afterward—things he never described for us, memories long suppressed, too heavy to keep on carrying around, things he didn't want to recall. Like the buddies he saw shot down or blown up.

What had happened was that Whitey, ever freewheeling, had unwittingly drained the dregs of the electric gallon of wine. He probably imbibed ten or twenty times the normal dose of acid. And he didn't know he had done that! Imagine being hijacked onto the heaviest trip possible and having no idea how that had happened! Your average *Homo sapiens* would have freaked out totally, believing he had lapsed into an advanced state of insanity and was destined to spend the rest of his days in a rubber room.

Here was Whitey, under LSD's influence for three days and nights, having those heavy visions and in between walking around in a world he had never before seen the likes of, with no idea what was going on, the why and wherefore of it, and yet he never freaked out, but kept returning to his central self and his quizzical view of a world he had always suspected was crazy anyway. "Well, we're just gonna have to see what comes of this."

When we left the A-frame for the return hike to Back Lake we all thought Whitey was up in the loft sleeping peacefully. So our minds were at ease and open to the winter night. Walking was a little like floating, we were so charged with psychedelic energy. It was as though we were inside another three-dimensional, living painting, maybe Van Gogh's "Starry Night"—in winter dress.

At one point I paused and looked up, and there were the galaxies of Van Gogh stars and the beautiful, sinuous trees touching the heavens, their tops festooned with stars. I gave way and flopped back into the soft snow, transfixed by the trees leaning over me, looking down on me, the stars oversized and brilliant among their branches, winking messages into my mind. I was caught up in a kind of ecstasy, to know that beyond the bullshit inside me and outside me I was *that*. I lay there gazing up, gone out of myself. The others passed by saying nothing, guessing where I was at. Their voices faded very slowly, over a long period of time. Once again I found myself reluctant to move and break the spell. I felt the cold of the snow as friendly and pleasant. The thought of the metaphysical horrors of alienation flitted through the empty space of my mind like some night bird and disappeared into the starlight.

I got word of Whitey's plight on the third day of his psychedelic journey and went right into Talkeetna, more than a little concerned. Christ! Who knew how many mics he might have absorbed? I found him sitting restlessly on the bench in front of the B&K Trading Post, looking as normal as a man could in his condition.

"Jesus Christ, Jungle Bob, am I glad to see you! I don't know what the fuck's going on. I been killing a quart a day and I still can't sleep. I stretch out and here they come, the curtain goes right up. I got no say in the matter. The curtain goes up, and here they come, the goddamnedest dreams, things I haven't thought about for years—and don't care to neither."

I took him back up to the lake, explained what had happened, and put him on the best grass I had, to calm him down. After an hour or so of marathon inhalations it started working. The psychedelic daemons and demons began fading and soon he started getting sleepy. I put him in a bunk and threw a blanket over him. He slept for a night and half a day and when he woke up he was all right.

"Jesus Christ," he said. "If that wasn't something!"

Men to match my mountains.

Whether the townspeople ever learned about the party with the electric wine and Whitey's accidental trip I don't know. They were used to seeing him discombobulated on extended benders and hangovers, so his time in town trying to recover wouldn't have alerted them to anything unusual. He couldn't have told them much because he didn't know much himself, and as for us, we weren't out to embellish their view of us as probably dope fiends by talking about what to us were just funny or interesting stories but to them would be incriminating evidence.

They had to know we smoked pot, but outside the pale of official warnings and jailings in the name of "killer weed" and the horrors it was alleged to lead on to, in actual everyday life most folks saw that all pot seemed to lead to was a lot of silly laughter, philosophical speculations, unusually strong libidinous inclinations, and a degree of overeating. They didn't feel any urgency to mount a campaign to rid the town of the marijuana menace, because they couldn't find any menace. Some of them undoubtedly knew that booze was the real troublemaker, the real killer. They were hip enough to see that the sweet scent of marijuana wasn't the odor of a smoking gun.

In any event, the two worlds bumped against each other a little but never really collided. In back of everything, underlying all the minor frictions, there was something we had in common, something we shared: living in that country, living on the frontier. The value of that. In the teeming cities and sprawling suburbs you can get lost, your identity lost in the crowd. Nobody but a few personal friends cares to know you, and they're a movable feast. You get lumped into one or another generality, mainly on the basis of your appearance: notoriously, the color of your skin, your job and income, your accent, the clothes you wear, and the like. In that world, hippies were thus easily categorized and lumped together under the aegis of mainstream generalities, mainstream paranoia.

But Talkeetna and its environs constituted a very small community. You could not become invisible, lost in a generalization; you would get to be known, especially since, as the old saying goes, "the woods brings out what's in a man or woman." Knowledge defeats prejudice, except for those so tightly locked into a creed, an ideology, they can't see what they see, only what they think they see. They think they're seeing the real world through the window of their consciousness, but the window has already been painted on, and what they're seeing is a crude caricature of the real world.

A generous air of freedom, or wildness, blows through a frontier community, a kind of laissez-faire of which the capitalist is ignorant. The capitalist system of mainstream America requires a passive, stable, obedient population to form its workforce, and the elites of that system have a myriad of ways, both subtle and gross, to ensure that such is the enduring status quo sustaining their privileged lives. The bush speaks a different language. The wind that bloweth where it listeth whispers freedom and independence into our inner ear. Frontier people are much more given to making independent judgments about you based on their direct intuition and observation of your actual behavior rather than on a priori generalities, stock responses, or your background.

Despite all the bad press about hippies (the last thing the Establishment elites controlling the media wanted was a *counter-cultural* movement, since it was through culture that they controlled the people), most Talkeetna folks took us at our face value and concluded we were all right. We were accepted as part of the community—and Talkeetna, with its small population, including the surrounding bush people, *was* a community. Because the people were independent-minded there were plenty of disagreements, discussions, and arguments about this or that having to do with the community and its territory, but a consensus almost always emerged.

We liked the town and its way of life and were willing to go to bat to preserve it against the forces of development that would turn it into Hoboken. Moreover, when disaster struck someone in the community, like when Anne and Big Tom Mercer's cabin burned down, the community responded. Benefits raised money, clothes, and food, and a revolving workforce of friends and neighbors quickly rebuilt their cabin. As I've mentioned before, communal cooperation and sharing were anciently a large part of what distinguished us as human and made our species an evolutionary success. It was generous cooperation, not cutthroat competition.

In this connection, regarding the great value of community to bush people, I should mention a study I conducted in the Open to Entry area around Chase during the winter of 1972–73. Under a grant from the National Endowment for the Humanities to the Alaska Humanities Forum administered by the newly formed Talkeetna Historical Society, I was commissioned as Project Director to survey the backwoods settlers in accordance with the state's adopted theme, "Land: Bridge to Community."

I traveled by snowmobile (provided me by the grant money: a boon, since the old Elan had died), snowshoe, and foot to all the outlying cabins in the area, interviewing the people in depth along the lines of such topics as "What were your motives in coming to Alaska and life on the land?" and "What has been the effect of the land upon human relations, especially as regards the sense of community?" I can tell you right now that virtually everyone interviewed held the same views about the land and the importance of community as I've expressed in these pages. The back-to-the-land movement in those days was strong and homogenous. That the "authorities" were able to squelch that, a drive with hundreds of thousands of years behind it, and concomitantly managed to get the lid back on the psychedelic movement, the two movements being commensurate, testifies to the strength and depth of the Establishment. Like an ideological Leaning Tower of Pisa it looked like a good shove would send it toppling but in fact it was anchored by ten thousand years in the ground of history.

9

Expeditions

Back Lake in winter with fog, indicating a sudden drop in temperature. Smoke coming from Bob's cabin.

Toward the end of winter and by early spring bush people often find themselves on lean rations, especially if the moose meat is gone. So that was one good reason to mount an expedition into rabbit country. "Rabbits"—the large snowshoe hares—are, as old-timers would put it, damn fine chewing. But the fact of their culinary qualifications was more the excuse than the reason for that expedition in March of '72, because in truth rabbits are also damn fine hunting.

With moose the hunt is over when the first one is downed. But with rabbits the first one is only the beginning. The hunt can go on for days, as did ours in the rabbit country up around Healy on the Parks Highway. Mention the prospect of camping and hunting snowshoes to six guys living in the bush and it's a sure thing they will go for it. Having a good reason to go—the lean time of late winter, wanting meat—makes it all the better: When love and need are one, and the work is play for mortal stakes (from Robert Frost).

March in the Susitna Valley can look both ways. It can face back toward winter or forward toward spring. Which is something along the lines of "in like a lamb, out like a lion," or vice versa. The March of 1972 faced toward spring and remained lamblike through midmonth. That, together with the idea of bringing home the bacon, did it. The word in the bush was that the snowshoes were peaking up around Healy. Most people know that snowshoe hares run in roughly seven-year cycles of abundance to scarcity and back again. In '72 they were back again. Success practically guaranteed. We would bring home the bacon for sure. —Actually, "bringing home the bacon" is an inappropriate expression as regards harvesting hares because their meat is so lean—"fat free"— were they your only food you could eat a dozen a day and starve to death in short order.

Folk sayings that last do so because they express, usually cryptically, some truth of experience, like "There's many a slip between the cup and lip," or even more to the mark, "Don't count your chickens [rabbits] before they're hatched [bagged]."

It wasn't that March suddenly turned from lamb to lion. Around the lake it was definitely facing toward spring. The Coldman was gone from these parts. "From these parts . . ." Aye, that was the rub. The Healy rabbit country was many miles farther north, and more significantly, or ominously, it was at a much higher elevation. When the Coldman retreats from Back Lake it's not the case that he immediately tips over and falls into a coma. His retreat is slow and variable, depending on such things as latitude and elevation and/or freak turns of weather. In March of '72, unbeknown to us, the Coldman was hanging out around Healy, with all the country north of Healy still to go. He was far from gone. In that high country he had regained his strength. And then some.

We packed our gear in keeping with the weather at Back Lake. More exactly, all the young bucks packed their gear—clothing, sleeping bags, how many blankets, and so forth—according to that yardstick. But not me, the lad who had made second-class scout and had never forgotten though sometimes failed to heed the watchword: "Be prepared!" So while most of the boys packed hurriedly and lightly, as if for camping at Back Lake, I who had been burned before by the trickery of the Big Eskimo in the Sky stuffed my best down bag into my pack, and my warmest long johns, wool socks and sweaters, windbreaker jacket, and pulled on my faithful "bunny boots"—those white, waterproof, triple-insulated bulbous inventions in which my feet had never gotten cold at any temperature. So when at Healy the Coldman landed on us like a lynx on a rabbit I was the only one who escaped unscathed.

I give myself credit also for having talked the other guys into agreeing we had room for my little chain saw—to save us time with the firewood, I argued, time better spent out hunting rabbits (and also, in my mind, to make it possible to build and feed a fire big enough to hold the Coldman at bay, just in case).

So the six of us—I, son Steve, Steve Cross, Paul Simon, Phil Pugh, and Buddy Kobell—piled our gear in the rear of the old Plymouth wagon, with a couple of packs tied down on the roof. The day was sunny and mild. We were in high spirits: camping out and going rabbit hunting! The occasion called for a little something extra. We all chipped in and came up with enough money for a couple of six-packs to add to our pleasure.

The Parks Highway north was a thin ribbon of asphalt climbing the long, easy slope toward the mountains. It was bare and windswept with gusts of snow and almost no traffic. The State advised anyone traveling that road to carry emergency equipment. The only gas stations or roadhouse accommodations were in Trapper Creek and Cantwell. In between you were on your own, and there were many solitary miles in between. *Machts nichts* as far as we were concerned. This was a joy ride. We felt invulnerable. Our wheels were old and untrustworthy, but the thought never crossed our minds that anything could come up that we couldn't handle. Six grown men. Six *bushmen*. So we sipped on our beer and joked and laughed our way north into rabbit country.

The Plymouth quit on us once. We piled out, investigated matters under the hood, soon had the problem diagnosed and fixed, then hurried back into the wagon, shivering. It seemed to have gotten colder, or maybe it was mainly the chill factor because of the wind blowing. You've seen those movies where the pioneers are pressing westward into Indian country and the camera focuses on some distant hills from which smoke signals are rising. The cold we felt while huddled outside over the engine was our first smoke signal, the first indication that we could be headed into an ambush.

It was dark when we reached the small village of Healy, itself dark because of the hour. It had been a long drive. We cruised beyond the village a ways and pretty much arbitrarily stopped at a spot along the road where, bordered by likely-looking brushy fields, there was a patch of scrub spruce, a lot of the stunted trees standing dead: good firewood. We would set up camp in this patch of woods and in the morning check around to see if we were where the rabbits liked to be. But even as we moved into the woods with flashlights we saw that we had hit pay dirt right off. The snow was pockmarked with rabbit tracks—and we wouldn't need snowshoes. Apparently, the winds swept the snow into the valleys.

The other thing we noticed as we walked into those dark woods under the clear and starry sky was that it was a lot colder than it had been at Back Lake. As noted, we had not only been heading farther north; we had been climbing all the way. And whereas the skies had been partly cloudy around Chase, here there were no such blankets muffling the cold. A front of clear, cold weather had settled over the Healy area.

We were busy the first hour or so setting up camp. We didn't have any double-walled winter tents with their small sheet-metal stoves. Such tents can be kept comfortable at almost any temperature. All we'd brought were tarps for lean-tos to keep off the frost and any possible snow. Paul happened to have a compass with a thermometer in one end. A flashlight beam showed thirty-five below. It would probably drop another ten or fifteen degrees by morning.

"Okay, boys," I said, feeling my mustache hairs already stiff with frost and pulling, "we better circle the wagons." We erected the three lean-tos in a semicircle facing the fire, which we kept feeding until it was about eight feet long, four feet deep, and three feet high. The lean-tos, set fairly close, would act like reflector ovens, "ovens" being more rhetoric than actuality.

When with the first rays of dawn I stuck my head out of the bag to look around I saw three figures huddled up close to the fire wrapped in their sleeping bags. I couldn't tell who was out there by the fire. But three guys hadn't been able to make it through the night in their reflector ovens and had resorted to desperate measures. I pulled my head back in like a turtle.

It's an ill wind, as they say in Tierra del Fuego, that blows no good. The good that came of the three guys shivering by the fire was that they had fed the blaze all night, thereby permitting the other half of our hunting party to stay put in their bags—not toasty warm, to be sure, but not freezing cold either. When I reached out to pull my bag higher, my hand almost froze to the fabric.

The Coldman stood astride our camp of intrepid meat hunters grinning and drooling icicles. "Thought you guys had gotten rid of me, eh? Well, think again, *chechakos*." His laugh shook through the patch of frosty woods like a snow flurry.

I had slept with most of my clothes on, which retained some heat when I unzipped the bag. But I had to move fast. The fierce cold brooked no delay in its attack, and my heat shields quickly failed. All resident BTUs beat a hasty retreat into the body's central bunkers. I slipped into my bunny boots and outer jacket, then over to the fire, pulling my mitts on over the inner wool gloves. The resident BTUs, thus reinforced, returned to their frontier stations with new vigor. Paul, Buddy, and Phil stood up, backs to the fire.

"Well, Jesus Christ, Jungle Bob," said Kobell, "we were afraid you might have perished. I don't think you even turned over once all through the goddamned night."

They were a little bleary-eyed but smiling. A minor run-in with the Coldman wasn't going to stop this hunt. Who's afraid of fifty below? The sky was clear. The sun would rise, and it was late March. Things would warm up some. Our ready hearts were beating the BTUs out of the bushes. We'd be on the move, generating heat, too intent on our quarry to pay much attention to the Coldman anyway.

Everyone was up. After a quick trip into the bushes to answer nature's call, braving our butts to the Coldman's pinch, we managed to boil a pot of water without spilling it or burning our hands. We dumped in some coffee and let it brew for a minute or two, then tossed in a handful of snow to settle the grounds. It hit the spot, rousing the last of the timid BTUs out of their bunker.

About that necessary and quick trip into the bushes, an interesting footnote, looking ahead to the third morning, was that son Steve had taken note of the fact that while everyone else had made the trip each morning, Simon had remained steadfast in his sleeping bag. By the third morning Steve's curiosity got the better of him.

"Hey, Simon," he started, "how come you don't have to go into the bushes in the morning?"

"Well," Paul replied, "I convert it to gas."

Necessity is the mother of invention. Alaskan ingenuity triumphs again.

The bread and peanut-butter breakfast was an interesting study. Both were frozen hard of course. We placed the end of the loaf and the peanut-butter jar close to some coals we raked out. The bread thawed, then half burned, and the one side of the jar thawed. We had a couple of loaves going. The slices were cut thick, the peanut butter spread on thick. We repeated the thaw-and-spread procedure, all the while sipping on the strong coffee, until everyone had his fill.

Then without further ado, as is said elsewhere on the planet, we shouldered our emptied packs and grabbed our rifles. Son Steve and I would hunt together, Buddy and Phil and Steve Cross and Paul making up two other teams. We'd cover more ground that way, walking parallel. We headed off into the brushy hillside, spreading out as we went. There wasn't a house or pasture or fence anywhere to be seen, nor any person or footprint. The whole world and all its rabbits were ours.

Tracks crisscrossed everywhere. Within five or ten minutes shots rang out. Snowshoes depend mainly on their camouflage. Surely they heard us coming, but nine times out of ten they would just sit there motionless near a blowdown or willow patch, thinking they were invisible I guess, which to any thick sight they would be. But the practiced eye of the experienced hunter could somehow make out their form. Even if they spooked, typically they would hop off only ten or twenty yards and then sit again. You could still bag them if you followed slowly. Knowing this, we carried .22 rifles instead of shotguns, which would have been necessary had they behaved like cottontails. A .22 bullet was much less expensive than a shotgun shell, and a shot to the head spoiled no meat and was merciful to the game. (All this Steve and I had learned at Lake Nerka.)

By the close of the afternoon when we quit for the day, we had a total of a dozen rabbits. We didn't tally who got what because at the end of the hunt the meat would be shared according to need—like I, with a wife and three kids, would be given proportionately more than Steve Cross, who had only his own mouth to feed. That also was the way of our primitive forefathers.

Our lunch break was typical of bush hunters. We gathered at a sunny spot near a cluster of spruce, whose dead lower branches were excellent for a quick, hot fire to melt snow for tea water (we always brought along a pot, tea bags, and sugar on a hunt like this). The tea was made strong, hot, and sweet. It was delicious washing down the pemmican power food. Toward the end of

March the Alaskan sun regains enough strength to cause the Coldman, even at these higher altitudes, to seek refuge in shady groves or lonesome hollows where the sun doesn't shine, waiting to emerge after sundown and reclaim his domain. By then, we were back at camp building up the fire, cutting more wood, and heating the premade stew for supper.

Anthropologists tell us that hunter-gatherer peoples needed to "work" only a few hours a day to fulfill their needs. The rest of the time was their own. Much of that time was given to singing and dancing to the drum. With darkness the cold descended. We threw on more firewood, and the showers of sparks whirling into the descending cold like a counterattack represented our defiant and jubilant spirits. In your face, Coldman!

The day's hunt was not *work*. Our merry band spontaneously fell into the ancient pattern. First Phil took out his harmonica and started a lively tune we all knew. Then someone picked up the beat with a spoon on a piece of wood. He was quickly joined by the others. Then son Steve started singing out the words, and again everyone joined in. Buddy grabbed a pot and a spoon, adding that sound to the drumbeat. Primitive impulses usually constrained by the civilized ego were loosed. Buddy got up with his pot and spoon drum and launched into an Indian-style dance in front of the blazing fire. Resistance was futile. Soon we were all up with our spoon-and-stick drums doing a circle dance in the firelight, singing into the silent darkness at the top of our lungs.

It crossed my mind and broke over my face in a big smile that should a state trooper happen by just then and glimpse the firelight through the trees, stop his car, and hear the drumming and singing, he would immediately call in for backup, draw his pistol, and sneak up on us, sure that we were either escapees from a lunatic asylum or some kind of satanic cult. Ours was definitely not civil behavior.

The hunt went on for three days, the weather holding steady. We had more than enough rabbits. In fact, we were pretty sure the

Plymouth wagon wouldn't hold them all. But a solution was in the offing. The night before we were to return, the Healy high school was holding a dance, with a live rock and roll band performing, and the lead guitar was to be none other than thirteen-year-old Jonathan Durr.

We got there just as the van with the band pulled up. The door opened, and there was the lead guitar on his very first gig. All those years of listening to his big brother play and watching his hands, learning like osmosis, and now it had happened. He was here. He stood on the van's step wearing a huge twenty-gallon Stetson and looking like he had just been pole-axed. The occasion, his first gig as a rock superstar, had left him dazed with excitement. He would be playing for an audience of maybe a hundred! It had taken a thing this big to bump the hunt off his agenda.

The van had a basket-type rack on top big enough to hold our overload of rabbits, and the band was willing. We went in and sat over on the side of the dimly lit gym, six grubby hunters trying to be inconspicuous amid all the high school spit and polish. We sat in the warmth and listened to the band and watched the kids dance under the colored lights. Then we left and returned to that other reality in the scrub spruce, darkness, silence, and cold.

The next morning we broke camp and went back. It had been a great hunt.

In the summer of that year another kind of itch needed scratching. We had heard of the McWilliams gold mine situated near the headwaters of Clear Creek. It had shut down only a couple of years before, so its buildings and apparatus should still be intact. It had been probably the largest gold-mining operation in the Upper Susitna Valley. It stuck in our collective imagination as an entity just about as fabulous as, say, an Aztec ruin in the Yucatán jungles. It needed to be found and explored by some hardy band of adventurers. We, the Back Lake rabbit harvesters, would volunteer.

But finding the McWilliams mine wasn't our only motivation. Water runs downhill. The headwaters of Clear Creek were several miles up in the hills north of us, at the base of mountainous terrain. We wanted to hike into the high country and see what it felt like. The Susitna Valley in the summer was densely wooded, with thick, tangled underbrush, almost a jungle. But the high country would be different, open and expansive, treeless tundra and rocks. We wanted to find out what it felt like up there.

It wouldn't be a mountain-climbing expedition, nothing like scaling one of the mountains of the Alaska Range. The landscape above the McWilliams mine could be described as foothills, with elevations of two to three thousand feet, well below the snow line but above the tree line and high enough to look and feel very different from the valley floor. I thought of the Scottish Highlands, and my sense of it somehow conjured up the old folk saying, "In the mountains, there you are free." Really, we wanted to experience the high country more than we wanted to explore the mine. There's some kind of moral in that.

It was summer, so we could travel light: nylon, netted pup tents, summer-weight sleeping bags and ground pads, a nylon tarp, an extra set of clothes, rain gear, cooking gear, fishing tackle, and of course the usual hunting knife, map and compass, waterproof matches, bug dope, and a coil of quarter-inch nylon rope. We each brought a stash of brown rice and a chunk of cheddar cheese. We would eat partly off the land—mostly, no doubt, fish from the creek supplemented with some wild plants and, since it was early August, berries. Besides the fish and rice and probably some spruce chickens and ducks, the mainstay of our diet would be smoke-dried salmon and pemmican, the old Indian standby. Pemmican is jerky pounded almost to a powder and mixed with fat, preferably bear fat, which doesn't get rancid. We had both the jerky and the bear fat, from a blackie that wouldn't scare off. We threw in some raisins for good measure and better taste. Pemmican is lightweight and highly nutritious—"power food." A patty the size of a small hamburger, which was how we made it up, eaten on a lunch break and washed down with sweet tea would keep a man going strong the rest of the day, up hill and down dale with a pack on his back. Of course, we were already in good shape from following the normal protocol of bush living.

We had heard that an old trail was still discernible on the far side of Clear Creek. Our "plan" was to find that trail and hike north parallel to the creek, fishing and camping as we went, until we spotted the McWilliams mine. We figured on maybe a three-day trek up to the mine. But what we didn't figure on was 1. either "the trail" had been reclaimed by the bush or we simply couldn't find it or it had never existed; 2. following the creek involved torturous ups and downs and frequent wading across the creek where possible (the water neither too deep nor too swift) in order to avoid some of the ups and downs necessitated by the steep gullies across our path; and 3. we weren't yet familiar enough with the weather pattern in the valley to know that typically August ushered in something like a rainy season.

This August was typical. It started raining the night of our first day out. We made camp, built a fire, and ate. The sound of the creek filled the air, but in the middle of the night I woke up and what I was hearing was more than the creek. It was a sound of water all right, but very close and a little different from the creek sound: raindrops pelting the tarp over my head.

The campfire had been doused out, not even a coal showing. A hard rain's a-gonna fall. For days on end. But at the moment I was warm and dry in my bag, my body gratefully resting, full of pleasant feelings after the miles of the first day. Take thought about the rain tomorrow. For tonight, it sounded good beating against the tarp and pattering on the trees and bushes in the darkness. Ah, to be dipped in sweet oblivion, to be absorbed into the night.

The thought of turning back never occurred to us. The rain let up some by morning, enough to get a fire going—if you knew how. We got into our lightweight rain gear and broke off a couple of armfuls of the dead lower branches of the spruce, still dry under the green canopy above them, and also some strips of birch bark, whose oils will burn even in the rain.

Cross and I strung up the extra tarp we'd brought for this purpose—to keep the rain off the fire and us as we squatted around the flames drinking the strong camp coffee and chewing on the salmon. We didn't see ourselves as a *Field and Stream* centerfold. Actuality was too pressing, commanding all our attention. Magazine images were irrelevant stereotypes from back in that other world of stereotypes. This world was always three-dimensional and original. Here and now, boys, here and now.

The rain gear turned out to be next to useless. By the first hour of pushing through the underbrush we were wet with sweat and feeling clammy. Some of us decided it would be better to pack the rain suit away and just let our clothes get wet. At least they "breathed." Being wet and cool from the rain was better than being wet and clammy from sweat. When we stopped for the night we'd change clothes and dry the wet outfit overnight by the fire. Crossing the creek, the water sometimes up to our waists, as the terrain dictated involved only the additional discomfort that the water was cold. We were already wet.

When our passage was down beside the creek we stopped at likely pools to fish. With every other cast it was "fish on!": healthy, firm-bodied rainbow trout and arctic grayling, some of them running to over a foot. We'd have them fresh for supper along with some rice. It was a healthy, tasty diet. At night we'd keep at least three small fires going in front of the tents for cooking and drying clothes. We rigged the protective tarp in such a way that it acted like a chimney carrying the smoke away. The going was strenuous because of the gullies—up and down, up and down—so it was very pleasant lying or sitting on our bags in the tents facing the fires, soaking up the welcome dry heat.

By the end of the second day of steady rain, everything was damp, if not wet. We hit upon a good spot of higher ground by a beaver pond and decided it would be best to camp there for a day or two to dry out well and hope the rain would let up. Everything was damp but our spirits. If you were of a philosophical bent of mind, as I've always been, you'd have to conclude that this sort of thing, a small band moving through wild country hunting and gathering, taking the bad with the good as nature decrees, was right for hominids, the good life we lived for maybe a million years before we went mad. Back in those days, the women and children went where the band went. I thought of Carol and my kids. They could do it, if they had been born to it. I felt they could do it now, if they had to. Hominids were built for it. Some indigenous peoples were doing it right now. The only splinter in the ass of that kind of progress now was Western cultural convention, which was debilitating to most of human nature.

Paul spotted a couple of ducks over on the other side of the pond. We had just finished the last of the squirrel stew, and those ducks were a call to arms. He and Buddy grabbed their rifles and sneaked around to the other side of the pond for a close shot. They let loose and got both mallards.

But the ducks, pushed by the wind, were floating out toward the center of the pond. Only one thing to do. Go in after them. Paul and Buddy doffed their clothes and with whoops jumped in. When they were out in the middle and had the mallards, a big buck beaver decided to confront the trespassers. He nosed out a ways toward them and slapped the water hard with his broad flat tail, then dove out of sight.

This opportunity could not be missed. What did Buddy and Paul know about beavers? Next to nothing. Son Steve and I were the "old-timers" on the safari and were heeded as being knowledgeable about the ways of the wild. When the beaver slapped the water Paul and Buddy looked around, all attention. I hurried to the edge of the pond and cupped my hands around my mouth.

"Hey, you guys! Bucky beaver's on his way. He thinks you're

trespassing. Better watch out he don't come up under you and snip your balls off!"

Perhaps you've seen one of the old Johnny Weissmuller Tarzan movies where he's moving through the water like a torpedo, maybe chasing a mean crocodile. He'd have lost the race to Paul and Buddy, who in this case believed they were being chased by the crocodile. Ain't gonna get my balls, you son of a bitch! Waves from their vigorous passage through the water lapped against the land, where the rest of us had collapsed with laughter.

The McWilliams establishment was still very much intact. It had been a big operation—bunkhouse, mess hall, shop, the whole nine yards. This hadn't been some grizzled old-timer with a plaid shirt, suspenders, and a long white beard patiently sifting sand. This had been modern technology at work, not romance. I could almost hear the machinery. We roamed around the premises.

What struck me most were the logs. All the buildings had been put together, very skillfully, with cottonwood logs, silky smooth and off-white, very handsome, and very unusual. In all my years in the Alaska bush I never saw anything like it. Cottonwood is a soft, perishable wood. Did they know they'd be in and out in short order? Bring in the machinery, get the gold, and scram. I saw they hadn't filled in the deep gouges they'd made in the terrain. Hit and run. Business as usual.

The rain had finally let up. And then we ran into another piece of good luck. We had planned on heading up into the high country at the McWilliams site, but we hadn't expected the bush equivalent of a red carpet for the ascent—a trail. But there was one, heading straight up to where we wanted to go. Why it existed we had no idea. Had some of the miners used it to get above the noise and business? Perhaps. In any event, we were glad to make its acquaintance.

After about an hour's climb, the underbrush started thinning out, the spruce got smaller and smaller, the tundra drier and drier, crisp little tangles with scattered red and black berries, and then we were above the tree line, and vistas of the enormous country opened up. Across the valley and the Susitna and Chulitna Rivers the Alaska Range reached into the sky and spread out to the north and to the south into the distance.

We took a lunch break, and something, my soul I suppose, was being nourished by the vast wilderness before my eyes as my body by the pemmican. We sat on rocks or sprawled on the tundra, not bothering to talk. What was there to say? A thousand voices speaking perfectly loud.

That evening we made camp on the tundra and were struck with astonishment when a huge flock of ptarmigan flew down on us, the air filled with the flutter of many wings. Some landed and waddled swiftly among the tents. They were in their splendid summer plumage, russet and white. Our astonishment left us befuddled, and we didn't bag a single bird before the whole flock flew away.

Our location above Curry on the Alaska Railroad was like a wide plateau with its own ups and downs. It was treeless but covered by tundra and rock outcroppings. Some hollows where moisture collected were dense with underbrush—willows I think. We flushed ptarmigan and managed to collect a couple for the pot. Some ducks too—we had gotten a few ducks along the way as well. Across from us we saw a really big bull moose moving along the side of a hill in his slow, dreamy gait.

We came upon a shallow pond ringed with rocks. In the high country you feel above the world, removed from all the bullshit. "In the mountains, there you are free." That was the feeling. And I thought one day I might come back up here to this pond and build a small house out of the rocks and live like any other animal in the wild.

This high-country expedition lasted about two weeks. The thought of retracing our steps back down Clear Creek with all those gullies was daunting. We were a little tired, truth be told. We went over to the edge of the plateau and looked down. The tracks and the Susitna River were just skinny lines way down there. The distance was probably about three thousand feet—but that was a great many feet less than the alternate route back. And once at the bottom, we'd be near Curry and if we timed it right we could flag down the evening train south; in those days the railroad ran north in the morning and south from Fairbanks in the evening once a day.

The first part of the descent looked pretty steep, but it was covered with alder we could use as handholds as needed—which would probably be a lot of the way. But we figured we'd reach the tracks in about an hour or two, three at most. It was very tempting, if a bit risky. So what else was new about bush life? The element of risk was intrinsic. And really, being young and healthy, we felt capable of tackling anything the bush had to offer, including the side of a cliff.

Naturally, it was rougher and tougher than it had looked. In some places it was hand-under-hand on the alders down a nearly vertical wall, feet swinging, looking for a supporting branch. The packs proved very detrimental to our progress. They kept getting hung up in the branches or bumping into a trunk and knocking us off a dubious balance.

Because of the tough, slow going it took us half the day to make it down, but that was a lot less than the week or so the other route would have needed—and there had been some risky stuff along that route anyway. At one point we had had to kind of swing across a cleft in a bluff high above the creek because our feet had run out of footing, a steep wall rising up and another steep one falling down. The swinging part was from the hand of one of us holding on to a root across the cleft to the outstretched hand of another of us on the other side. I know that was how I got across. What I don't know was how the first guy got across. I don't think he jumped, leaping to the trunk of a tree or alder on the other side. But maybe that was how he did it. I'm pretty sure he didn't fly.

It wasn't cliffs all the way down, but it was steep all the way except for the one plateau about midway. A beautiful, pure, isolated lake lay among the hills of the plateau, with clusters of spruce here and there, like a park. And I thought that here too would be a place a man could withdraw to; and a few years later our buddy Dan did build a cabin near that lake, accepting the long, steep climb up from the tracks as a fair price to pay for the perfect solitude and beauty of that spot.

It felt a little strange being down at the tracks at river level. We looked up to where we had been and it seemed a long ways removed, like a different world. Our packs off, we sat around and munched on the pemmican while we waited for the southbound. We felt pretty good for having made the trek, something none of us would ever forget. But son Steve allowed that he was looking forward to the night when he'd be sleeping spoon-fashion up against Anna's sumptuous ass.

"So you like that stuff?"

"Hey, are you kidding?"

Here came the train, pretty much on time. We flagged her down, threw our packs up into the baggage car, and climbed aboard, strangers from a strange land. Among the other passengers, we felt we had been to a place most people couldn't even imagine, except that maybe something like the high country appears in their dreams.

10

Risky Business: Chain Saws and Snowmobiles

View of the outhouse and cabin.

Having a snowmobile made our lives easier, just as having the chain saw had. I wasn't enamored of technology as a general phenomenon of modern life (you think of all the "weapons of mass destruction," degradation of the environment, pollution, etc., etc., made possible by mushrooming technology). But give the devil his due. The chain saw and snowmobile did make some elements of bush life a lot easier.

Yet there were side effects, some of them severe to potentially fatal. I've never been fully convinced that we should have brought these technologies into our lives. I think of the Taoist sage Lao-tzu, who refused the bright young man's technology of pulleys and gears designed to make it easier to draw water, saying something to the effect that it is well to resist the beginnings of corruption.

Logging is recognized as the second most dangerous occupation after commercial fishing. Through all the years of our bush life, one way or another we had to get building logs or firewood. While the chain saw made it easier and faster it also made it more dangerous. The saw itself, mishandled, could be lethal—a wrong move, a slip, and there goes a foot. Should that happen when a man is out working alone, it would likely be curtains. Then too if a tree gets hung up the chain saw makes it possible to bring it down in sections, but the necessary cuts from below and above are tricky and difficult, and the tension of the hung-up tree could be released with bone-crushing force catching you by surprise. With a hand saw and ax everything goes slower, and moreover you're not apt to tackle the real big trees.

With a snow machine, building logs can be skidded to a site rather than carried on pairs of shoulders, and a sled behind the machine makes bringing in firewood expeditious, as was the case at Iliamna. We'd head out usually about midmorning, chain saw and axes aboard, sled attached, and cruise slowly down the snowmobile trail, kneeling and looking for a good quarry, ideally a standing dead spruce close to the trail that we could fell, again ideally, parallel to the hard pack so that we wouldn't have to push through deep snow to get at it.

We'd limb it with the axes and saw and cut it into lengths of about eight feet to be carried back to the sled. I had made a good tough sled out of a birch log with a natural curve upward for the bow. I ripped the log down the center, flattened top and bottom, and inset sturdy cross pieces on top. The solid hitch to the snow machine was a carefully selected Y-shaped branch of birch of the right width to bolt to the sled's sides, with a hole for a bolt-and-nut rig to fit the trailer hitch on the snow machine. We'd stack the logs as high as possible, tie them down, and off we'd go. Three of us—Steve, Jon, and I—could bring back a lot of firewood in a few hours. It was good, invigorating, satisfying work. Our cuttings for firewood and building logs were so selective and scattered that pilots flying over said the woods around Back Lake looked untouched.

A snow machine also provides independence from the railroad and its uncertain schedules. A truism based on repeated experience was that the colder it got, the later the train would be. So often in the dead of winter we would have snowshoed to Chase in plenty of time to catch the southbound into Talkeetna only to have to wait beside the tracks an hour or two while the temperature dropped out of sight. Standing by a big fire helped dispel both the cold and the dark, and even under such trying conditions some part of us marveled at the giant, silent stars and, often enough, the ghost dance of the mysterious northern lights. Nevertheless, time hung heavy standing around, stamping your feet and peering north for the train's light, especially if you were alone.

So with a snowmobile I could get to Talkeetna pretty much when I wanted or needed to: "pretty much" instead of "whenever" because the variables involved were significant. The machine could and often did break down, for instance. Sometimes we could fix it on the spot, change a belt or spark plug along the trail. But subzero temperatures made even that a challenge: You can't handle tools efficiently with mitts on or with hands stiffened and hurting from frostbite. And snowmobiles, even the long-tracks, can get stuck bad. It's easily done. After a big overnight dump of snow, with it still coming down, you have to try to keep the trail open. You have to make the run from the lake to the cat trail and on down to the gravel pit at Mile 232 of the railroad, at which point you could count on enough traffic from the other bush dwellers to open the trail the rest of the way to town. But making that trail-busting run could involve more than simply sitting there and putting in the time.

You could get stuck good and proper. The original trail you're trying to follow has become only a winding indentation. If you make a turn either too sharp or too dull you could get sucked into the really deep stuff bordering the trail. And that's a backbreaking bummer. You have to stomp down the waist-high snow back to the trail and also all around the machine so that like the mother who lifts a car off her child you can lift and move the rear of the machine and then the bow into a position that would bring it back onto the trail—if you can get it to move at all.

Two people can do it, one pulling and lifting from the front, the other working the throttle and pushing from the side. Alone means getting in front and pulling your guts out to lift the bow onto the snow you have stomped down, then going to the side, working the throttle just right, and pushing with all your strength. Which might not work until maybe the third try. By then you're wet with sweat, and supposing you're on your way again, the snow is curling up over the windshield into your face because you have to kneel and use your body weight to help the skis make the turns.

A little trick, itself a little risky, when the machine is stuck hard and you're alone and can't get moving with muscle power only— the pulling, lifting, and shoving—is to insert a twig of precisely the correct thickness into the opening made in the thumb throttle when depressed to give the engine gas. The idea is to get the machine's power working for you as you pull and lift at the front. Yes, that's right, you anticipate me: If the twig is too thin it won't keep the throttle opened enough to turn the track, and if the twig is too thick, gunning the engine too much, when you're up front pulling with your body weight the track might find the traction to leap forward and pin you down. Then you've got to wiggle out from under fast and dexterously pluck the twig out as it goes past, thereby stopping the machine. And so on and so forth.

The best way to get unstuck, I finally realized, was to carry a snow shovel with you when you thought conditions were such that you might bog down. You could clear the snow out from in back and in front more easily, even the pile bunched up under the cowling. The only time the shovel wasn't much help, the worst of times, was if you broke through the top layer of snow on the lake and sank into the perfidious overflow: water and slush. The more you shoveled, the more rushed back in.

It takes at least two men working hard to get a machine out of overflow. And if it's cold and getting colder there's no quitting, because the slush without its insulating cover of snow will freeze pretty fast, locking the machine into maybe six or eight inches of ice. Not a pleasant thought. I won't describe what can be done about that because, thank heavens, it never happened to me or anyone else on the lake. I suppose your options are: Wait for the spring thaw;

spend the rest of the winter patiently trying to chip it out; or bid the doomed machine farewell, pull off a robbery, and buy another one.

If you're alone and in overflow your only hope is a good-quality come-along and a length of stout rope or chain long enough to reach a tree on shore, devoting the time and energy necessary to ratchet all those tons up onto some solid footing (overflow exerts a diabolical reluctance to release its prey). For years when we had to run down half the lake to reach the cabin from the trail's end I carried a come-along with me and learned early in the game to stop the snowmobile at trail's end and walk out a ways testing, no matter how benign the snow looked out there on the lake. (We've since punched through a trail that runs overland to our cabins, thus avoiding the lake when overflow conditions are suspicious.)

Neither the shovel nor the come-along could have saved me the day I nearly didn't make it to the cabin. I had a load of groceries and supplies on the sled, and a heavy, wet snow had come down while I'd been in Anchorage shopping. I wanted to get the load back to the cabin before the food would freeze. The temperature was falling. I knew conditions were marginal ("conditions" are the traffic cops of the bush), but I was willing to bet on the margin. I went for it. The miles up alongside the tracks were trouble-free; someone had broken out the trail just a little while before. But the heavy snow was still coming down, and I couldn't make it up Gliver Hill from the Gravel Pit at Mile 232. The track started spinning out about halfway up. Shit! Piss! And corruption! I knew what had to be done and it was not a happy prospect.

I unloaded half the sled, which involved untying some knots with bare hands. After thawing my hands in my armpits, I shoveled a circle of snow away around both the Yamaha snowmobile and the lightened sled, then inched the rig around till it faced downhill. I drove back down the hill and, maintaining speed and using body English, managed to turn around through the deep stuff at the bottom without getting stopped. Then gunning it in low gear I hit the hill again, passed the other half of the load, and got to the top, there to unload and perform another shovel-and-pull turnaround. Then down to pick up the other half, and so on back to the top to redo the whole cargo. I was wet with sweat despite having doffed my outer layer of clothes. The light was fading, the temperature dropping.

The rest of the trail was unbroken through the new snow. It would be up to me and the Yamaha. I was on my own. I had enough sense to be concerned but not enough to try retracing the way back to town. I wanted to get home with my supplies. I was determined.

That wet, heavy snow was deep enough now to pile up in front as I pushed through. A finer, lighter snow would have fanned away off to the sides, but this stuff kept piling up and stopping me about every hundred yards. I'd get off and work my way to the front end, the snow now, even on the trail, almost up to my knees, and shovel a passageway ahead to get started again. I was careful to remove the snow packed under the nose of the cowling before starting up again. This exercise had to be repeated several times along the cat trail. I was aware that my strength was starting to give out. Okay, I'd call forth the adrenaline reserves as needed.

I wasn't especially cold despite the sweat and falling temperature because I was working so hard. But I knew that as I lost strength the cold would be gaining it. As the temperature dropped, the wet, heavy snow falling tended to dry out and lighten up a bit, which was nice but of little help to me because the foot or two already on the ground remained wet and heavy, just a little stiffer and more resistant from hardening up.

I couldn't negotiate the turn off the cat trail onto the mile-and-a-half spur trail to the lake. Fortunately, quickly realizing the machine couldn't do the turn, I had stopped before it plowed into the really deep snow on either side of the plugged trail. Why hadn't the turn been possible? Something was wrong. I shoveled the snow away from a side of the Yamaha and lay flat to check out the situation underneath. As I suspected, the heavy snow had packed in between the tub and the track more and more densely until the track was actually stretched into a half round, which was why I'd had to kneel and use a lot of body English for even the gentle turns along the cat trail. It was like riding on the edge of a dime. I tried cleaning it out. That was difficult because the snow had become half-frozen slush. And it clogged up again right away anyway. Also, I was sure the skegs on the skis were clogged and unable to dig in for a turn. I shoveled and stomped and tried again, but at the first bend in the trail the same thing happened.

The Back Lake trail was all bends and sharp turns. I knew there was no way I could make it pulling the sled load. I would have to disconnect. Easier said than done, but done it was, the adrenaline squad rising to the occasion. I was breathing hard and encased in a cold, clammy sweat. This was not good. Hypothermia was waiting in the wings, ready to play lead. A rough camp might have been a possibility an hour ago before I'd started tiring. Now I was giving out, and it was getting darker and colder. I doubted I'd have the strength to plunge around in the deep snow collecting enough spruce boughs for a bed and dead branches for a fire. I'd need a pretty big fire to keep from freezing once I was immobile—an all-night fire, a long night at that.

No. I had to keep moving or hypothermia would set in fast. They'd find me stiff as a board the next day. The food on the sled would freeze, but that was the least of my worries. When the Yamaha failed to negotiate the next bend I abandoned it too. It was survival time. I started pushing ahead, running on empty, even the adrenaline squad failing. I took several steps, then rested until I started feeling the cold. It wasn't a light fluffy snow you could move through easily even when knee deep. It took effort to push ahead through this heavy stuff. Bad enough. And then things started getting worse. The tendon on the outside of my right knee began to hurt. I had damaged it years before when hiking the Appalachian Trail, and ever since, if I got real tired and had to use my legs hard, it would start complaining—louder and louder if I ignored it and kept going.

So now there was pain added to the mix, and the possibility the knee would give out before the rest of me did. I slowed my pace: three or four steps, then rest. It was getting colder as it got darker. Only about a mile left to go. I should be able to make that. I would have to cater to my right leg and ignore the insistent desire to plop down into the snow and rest long and deep. People who succumbed to that often never got up again.

It seemed the Coldman was hovering around me the way vultures circle a man on his last legs. I kept moving under power of sheer will. If death was in the offing I'd accept it—this was a good day to die—but I'd go down fighting.

I made it to the lake, but now a life-or-death question confronted me. Had this snowfall been heavy enough to cause overflow? I was sure there was some overflow out there, but the snowmobile trail down the lake had been packed hard and formed a kind of ice bridge several inches thick, enough maybe to have remained above the overflow adjoining it. If not, I'd be done for. Couldn't slosh through the stuff, and couldn't push through the deep snow in the woods. Only half a mile to go. Sheer willpower could do it.

I moved out onto the lake, and my leg gave out and I fell into the snow. Could I get back up? Yes. I could. The snow melted on my face and ran down my neck. Some had gotten inside my mitts. Maybe I could resuscitate a couple of the adrenaline squad, like a dead-tired horse who smells the stable.

I collapsed two more times but the third time was through the door of my cabin and into the arms of my worried family.

Eat your heart out, Coldman.

FREIGHT TRAIN ROULETTE

Winter trips to and from Talkeetna by snowmobile were a bit hairy, even putting aside the possibility of getting into the kind of fix I just described, because circumstances forced us to play what we called "freight train roulette." We ran alongside, and sometimes down the middle, of the tracks half the way. Especially when the snow was deep, it was a big help to travel the railroad right of way, because it was plowed. But there was a price.

You had to keep looking back for the ominous headlight of a train. We knew the passenger-train schedule and tried to work around it, though the train could be late an hour or so in either direction, and we had to take that into consideration. But it was the random freight train we worried about most. They couldn't stop on a dime or within a country mile. Avoidance of contact was up to us.

When we saw that light coming we pulled over as far as we could to the side, stopped, and walked several yards toward the oncoming light. We had heard that it had happened that a freight with a loose cable hanging from one of the cars had cut someone standing to the side right in half, and we'd also heard that something projecting from a car could hurl or drag a snowmobile. So you wanted to be upstream of your machine when the freight was rumbling past, upstream and a few feet down the embankment as well. This was always somewhat harrowing—all those tons of steel rumbling interminably by.

But the real challenge was returning north out of Talkeetna. Except for the brief time the Talkeetna River froze solid enough for snowmobiles to cross, the only way across the river was via the bridge. The bridge was there for the trains, not for snowmobiles. We had to hop the rail and go fast, clopping over the ties right down the middle of the tracks.

Of course, we stopped at the bridge first, turned our machine off, and looked and listened. Unfortunately, a southbound train approached the bridge around a long curve: You couldn't see a headlight way off. You hoped to discern its beam in the air if it was dark, as it usually was. This precautionary stop, look, and listen was an uncertain safeguard, and if you were in the middle of the bridge when the light rounded the bend you were out of luck. You could save your hide by hanging over the side, but your machine would be totaled. Which happened to our friend Brad Smith, and almost happened to me.

Whitey and I were headed out of town back up to the lake after an extended period of merrymaking at the Fairview. We had enough of our wits about us still to inquire of the guys in the station house if a freight was coming. Yes, they said, a northbound was about fifteen or twenty minutes down the tracks. It was cold out, and we didn't feel like waiting till the freight passed.

"Hell," said Whitey, "we'll jump the rail right here where it's easier [because of the station's platform being level with the top of the rail] and zoom right down the middle. Probably be at the Gravel Pit before the freight catches up to us."

"Sounds good," said I. After a certain number of liquid refreshments caution walks the plank because you become indestructible.

So this plan was the first sign that some of our wits were no longer about us. We should have gone back to the Fairview, had another drink, and waited for the freight to pass. The second, and determining, sign was that we both forgot about the squeeze play of the inner rails just before the bridge. We jumped on the Yamaha and tore down from the station right into the squeeze play. The converging inner rails brought us to a sudden stop, with my head hitting the windshield and Whitey's head hitting my back. We were locked in tight, the skis caught under the rail's lip and now somewhat pigeon-toed. The Yamaha had reverse, but neither that nor our efforts to free the skis availed.

I ran back to the station house where Glen Valentine and his crew were sitting around drinking coffee. They were not kindly disposed toward the "up the tracks hippies," I knew. When I burst through the door, they looked up surprised and said nothing. I glanced at them and hopped over to the corner where stood shovels, picks, and a heavy-duty six-foot pry bar.

"I need this," I said, grabbing the bar. I didn't wait on a response and was out the door before any of them recovered their composure. Running back to the machine with the bar I met Whitey hot-footing it back to the station house.

"They gotta stop that train," he said in passing.

I kept going, got the chisel tip of the bar under a ski, and popped it loose, then the other one. Now, baby, I said silently, start right up. It did. I backed her up, then with the old adrenaline surge of strength lifted the front end over the rail and bumped the machine across and safely to the side just as Whitey came huffing and puffing back with the news that the freight was already too close to be stopped in time. Then he saw the machine safely to the side. He clapped me on the back.

"Goddamn it, Jungle Bob, that's nice going! —Where's that jug? We need to calm our shattered nerves."

I pulled the whiskey bottle out of my pack, and we sat on the machine passing it back and forth and sure enough, in a minute here came the freight, a long one that hadn't had to slow down for Talkeetna and couldn't have stopped for us. We raised the jug in salute as it went roaring by across the bridge.

Then I ran the pry bar back to the station house and leaned it next to the door, not bothering to offer explanations. We aligned the skis and headed up the tracks, wide open right down the middle, in the wake of the freight. We wouldn't even have to look back. Whitey clapped me on the back and let out a whoop. "Ride 'em, cowboy!"

Another freight train incident I heard about came much closer to being tragic. The story goes that a fellow from Anchorage almost got run over. He was cruising up the tracks between the rails when his machine quit on him. While under the cowling working on the problem he heard a train whistle. As luck, destiny, or bad karma would have it, an unscheduled freight was approaching Talkeetna northbound, and he was only a mile or so north of the bridge.

Maybe hearing the train coming caused him to hurry and force something under there. In any event, his left hand got stuck fast.

The train would be upon him in a couple of minutes. He pulled hard, but the hand was caught good. With his other hand he felt for his belt knife, thinking at the last minute he would have to cut his hand off to save his life. But he was a big strapping fellow, very strong. When the train was crossing the bridge and closing the gap his adrenaline squad leaped into action, and he lifted the machine and fell over backward with it, clear of the tracks. When he got his hand free it was cut and badly bruised but still attached to his arm. All's well that ends well.

One other snowmobile/train incident is worth telling to round out your sense of what bush snowmobiling was like. Son Steve has written a book titled *Wise Men Don't Smoke Dope on Snowshoes*. I could add an addendum: *And They Shouldn't Smoke Dope When Bombing Down the Tracks on a Snowmobile in a Snowstorm*. Which was what I did one day.

It was a wild ride alongside the tracks through the driving snow. I was stoned and enjoying myself. Visibility was minimal, and I heard nothing but my engine and the wind whistling past my ears. Then without warning, coming at me maybe ten or fifteen yards ahead was a train's headlight up there piercing the whirling snow. Instinct and lightning reflexes took over. I turned the skis hard to port and rolled down the embankment out of the way. I lay there sunk in the snow under my machine as endlessly the tanker cars rumbled and clacked by. I was more careful about that sort of thing from then on, as you might imagine. (I won't burden you or me with my struggle to get the machine back up to the tracks.)

Railroads are not usually associated with the idea of wilderness, but the fact is that the Alaska Railroad runs through a lot of it. The railroad was a prominent factor in our environment and featured importantly in our life in the bush. Nowadays it's not so significant a factor because a trail has been put in down from the track embankment, and walkways have been attached to the bridge over the Talkeetna River and Billingham's Slough wide enough to accommodate snowmobiles and four-wheeler ATVs. The days of playing freight train roulette are behind us now. I have to admit it's getting better, a little better all the time.

But there are still the moose to contend with. When the snow is deep they, like us, prefer a packed or plowed trail. It's a bummer when you're heading home or to town if up ahead you spot the rump of a moose, legs going, head wagging from side to side. Like it or not, you have to be patient. You can't just bull ahead with roaring engine and drive the critter off the trail. They don't want to go. If you push them they'll gear up to a trot for a mile or so, then tire and turn to confront you. If you keep pushing at them the odds are ten to one their ears will go back flat on their head, their ruff will go up, and they will charge. It happened to several of us bush rats. No one to my knowledge got seriously hurt, but windshields have been smashed and cowlings broken.

So it's best to practice patience. But the night when I was heading home from Talkeetna for the first time on my new Yamaha, courtesy of the "Land: Bridge to Community" project, I was reluctant to put my patience into practice when the dark rump of a moose emerged out of the snowfall. Steve Cross was right behind me. We were riding between the rails, big snow mounds on either side from the plowing. Which was why the moose behaved so obstinately. They couldn't feature getting bogged down in a snowbank just because some noisy hominid was in a hurry and wanted them out of the way.

Every time I pressed up close to the moose, he stopped and turned in hostile fashion. I too stopped until he got going again. At this pace, it would be hours getting home.

"Screw it!" Steve called out. "Let's go back to town and wait an hour or so."

Good advice but unlikely to be heeded by an impatient man on a fast new machine. I was watching the moose closely. Now and then he would weave over to the left side away from the center. I figured if I edged up as close as possible without making him stop and turn, when he wove over to the left side I could gun the powerhouse under me and whiz on by with a foot or so between us. If I went for it from the critical close position the moose wouldn't have time to react before I was past him. That was the plan.

It would be close. But you know what they say in Tierra del Fuego: A miss is as good as a mile. The moment came. The moose swerved to the side, I hit the throttle, and as I tore by him, leaning way over to the right side of the Yamaha, out of the corner of my eye, I saw his front legs up in the air, hooves flashing. But they didn't connect. I stopped a ways on the other side of him, where my momentum had taken me. I looked back.

"You going to give it a try, Steve?" I called out.

"Ain't got the machine could do that, Bob. I'm heading back."

I waved okay. Steve swung around, and his red taillight disappeared into the whiteness. My breathing soon slowed down and I cruised on home in high spirits, wheeling and dealing way faster than usual along the trail through the woods, my headlight sparkling on the tunnel of fantastically sculpted white forms opening ahead through the surrounding darkness.

11

The Fire

Hamming it up with the chain saw.

(September 1973)

We had made many improvements around the lake during the summer of '73, bedrooms added on, docks built, double windows installed, furniture constructed, vegetable gardens expanded and planted. I added a bedroom for Jon, Sal, and Beth, a closed-in porch, had a second bedroom well under way, chinked the entire cabin tighter (no more forty-below drafts chinked with rags or paper towels), and had built a sauna attached to the bedroom at a right angle. My idea was that the bedroom would serve as a dressing room for the sauna, with a door between the two and another opening from the sauna for the short dash to the dock and the lake.

As an idea the attached sauna was good, and in practice it was very convenient having the warm bedroom to undress and dress in through the cold months. The flaw in the plan was that saunas by definition require very hot fires to bring the temperature into the 180-degree range. As a result, saunas sometimes burn down. If they are off a ways by themselves, the loss is not too great, but if attached to the main house a sauna on fire can take everything with it unless people are right on hand to dowse the incipient blaze.

On the afternoon of the twelfth I took a good long sauna—
"My last for a while," said I. We were all packed and ready to
start the trip down the long and winding road to New York to visit
family and friends after five straight years in the bush. The cabin
was scrubbed down, and the staple foods like rice and beans were
all packed away in shrew-proof containers tight enough also not
to emit any bear-enticing scents. We'd been able to save only a
thousand dollars for the trip, but as usual we would camp out
most of the way and fix our own meals, which would greatly re-
duce expenses. We knew how to do it.

We were about to canoe over to Steve and Anna's cabin for dinner when Paul and Mona showed up and asked if it would be okay
for them to take a sauna. Carol, always the more cautious of the
two of us, hesitated; everything was so ready for us to leave in the
morning. But ours was the only sauna on the lake, and we had
made it available to the whole gang. The sauna is a marvelous experience when done right; you come out of it feeling washed in the
blood of the lamb—relaxed and rejuvenated, just about born
again. We were a tight community. I was pleased to share the
sauna.

"Sure. Go ahead. It's probably still hot in there. —Don't forget
to close her down when you're done."

Over at Steve's after dinner, legs well stretched out, relaxed to
the edge of dozing, I felt mildly annoyed that something was
drawing me out of my pleasant mental haze. Carol, as I rolled my
head toward her voice, was turning from Steve's big bay window
overlooking the lake, her eyes widening with realization.

"Oh, my God, Bob!" Her voice was rising as she turned toward me. Things seemed to have gone into slow motion.

"Bob! The cabin's on *fire!*"

My body was moving before the first shock passed through it. I
went to the window. Across the dark lake great sinuous flames were
rising out of the sauna roof. They leaped into the darkness and
sent orange reflections flickering over the lake. Two figures were

silhouetted running. They were shouting. Steve and Jon were out the door and headlong down the steep trail to the canoe, me right behind them, Carol and Anna following. No flashlight among us, and leaping down, I turned an ankle on a root. A sharp, hot pain shot up my leg, but I ignored it.

We dug the paddles in and made that canoe move, and as we neared our dock we saw that the figures, no doubt Paul and Mona, were dashing from the lake with buckets of water—which didn't appear to be giving the fire any pause. The flames were growing. We had been yelling our lungs out all across the lake, rousing everyone, and now we saw lights and canoes coming.

In my total consciousness, clear and without emotion, the words came: "It's gone." The logs had been drying out for years; the fire was already big; we were isolated and had nothing but buckets to fight with.

Carol and Anna were coming around the end of the lake, cutting across the marshes and the channel, wading up to their waists in the cold water. Sally stayed behind, watching over Beth. Carol was calling out, "The money! Get the money!" The cash was in one of my books in the main room, which was not yet aflame. But when I opened the door a blast of intensely hot, thick smoke knocked me back gasping. The room could ignite at any second. I tried getting in low nevertheless but stumbled back out after only a few feet, unable to breathe or endure the heat.

My Winchester 30.06 was hanging on a peg just inside the door. The stock was very hot but I reached up and snatched it, burning my hand, and threw it across the porch and into the grass. Steve Cross and Jon both tried to reach the book but couldn't. Then Steve insisted upon going in although I told him not to. He crawled along the floor, trying to keep his head beneath the heavy smoke. He penetrated farthest into the room but almost passed out when he tried to reach up for the book. Thank God he knew the cabin so well he was able to find the door although blind and semiconscious.

Everyone from around the lake was fighting the blaze except the Kobells, who were away. They ran into the water so as to be able to fill the buckets with one swoop, then ran back to empty them into the flames—as good as trying to stop a grizzly with a bean shooter. But we kept at it, the adrenaline charging our bodies with the urgency to act.

Then Steve was up on the bedroom roof next to the sauna. He was pouring the buckets handed up to him directly down into the flames through the burned-out gaps in the poles and sod. It seemed to be working; the flames seemed subdued. "Keep 'em coming! Hurry!" Steve shouted. But either the fire burned out a window or someone thought to break it out to throw water into the bedroom. The flames caught new life from the rush of air and shot up through the roof. I feared for Steve. The room beneath him was filled with flame, and the poles under the sod he stood on could collapse.

"Steve, come down! Now! It's no good." My words rang with force above the confusion, and he jumped down.

The tool cache, about six yards from the cabin, began to smoke. A few of us darted to it, ducking and shielding our faces from the blaze, and soaked it down. Any of the spruce or birch trees that close were either on fire or scorched. A finger of gray smoke shot out of the broken limb of one of the birches whose side facing the fire was charred black.

Suddenly the fire encompassed the entire house. The windows blazed out at us like the multiple eyes of some sacrificial deity or demon. The log structure stood intact, all details firm and clear, but engulfed in writhing flames. The sight was both awesome and terrifying. We watched it, transfixed.

Bullets and shotgun shells began exploding inside. The windows were out. Parts of the walls and roof were collapsing, sending spirals of sparks up into the darkness. I yelled to everyone to move away and stay low. No one had gotten hurt so far, and that was a mercy. I had a bleeding welt over my right eye where a half-gallon bottle filled with oil had struck me when the boys were flinging all flammables away from the cabin. I barely felt it hit and paid it no mind until the blood started running into my eye.

We all moved back down the path into the dark, cool woods and sat on the ground watching the immense blaze while the shells exploded. All our guns except my rifle were in there, mine and my sons'—three shotguns, one of them a fine old L.C. Smith double-barrel, with two sets of barrels with different bores and a handsomely engraved walnut stock that a wealthy colleague had given me years ago at Syracuse University, three .22 rifles, a .22 handgun, and the Ruger .44 Magnum Blackhawk six-shooter that had probably saved my life when that bull moose had charged back at Iliamna.

All that we owned in the world was in there except my tools and snowmobile—all my best books that I had taken with me when I resigned my professorship, including the valuable "William Law Edition" of Jacob Boehme's works translated into English, four quarto volumes expertly rebacked in calf, seventeenth-century paper and print, fabulous fold-out engravings illustrating Boehme's metaphysics; our sealskin parkas with ruffs from the first wolverine Steve had trapped at Lake Nerka; several of my best paintings; the stereo music system (powered by a small generator); the bear rugs, the tanned marten and fox furs from my trapping days; the handmade gifts from our friends around the lake; all the furniture I'd made of spruce and birch; the cupboards and closets I'd just completed; the stoves and lamps; the cabin itself, four years of hard, satisfying work, growing from the one sixteen-by-twenty room we wintered in that first year to its final comfortable form.

As I sat there on a damp mossy log Carol came over and sat by me, taking my hand. All the women and girls were sobbing. I saw tears in the others' eyes as they looked at us. Steve and I had first found this little lake in the spring of 1970. Ours had been the first cabin. No one had to say anything. Everyone knew what had happened.

Later, our home reduced to a mass of glowing coals, burning log ends, and black twisted metal, we stood out on the dock keeping watch to see that the fire hadn't spread. A light rain began to fall, relieving that concern. We were wet already from plunging into the lake with the buckets, and too numbed to care anyway.

The drone of a plane approached, coming in low. Some pilot must have seen the huge glow in the sky. The plane buzzed over, its wing lights bright in the darkness, circled once, then came in for a landing. I figured it must be Don Sheldon, a man of many rescues with an instinct for encountering catastrophe. The Cessna 180 taxied to within hailing distance, and the pilot cut the engine, gliding closer. Don stuck his head out. "Is everyone all right?" I called back that no one was hurt and then was about to indulge in a little Hollywood macho by asking had he remembered the marshmallows but canceled that bit of heroics as childish. This was no movie. I did, however, ask him if he happened to have a jug on board.

"No, by golly," he replied, "but if I did I'd sit down and kill it with you." (Don Sheldon normally never touched alcohol, and I understood his remark in the kind and feeling way it was intended.) Before he took off, he assured us that we could count on him to help in any way he could. People on a frontier know what it means to have their bush home burn down.

I stood at the end of the dock gazing into the darkness. I didn't feel the light rain falling. I didn't feel anything now that it was over. Behind me the mass of coals was slowly dimming under the rain. We had nothing left but the clothes on our backs, some tools, the snowmobile, and my 30.06. I turned the palm of my burned hand up to the cool rain. What was trickling into the corner of my mouth now was more blood than water, from the welt on my forehead. The cabin and everything in it was gone. I could hear the others talking quietly now that it was over and the adrenaline had drained away. I stood there at the end of the dock with my right hand opened to the rain and the taste of blood in my mouth. The night was very dark. Now what? No home, no money. I had no idea.

12

Cabin Raising on the Last Frontier

Bigger and better.

It had been a bad night. Upstairs in Steve and Anna's bedroom Carol and I hadn't really slept at all. Sitting up in the bed we held hands but didn't talk much. A window opened onto the lake, and we watched the orange glow on the other shore getting smaller and dimmer and by dawn go out.

It was on both our minds: We might have to go back to academia and suburbia, leave the woods, abandon this powerful life, go back to quiet desperation in the world where nothing is true like ice, like fire. But how could we possibly muster the spirit and energy to start all over again here in the woods? We weren't ready to make decisions or even talk it over rationally. The loss felt heavier now than it had when we were fighting the fire, even while knowing it was useless. We lay there in silence, holding hands.

Next morning after breakfast we were all sitting around downstairs, feeling at a loss. My right eye beneath the ugly welt on my forehead was almost closed and turning colors, my ankle swollen and complaining, my clothes charred and dirty, my pockets empty, my future blank. Everyone else looked a little beat-up and bedraggled too. Paul and Mona had showed up earlier, woebegone, probably not having slept either. Apologies were unnecessary. We knew how bad they felt. No one had much to say. Our spirits were at low-water slack.

A knock came on the door. It was Whitey. The news had traveled fast. He shot us that quick glance of his from under his brows, Walter Huston style, and knew at once where we were at. He sat down and took the coffee Anna brought him and started talking.

"We'll get going on it right away. Tomorrow. No point sitting around feeling bad. People will be showing up. We'll get ready for them, put up all the tents we have, set up a cook tent at Paul and Mona's—spruce poles and plastic, it'll go up in half a day. Their place will be mess hall and general headquarters. We'll run the operation like a logging camp. Up at seven, breakfast at seven-thirty, on the job at first light. Midmorning and midafternoon breaks, coffee and rolls, maybe cake or pie. Sandwiches and hot coffee available at all times." He smiled at Carol and Anna. "You ladies is an important part of this operation." Then he turned to me. "You know, Jungle Bob," he said, grinning, "you've got to feed the crew first class. You must never let them weaken."

In an impasse, there is a way. Whitey saw the dark tunnel of funk we were in, and he was showing us the light at the end of it. His spirit and strength of experience flowed out of him unconsciously and into us. Just like that the tide had turned. I felt life flooding back.

Hell, what a number! To go right at the rebuilding, mount up again right after being thrown hard—and not for the first time either. It could be good, with Whitey and who knew who else might show up. The core crew was on hand already. There was myself and Steve and Jon and now Whitey right off, and Carol, Anna, Mona, and Linda; even the kids could be counted on to pull an oar in our lifeboat of the undefeated. Paul, Buddy, and Steve Cross I knew I could count on too. These were all good hands, an experienced crew. Add a few more neighbors and friends and it could be done, even this late into autumn. Wasn't this the Great Land? Men to match my mountains.

So maybe you've lost an eye and a leg and your skin is scarred and leathery from wear and tear in sun, wind, rain, ice, and fire. That's all right. Think of an old bull moose with his scarred-up hide and broken antler. He has your respect, he's weathered the storms, and you know it's all right because it's part of the natural world. Disaster can knock you down, but you're built to take it and get up again. Dangers can steady the nerves, hard knocks can strengthen the spirit. A broken bone will heal stronger than it had been before the break. But ah . . . the relentless pressures and stress of mainstream existence eating at your heart and soul can secretly hollow you out even while the shell of you continues to look smooth and smiley, like a birch that goes rotten from the inside out. I wasn't thinking this, I was feeling it as Whitey talked. And then much later when I did come to think about it all that way it got focused in Emerson's lines, which I knew by heart, from "Self-Reliance":

> *Cast the bantling on the rocks,*
> *Suckle him with the she-wolf's teat,*
> *Wintered with the hawk and fox,*
> *Power and speed be hands and feet.*

Half an hour later big Denny Dougherty ducked through the door, his intense blue eyes taking in the room from under his watch cap. He sat down on the floor cross-legged and looked at me. "When do we start, Jungle Bob?" Not waiting for a response, he jumped to his feet, arms akimbo. "Let's make it the best damn cabin in the Susitna Valley!—except for my place of course." He liked to chuckle at himself when he did or said something untoward.

Steve picked up fast on these upbeat notes circulating through the room.

"Hey! We'll put on a benefit smorgasbord at the Fairview next Saturday night. By then everyone will know about the fire. Dad and me and Jon will do a gig of folk songs, with maybe a few of our own thrown in about this life—what they all know. I bet we'll raise enough money for food and building supplies too."

My two sons and I still knew dozens of the old songs I used to sing them to sleep with. We all played guitar and I the five-string banjo too. (The banjo was lost to the fire, but fortunately my guitar had been over at Steve's.) We would show the people a good time for their donations. The town and bush people had come through for Tom and Anne Mercer when their cabin had burned down a year or so earlier. It was the frontier way, as it had been the way of our hunter-gatherer forebears: compassion, cooperation, and sharing. In this regard, the Talkeetna-Chase area was a loose-knit but genuine community of ancient lineage.

Life was definitely flooding back into me. When I glanced over at Carol, sitting there with Beth on her lap and Sally leaning against her, I saw color in her face.

"Beth and I will get the moss just like with the first cabin," bright-eyed Sally piped up in tune with the song of resurrection being sung. "Sure," said Beth, and Carol drew her daughters to her and kissed them. Their words were like the first robin song in the spring.

I'd always liked the design of Steve's cabin, with its upstairs bedroom. I liked going upstairs to sleep; it was like rising above the concerns, leaving them behind. When Steve had first proposed his cabin idea I was hesitant. It seemed complicated; we'd lose time trying to figure out how to do this or that, and we had other cabins to build that summer. But I told him, "Sit down with pencil and paper and work the whole design out, every detail, all the angles and dimensions, and we'll see how it looks." It looked good, we built it, and it was a fine cabin.

"You know," I said, "I'd like the new cabin to be along the lines of Steve's—with the upstairs bedroom. Bigger of course. We'll have to sit down and draw up the plans, using Steve's place as a model." We were off and running.

"Count me in on that," Denny said. Unpracticed in procrastination and unfamiliar with delay, he went to the table, grabbed the pencil and paper, and started the blueprint. Steve and I pulled up chairs on either side of him, Whitey looking over our shoulders, and heads together there and then we drew up the design of a bigger and better cabin than the one the fire god had taken: eighteen by thirty-two, with a ten-by-fifteen upstairs bedroom, a cubbyhole, and a porch, also notched corners this time, even though it meant longer logs and more work, but because of the constraints of time, instead of pole-and-sod roofs we'd use milled lumber bought with the proceeds of the benefit at the Fairview. The plans were in place; a crew of able-bodied men and capable women was on hand, with more to come. Yes! We were ready to raise a cabin of some distinction in the Susitna Valley. You could almost hear the energy buzzing in the room.

A cabin raising in the bush was still, in 1973, as it had been throughout the nation's frontier experience, a communal affair. Just about everyone in the area tried to help in any way they could no matter how pressing their own work demands nor how extreme their [semi-] voluntary poverty. A few left off building their own cabin to put in some time helping us. Several who had little enough of their own packed in clothing and food.

The women, including a few volunteers, were kept busy helping Whitey the bull cook with the three squares and the snacks for the daily breaks. Men putting in long hours working hard outdoors develop prodigious appetites. One time Carol was about to dip into what she assumed was the serving bowl of potato salad on the table and realized just in time that that huge mound of salad was the private portion of Big Jim Carlson, one of the volunteers.

Besides helping Whitey, doing dishes, and so forth, the women often lent a hand draw-shaving the bark from the logs and also with the chinking job. Sally and Beth went out on daily expeditions to collect moss for the chinking before it froze. A cabin as large as the one we planned needs a lot of moss. The girls thus freed the men from that time-consuming job. And they felt good about doing it, pitching in. There were no slackers at Back Lake. Everyone was into it, wanting to contribute. There was no forced labor.

Those first several days as more help showed up we had a serious feeding problem. No one had connected with an early season moose. There was no meat on the lake. We were waiting for cold weather and snow. Everyone contributed what they had, wholewheat flour, beans, rice, and the like, but Whitey shook his head, insisting that you can't feed loggers a vegetarian diet; they needed power food, wild game. Moose that year were scarce in the valley, spruce chickens too, and the rabbits hadn't even begun to build up in their cycle. The few salmon brought in didn't go very far. We needed to raise some money, and we needed a moose.

The benefit in Talkeetna went well. Half the town showed up, sitting around the bar and on rows of foldout chairs from the grammar school. My sons and I poured on the coal, singing and playing song after song with gusto. The vibes in the building were very high. Don and Roberta Sheldon sat in the front row and started a chant: "Yeah Durrs! Yeah Durrs!" The Durrs had gotten clobbered but weren't quitting, and the town was applauding that. Several hundred dollars were raised—and our morale too. To be part of a community like that is a great boon on more than just the material level.

Carol and I lost no time in making a trip into Anchorage for supplies, mainly food—a fifty-pound bag of onions, a crate of carrots, twenty-five pounds of brown rice, twenty-five pounds of beans, a crate of eggs, and three hundred pounds of potatoes, all but the potatoes purchased from a wholesaler who was glad to help. The potatoes we gleaned from the harvested field of a Matanuska farmer, with his blessing, the two of us bent over going down the long rows of turned earth, like a scene out of Van Gogh.

In Talkeetna before heading on to Wasilla and Anchorage, we had run into Jesse Cartwright and Jimmy Rowe, friends of ours. They volunteered to go after a moose for us, with Sheldon offering to fly them to a hot spot. But moose, like gold, are where you find them. The boys hunted hard, despite a case of dysentery for Jim and a turned ankle for Jesse, but they had no luck.

In the meantime Whitey had sent into Talkeetna for meat. All they could come up with was several pounds of . . . sliced bologna. For the next few days, we ate not only bologna sandwiches, but hot meals oriented around the humble cold cut: creamed diced bologna, fried bologna, bologna stew, and any other form of disguised or amalgamated bologna Whitey could devise. Some of the crew vowed they would never again eat bologna, not even on a sandwich.

I was worried that we'd be shut down before the first tree was felled. Whitey was right. We needed moose meat to build meals around. I let Sheldon know. As soon as he had an opening in his flying commitments he would fly someone into the high country where the bulls lingered until the snows drove them down. That someone would be son Steve. He was the best and "luckiest" hunter I knew. I was mindful that at Iliamna he had bagged three moose. It was as if he had a sixth sense for moose, could nose them out. I'd miss him on the job, but getting those hundreds of pounds of top-quality meat into camp was first priority.

We put a pack together for him with everything he'd need for a hunt of several days, though I was hoping he'd connect sooner than that. If anyone had the right karma, he did. I imagined the moose up there, when they got wind of his coming, standing in a circle resignedly drawing straws to see which of them was to be harvested. They knew it was a foregone conclusion that he would take one of them, and this way all the others would have no reason to be nervous.

Aware of our situation, Sheldon squeezed Steve into his schedule the following evening. I'll let Steve tell the story of this important hunt, starting with the takeoff from Back Lake:

Sheldon taxied slowly to the south end of the lake, then turned the nose into the north wind and poured the coals to her for takeoff. As

we went roaring past the cabin site the gang on shore were all wav-
ing and giving the thumbs-up: Go get 'em!

As soon as we cleared the trees Don banked west and made a line
for the southern edge of the Alaska Range. The Susitna and Chilitna
Rivers, along with mile upon mile of uninhabited forest and swamp,
passed below. The first probing finger of civilization, the newly completed Parks Highway, wound its way northward to Fairbanks. It
looked so insignificant way down there, a pencil line drawn across
the vast territory, it made me remember that most of America had
also been wilderness not so long ago.

We flew for about forty-five minutes. "Kahiltna," Don said as we
crossed the foot of a great glacier. Then he enunciated in his exaggerated midwestern accent to make sure I understood: "Kuh-hilt-
nuh." I nodded my appreciation.

Over the roar of the engine he counseled me. "You want to get a
fat barren *cow*. A fat, barren *cow*. They're the best. That fat will lay
along their backbone an inch thick."

We circled over a number of small, swampy lakes and finally
landed on one much like our own lake, but surrounded by boggier
country.

"Remember, a nice fat barren *cow!*"

Daylight was beginning to fade by the time I got camp set up.
Not that there was much to it: a two-man cheapo non-rain-repelling
orange baggie that was sold as a tent to me by one of our country's
finest retail outlets.

The lake was shaped like a mitten, with the end of the thumb
jammed up by a substantial beaver dam. I was camped on the upper
inside part of the thumb. I decided to traverse its hundred yards and
cross the dam to the other side. A beaver slid into the blackness of
the water and left a silver wake in the afterglow behind it. Twenty
minutes later I was standing on the other side of the thumb, looking
across the water to the point of land where the tent was. Something
there looked out of place. I didn't recall a big stump or any such
thing being there, but then that wasn't likely anyway. It wasn't

as though this was familiar ground. I stared and stared at the stump, or whatever it was. For five long minutes there was no movement. My eyes began to see things that weren't there, and I had to look away for a moment. As I strained to see in the fading light, an almost imperceptible change danced across the shape, and I was sure the thing had moved.

They don't teach you this in hunting class, but this was not a casual hunt, so I raised the rifle at the shadow and fired. As the boom resounded around the lakeshore, the shadow took off into the woods.

So there I went as fast as I could back around the thumb to the camp. It took me a good five minutes to cover the distance. My hope was that the moose had been hit hard enough to bring her down quickly—or not hit at all. A wounded moose in the half dark was not a happy thought. There was blood on the ground. It led to a game trail in the grass nearby. The pale grass of autumn back-lit the blood as if it were illuminated. I took off running flat out, conscious of where the lake lay behind me. Getting lost for the cause would be an unwelcome, stupid happenstance. I admit I was a little panicky about maybe losing the moose, something I'd never done before. It had been a shot I wouldn't have risked under any other, less pressing circumstances.

I ran hard about three hundred yards, able to follow the blood on the grass surprisingly easy, thankful that the moose was sticking to the trail. I'd have probably lost her through the tangled underbrush.

The sound of hooves pounding up ahead told me I had almost caught up with her, so I ran even harder. The trail hooked to the right and I made my mental adjustment as to the location of the lake. Then there she was, fifty feet in front of me, just standing there. I was out of breath and shaking from the exertion. It was with great relief that I watched her drop after a single shot. Then the silence rushed in.

The first order of business now was to find the lake. A small rise to my right might reveal where it was. I ran up to the top and was cheered to see the last light rippling on the water a quarter mile away through the trees. I gutted the moose and slipped off some of her hide that night in the company of an owl: a nice fat barren *cow with fat an inch thick along her back. Tomorrow would be soon enough to cut the carcass up and pack it to the lake. I wasn't expecting Sheldon until at least the day after, so I could do the job at my own pace.*

I spent my time after the packing out pleasantly enough, playing whistling games with a group of curious swans, eating moose liver, and watching for bears.

Sheldon didn't return until the morning of the fourth day. The Cessna was a welcome sight as it banked and came in for the landing. Don cut the engine and stepped out onto the float as the plane glided into the marshy shore.

"What did you get?" he asked, somewhat apprehensively, as he eyeballed the mountain of meat.

I gave him my best Davy Crockett grin. "A nice, fat barren *cow!"*

Imagine my surprise when instead of giving me a well-deserved "attaboy," his face turned red, smoke poured out of his ears, he went into a full-fledged, Yosemite Sam shit-fit.

"Get that friggin %$#@(*!!!! thing in here! Now! Move it! Goddamn it! Hurry your ass!"

And so on. For five minutes he screamed at me like that as I hoisted each one-hundred-pound-plus piece of moose onto my shoulder and sloshed into the lake up to my waist to hand it up to him and run back for another. ("$#@!!&A%!") My lungs began to burn. My legs weakened. Sweat poured off me. And still he refused to let up. We (I) loaded that entire moose in less time than it takes to say "Sir-yes-sir!"

I was reasonably angry as we got back into the air, and just looked out my window at the ground below. After about ten minutes I heard him start chuckling softly. He reached over and tapped me on the shoulder.

"I guess I neglected" (nee-gleck-ted) "to tell you we switched units."

Switched units . . . Game units. That explained it. The nice fat, barren cow *that was legal in the units we were flying over on our way out was, evidently, illegal in the one he'd finally landed me in. He could have forfeited his plane and gone to jail if we'd been unfortunate enough to have been caught by the Department of Fish and Game.*

I looked over at him and he was grinning. "You did good," he said quietly. And on that note we headed home.

All's well that ends well.

The day Carol and I returned from town, Steve was already back at the lake. As we approached the "mess hall," he was lounging with exaggerated nonchalance in the doorway, grinning broadly and looking with some deliberateness over to the left of the cook tent. We followed his eyes to where the deep scarlet moose quarters hung heavily from a pole between two spruce.

That called for a celebration. We stopped work for the rest of the day. The back strap was big and good to go. Add to that onions, baked potatoes, and a vegetable and you have the wherewithal to gladden the hearts and strengthen the sinews of loggers. And then coffee and blueberry pies—Back Lake blueberries—to sweeten their dispositions. The crew was ready now for the weeks of hard work ahead.

After the meal, full and content, we all sat around Paul and Mona's cabin, close pressed to one another in the small room, passing joints and listening to Steve sing some of the songs he'd written about life in the Alaska bush, the life most of the others were leading too, the life we didn't want to lose. Then as the sun drifted behind the trees on the west side coolness descended with the dusk and the people wandered off to their tents. Soon the lamps were lit in the tents of various colors, and as the heavens were hung with stars the woods were hung with Japanese lanterns.

During the night it clouded over and started to rain. It roused me, and I listened to it dripping from the eves of Steve's place. It

was September. Soon that rain would mix with snow and soon after that it would be all snow. A little rain could not be allowed to
stop the work. Rain or shine we would be at it tomorrow. Behind
the screen of rain the Coldman was building up strength. He was
the man, not the Rainman, who could stop us.

The birch had turned gold and amber, and the leaves of the
high-bush cranberry sprinkled the woods with deep vermilion. We
had been hoping for one of those rare autumns of crisp mornings
and mostly sunny days. But the fall season, starting usually in August, was typically the rainy season, and more than half the time
we worked in the rain or in the kind of raw, drizzly weather characteristic of the valley through September. Some years we got rain
and drizzle until in October it started turning to wet snow.

It's an ill wind, as they say in Tierra del Fuego, that blows no
good. At least the rain and drizzle meant cloudy skies, which
meant milder temperatures. The rain wasn't constant, but working
in the woods, pushing through the drenched underbrush, we were
always wet or at least damp. But what luxury entering the mess
hall, feeling the dry warmth of the wood fire, smelling the hot coffee or whatever sumptuous meal Whitey and the women had prepared! As Blake taught, everything is known by its contrary. The
perpetual comfort of urban and suburban life leaves people petu-
lant and craving living bodily experience.

Despite the hard work, most of the crew stuck with us to the
end. I remember Grady Taylor with great fondness and admiration. I met Grady in the course of conducting those interviews for
the report on "Land: Bridge to Community" mentioned earlier. I'd
heard of some guy living alone up on the bluff above Mile 244 of
the railroad. I put in a whole day trying to reach him. I followed
his snowshoe float up the steep bluff, figuring he must have had a
real need for the spectacular view of the rivers and the mountains
beyond and also that he must have the legs of a mountain goat and
the back of a mule to be hauling gear and supplies up that bluff.
When, breathless, I reached the top, expecting to find his cabin sit-

uated to take full advantage of the view, instead the float went off into the bush for another two or three miles. This guy, I was thinking, must really have wanted privacy. My curiosity was piqued, and I pushed on.

When I finally reached his diggings that's just what they were: He had dug a trench about ten feet long, four feet deep, and four feet wide, fixed spruce poles tent-fashion over the trench, covered them with two layers of six-mil plastic, and moved in.

Grady wasn't there when I arrived. I noted his snowshoe float heading off inland and figured he might have gone hunting or after wood and wouldn't mind my waiting and resting in his humble abode (in this case, "humble abode" wasn't just a figure of speech). A small rectangular cast-iron stove was banked, a pot of beans slow-cooking on top. On an earthen seating and sleeping platform at the far end were a pad and pencil and several books by his sleeping bag. Leaning against the dirt wall was a pair of homemade snowshoes he had been working on, crude affairs of willow bent to form and held there with manila cord, which also made up the cross-thatched webbing. Maybe, appearances aside, they could do the job; maybe he was on another pair right now.

No question, Grady Taylor was an interesting young man. College educated and son of a professor, he had come to the Alaska bush with a purpose. He wanted to find out how little it took for a man not just to survive but to live contentedly. You can't get much closer to the bare facts than living alone in a ditch in the wilderness. In a sense, as regards driving life into a corner to know what it essentially is, Grady was going Thoreau one better. By my reckoning, he was a true philosopher: He would prove his philosophy on his pulses, not only think about fundamental questions of human life, but act upon his conclusions or theories. When eventually we met for the interview, it was apparent that we saw eye to eye on a lot of things.

Grady was a tall, quiet-spoken southerner. When he heard about my cabin burning, he appeared upon the scene the third morning and stayed with us to the end. He was a good worker and a pleasant presence. I imagined the counterculture could boast many a young person like Grady, dissatisfied with the comfortable material existence of the affluent society, hungering for a reality that could touch the depths of his human nature. Like the rest of us, really, he was after *life*. That had meaning.

Another stalwart member of the crew I have to mention was Steve Mahay. He and his wife Chris had a cabin on the ridge above the railroad tracks and the river. Steve wasn't counterculture; we didn't share those kinds of values. But we did share the frontier life, and that appeared to be a stronger tie than the controversial politics of cultural persuasions.

Steve walked the four miles to and from Back Lake every day. He had short hair and was gearing up for a business career in Talkeetna, but there he was among us swinging an ax, wielding a chain saw, getting soaked, and helping to raise a new home for the mad professor and his family. Steve went on to become a sportfishing guide and owner and operator of a successful riverboat service out of Talkeetna. We don't travel in the same circles, and he doesn't live in the woods anymore, but whenever our trails intersect we meet each other as old friends.

A few of the volunteers had been strangers to us until they appeared at Back Lake to help. Wandering around Alaska, they had wandered into Talkeetna, heard about the fire and the cabin raising, and decided probably that that was something they'd like to get in on. We never asked these people who they were, where they came from, or why they wanted to be here in the land of hard work and inconvenience. We just put an ax in their hands and welcomed them as part of the gang.

Big Jim Carlson had probably been a drifter. He was loud, unrestrainedly friendly, good-humored, and possessed of a gargantuan appetite (it was his helping of potato salad Carol had almost mistaken for the serving bowl). Another young fellow whose name ended in the syllable "slaw" we dubbed "Coleslaw." I don't remember his actual name. He was skinny and tall and somewhat comical but a willing worker. He seemed to enjoy having a nickname and hanging out with us. Another chap, quiet to the point of taciturnity, had a severe facial tic and a speech impediment. We cut him all the slack he needed, and it was obvious he, like the other newcomers, enjoyed being part of what we were doing.

We scouted the woods for the best "sticks," as we referred to the giant spruce we were after. I think "sticks" was something like whistling past the graveyard or trying to diminish the intimidation of your opponent's size by calling him a punk. We were after the sill logs first. These would be the bottom course of the cabin; all the other logs would rest upon them. So the sill logs had to be the best we could find—big sticks, maybe sixteen inches at the butt and twenty-two or thirty-six feet long for an eighteen-by-thirty-two-foot cabin, counting the additional four feet needed for notched corners and overhang.

Such trees, although I'm sure they stood unconscious of their superior stature among their fellows, were nevertheless awesome, majestic to behold, like the alpha bull moose or caribou or the grizzly monarch rising from the tundra ten feet into the air it sniffs. So in terms of our regard, we didn't take these trees lightly, though we lacked the ancient words or rituals that would have enabled us to express what we dimly felt about them. And returning to the stubborn material plane, we didn't take them lightly on that level either because they were very heavy, very big and hard, and potentially very dangerous. Not only admiration, even reverence, was called for but also careful respect. More than one man in the Susitna Valley has forfeited his life through an act of carelessness when logging.

That first rainy morning I stood with my chain saw at the base of one of those selected behemoths. Whenever possible we chose a standing dead tree if it was straight and sound, because it would be much easier to handle, weighing less than half of what it would if green. But such prime specimens were scarce back then before the spruce beetle infestation that now makes them fairly easy to find. Felling a tall, heavy green tree, as I say, requires care. You don't want it to get hung up or strike another tree in such a way as to cause the butt to backlash or bring down a heavy branch, possibly onto your head. So making the felling cuts was my responsibility.

You must carefully gauge the tree's lean to see if the direction it's prone to fall in presents a clear slot. A tree may appear perfectly vertical from some yards away, but I learned to press up against the trunk and look straight up from two or three positions around its circumference. This procedure will reveal even a very slight lean. Then you have to eyeball the slot into which it will fall to be sure it won't crash into any of the surrounding trees or branches. Spruce are "thin," unlike birch with their many wide branches, so the slot you aim for can be quite narrow. But then it's up to you to calculate your front and back cuts accurately so that the tree lands precisely in the open slot. Most trees will obviously lean to the south because the sun fosters the heaviest growth of branches on the south side, but when the stick you want appears to be without any lean it's best to perform the procedure just described.

During the winter of '72, before I started practicing the procedure just described, I nearly got clobbered because of a faulty estimate of a tree's lean. I had almost completed the back cut when instead of starting to fall away from me the trunk settled back, pinching the saw's bar. The tree's proclivity was exactly opposite of my calculation. It stood still on the "hinge" of my mistaken notch. My snow machine and sled sat about ten yards back from the tree, opposite to the direction the tree was supposed to fall in. We were poor; I couldn't afford another machine. Foolishly, I made a dash toward the machine to move it out of the way should the spruce topple off the stump. Halfway there I heard a whooshing sound and felt a hard rap on my right shoulder. The trunk crunched into the snow a couple of feet from me, a small branch whacking my shoulder. It missed the machine but fell across the sled, driving it into the snow without breaking it. Talk about luck. Both my head and machine were preserved from obliteration by a margin of only a couple of feet.

Ten of us were standing around looking at that first tree we'd picked out. Could we get a thirty-six-foot log to the lake, about thirty yards from where we stood? There was no path. We'd have to bull our way straight through the underbrush, the tangle of berry plants, the unseen deadfalls in the way. The log on our shoulders wouldn't bend around obstacles.

"Well," I said, "we could cut it in half—allowing the feet needed for an overlapping splice. Get it to the lake in two trips."

I didn't like the idea, and neither did the others. It would be a shame to take it any way but whole. Were we thinking of the tree's integrity or maybe its dignity? Something like that, I'd say, with guys like these. They weren't commercial loggers seeing a tree as only so many board feet of lumber, and none of them was Blake's fool for whom a tree is only a green thing standing in the way.

We decided we'd at least give it a try getting it to the lake in one piece. Drops of rain were falling from our noses, but we were in good spirits, even a little high, and maybe a little proud of ourselves for *seeing* this majestic tree. A good feeling. There was a lot of kidding around going on, a camaraderie thing. Men enjoy working together, on something like this especially.

I went through the sizing-up-the-lean procedure, laid my plans, made my cuts (I could have said "reluctantly" except I knew even then that the woods understands this), and with slow deliberation and massive force the spruce came down into the slot I had calculated. The guys cheered, grabbed their axes, and started limbing. That done, we lined up along the trunk according to height, so that the weight would be evenly distributed on our shoulders.

I looked down the line. These were all young men in good shape, most of them toughened to woods life, among them Denny, who prided himself on his strength, and son Steve, Steve Cross,

Paul Simon, Buddy Kobell, Grady Taylor, and Steve Mahay, all of whom I knew to be sturdy and strong. Big Jim Carlson I would have bet on too, but young Coleslaw I had my doubts about. I wondered if his shoulders were broad enough for the log to rest on and if his spindly legs could bear the course without buckling, but if so there would still be nine of us to carry on. In any event, could we do it? They saw the question in my eyes, grinned, and shrugged. Nothing ventured, nothing gained (an old saying in Tierra del Fuego).

"Okay, guys." Spaced evenly along one side of the log, we all bent to the task. "On the count of three. One. Two. *Three*." And the great log came up onto our shoulders. "Let's move out!"

Denny, as the tallest and by his own proclamation the strongest, was first in line at the butt end. If we made it to the water he would have to walk right in to at least waist level, then angle a bit more parallel to the shore so as not to get pushed in over his head by the momentum of the guys following. I was last in line, under the lighter end of the log, which suited me fine. When I was in far enough for the entire log to be over water, I would call out for everyone to heave (more accurately, drop) the log into the lake.

That was the plan. Now for the execution. As we started out toward the lake, my entire body strained under the load. My legs trembled, and my shoulder hurt, even though padded with a folded bandanna. We had estimated the clearest route but nevertheless had to push through the brush, branches whipping into our faces. At every deadfall to be crossed a groan went down the line as each man stepped up and over, feeling as though the entire tonnage was momentarily on his shoulder. Down the line from me, Coleslaw's legs looked like twanged rubber bands, but the spunky kid kept going and wouldn't go down. Then there was a series of gasps as each man entered the icy water and then another chorus of yelps when the dropped log drenched us with spray.

But the deed was done. The great log floated free in the lake. We all fell back onto the shore, breathing hard, temporarily drained of energy. Jon had been waiting in our canoe with its new one-horse outboard. He tied a line from the stern onto the narrow end of the log, started the trusty little outboard, and slowly towed our prize to the cabin site.

Up and at 'em, boys. This ain't siesta time. Down to the site we went to haul the log out of the water and rest it on the cradles Whitey had engineered so that the draw-shaving could be done at the waist-high level. (By September, the bark had set and wouldn't slip.)

This first sill log, the shaving completed, was a thing of beauty, piebald with tan, brown, and russet markings on the slick, yellow inner trunk. (Shaving leaves irregular patches of inner bark in place. I always liked the looks of a shaved log better than one that had been peeled.) The air was sweet with the scent of sap. While we worked the rain let up. We were wet but not cold, because of all the exertion involved. Then, like a sign of heavenly approbation, the sun came out to warm and dry us some while we axed flat surfaces on the log and lifted it onto the footings already in place. Our first log. A cabin was being raised, bigger and better, on the cleared-off site of our original home, like a phoenix rising from the ashes.

The drill just described was repeated, log after log, through the days and weeks following. Several more people showed up, most to put in a few days before returning to their own preparations for the coming winter. We enjoyed a short spell of Indian summer, when we could lounge around at the site during the breaks soaking up some precious sun.

On one of those afternoons I was out scouting for good trees around the north end of the lake. Things had been going well. I felt relaxed, walking slow and easy near the shore. The long marsh grasses across the way were warmly lit and waving in a gentle breeze, sensuous and slow. I sat on a log there at the lake's edge, the sun warm on my shoulder. I looked up at the treetops shimmering and dreamily swaying, way up to where the last lone leaf or two gave way to all that blue. I loved this beautiful unkempt land, and as I sat in the soft stirring silence I felt at peace and at home. It was so right. I lost myself and disappeared into it in some kind of ecstasy, taken up into a bliss I knew absolutely was at the heart of life and death. That night, lying in my bag mulling it over I recalled the metaphysical horrors and almost chuckled aloud because I knew I was way long past that now.

But there was no getting past the fact that the Coldman was up and coming. The intermittent rain was changing to intermittent snow. By the second week into October wet snow was sticking and ice was forming in the coves of the lake. The birches were bare, black branches against gray sky. We worked in sweaters or jackets and wore gloves now. At break time everyone crowded into the Simons' cabin to warm up. I knew we were nearing the end. The cabin couldn't be completed before the snow and cold stopped us.

We had gotten as far as finishing the downstairs roof (temporarily covered with six-mil plastic because it had been too cold for roll roofing or shingles). Sheldon was delayed coming in with the lumber we needed to roof the upstairs bedroom. When his Cessna 180 buzzed over, the lake was half covered with ice. He circled once, wagged his wings, and headed back to Talkeetna. We watched him go, and that was that. There was nothing more we could do.

Tents were taken down, packs shouldered, and good-byes said with many a handshake among the men and hugs among the women and girls. Then they hit the trail to the tracks. A few of them—Coleslaw, Big Jim Carlson, the silent fellow with the bad facial tic, even Grady Taylor—we never saw again. Their lives took them away from ours. But it had been a special time we had shared. They were all well remembered, these men and women who had appeared when we needed them.

We would winter with old friends on their farm in upstate New York and see our families and other friends after five years away.

When we returned in the spring, about the time the loons and gulls and loud-mouthed grebes came back to the lake and the frogs and all the birds started singing their mating songs, and the ravens too croaking, black against the spring sky, and of course the bears, we would finish the cabin and go on with life in the Alaska bush.

In my personal dreamtime, early in the morning of the day we left a wolf howled loud and clear from the south end of the lake, close to where we had heard the two moose splashing the morning after the day we first found the lake back in the spring of 1970.

Epilogue

We used to say that if you manage to survive your early days in Alaska, then you've got it made. That's when you're most likely to make your big mistakes, the ones that can kill you. Thirty-five years later, experience has modified that motto to something like this: If you manage to survive your early days in Alaska, well, nice going, Sparky, but in the Alaska bush you're never out of the woods.

That thought aside, things have definitely gotten easier for us. We no longer have to play train roulette just to get to town, thanks to the Alaska Railroad for providing a walkway across the Talkeetna River bridge and a trail alongside the tracks. Our chain saws are all in good working order; sharp and ready to eat wood. Even the difference in wood stoves is like day to night—better casting, better design, efficiency galore. Snow machines are far more dependable now than they used to be. And, perhaps most important, we're not as stupid as we used to be. It's been a long, long time since we've been stuck in overflow.

The Alaska we first knew at Lake Nerka in 1964 is gone forever. Snowmobiles, ATVs, cell phones, and worldwide marketing have changed the nature of even the wildest places.

The old-timers we admired, Whitey, Rocky, Beaver, Sheldon, as well as the old folks at Pope-Vannoy Landing—Grant, Art, and Patty—are long gone too. Genus Popeius is still kicking, still living in Intricate Bay. Sometimes it's hard to swallow, but through no design of our own, we've become the new old-timers.

The cabins in our neck of the woods are, for the most part, standing empty, occupied only by the occasional passing bear. Almost all the faces we used to see have moved on. Some had kids and needed to get onto the road system so they could go to school. (Home schooling is fine, but there is the thought that kids need to interact with other kids.) Some couldn't make a living, and some just lost interest.

Not us. We three Durr men continue to live on Back Lake, each in our own cabins, immersed in the quiet, visited by moose, bears, loons, otters, foxes, and wolves, while we work on our various schemes and artistic endeavors. The din of progress is just beyond the next hill, but thanks to the mighty Talkeetna River, and the state's budget mess, there's been no road development here.

And, yeah, we've got TV now. It's not all bad.

Sally is now Sarah (girls become women) and lives with her family in Talkeetna. Beth lives in Oregon with hers, but comes north every summer for a little fix of Back Lake.

Carol died of cancer in 1996, at home in Talkeetna with her family beside her. We love and miss her, and no matter how our great Alaskan adventure plays out in the end, we couldn't have done it without her.

Steve

What would the world be, once bereft
Of wet and wilderness? Let them be left
O let them be left, wilderness and wet;
Long live the weeds and the wilderness yet.

GERARD MANLEY HOPKINS,
"Inversnaid"